*Classic New Hampshire*

# CLASSIC NEW HAMPSHIRE

**Preserving the Granite State in Changing Times**

*Linda Landry*

University Press of New England

*Hanover and London*

University Press of New England, 37 Lafayette St., Lebanon, NH 03766

© 2003 by University Press of New England

Printed in the United States of America

5  4  3  2  1

*Library of Congress Cataloging-in-Publication Data*

Landry, Linda.

Classic New Hampshire: preserving the Granite State in changing times / Linda Landry

  p. cm.

Includes bibliographical references.

ISBN 1-58465-349-3 (pbk.: alk. paper)

Winnipesaukee Flagship Corp.—Ballet New England—Deerfield Fair—Strawbery

Banke Museum Dunaway Store—New Hampshire Daughters of the American

Revolution—Canterbury Shaker Village—Lake Umbagog National Wildlife Refuge—

New Hampshire Historical Society Tuck Library—Pats Peak—Mount Washington

Hotel—New England Marionette Opera—Story Land—Currier Museum of Art—Miss

New Hampshire scholarship program—UNH Violin Craftsmanship Institute.

F31.L36 2003

061/.42 21                                                                                          2003010005

# Contents

# Acknowledgments

The people who helped me to complete this book are too numerous to list individually, but I am very grateful to the staff, volunteers, and friends of the following organizations:

Audubon Society of New Hampshire
Ballet New England
Canterbury Shaker Village
Currier Museum of Art
Deerfield Fair Association
Lake Umbagog National Wildlife Refuge
Miss New Hampshire Scholarship Program
Mount Washington Hotel and Resort
New England Marionette Opera
New Hampshire Daughters of the American Revolution
New Hampshire Historical Society
Pats Peak
Society for the Protection of New Hampshire Forests
Story Land
Strawbery Banke
Tuck Library
UNH Cooperative Extension
UNH Division of Continuing Education, Violin Craftsmanship Institute
Union Leader Corp.
White Mountains Attractions
Winnipesaukee Flagship Corp.

A special note of gratitude goes to the public relations people in these organizations who arranged interviews, provided me with books and documents, tolerated endless questions, and reviewed my work for accuracy; and to the librarians and archivists who burrowed deep to find whatever I asked for (however obscure it was).

I also want to thank my editor, Phyllis Deutsch, for her unwavering support of this project and the New Hampshire Writers' Project. Thanks also to Linda Rousseau for planting the seed, Heather Frye and Karen Davis for their moral support, and my family for their interest and indulgence.

And, finally, this book is dedicated to my husband, Dirk, who has always encouraged me to follow my dreams—all the thank-yous in the world would never be enough.

L.L.

## Author's Note

One day when I was browsing through the special collections of Tuck Library, I found the following poem on an early-twentieth-century postcard:

Here's to the state of granite and wealth
of the fir tree, green pastures, and beauty, and health.
Where the weak grow strong and the strong grow great.
Here's to New Hampshire, the best-loved state.

It sums up perfectly why I wrote this book. My parents were New Hampshire natives and I spent most of my childhood here, growing up in Portsmouth and attending high school in Concord. When I left New Hampshire at eighteen to go to college, I always intended to return, but opportunity took me elsewhere. Finally, three weeks after my fortieth birthday, I moved back. In all that time, I had never forgotten this place and, over the years, had come to see how it had shaped me. I was always proud to be from New Hampshire, even though I sometimes had to explain exactly where it is.

In the last few years, the state has changed quickly and, in some places, quite drastically. It is my intention in this book to document something of where we have been, through the voices of people who are leading us into the future. It's a personal work based on my own experiences with each institution. There are hundreds of New Hampshire organizations—each with its own story and contribution to our traditions—that easily could have graced these pages. But after researching many, I selected fifteen that captured my personal interest and that I felt symbolized a particular aspect of New Hampshire's identity and character.

The chapters sit side by side, contributing in their own way to the whole, with none being greater or less than another. You may notice a seasonal element—the chapter sequence follows the year I spent working full-time on this book. It's not so much a collection of histories, although a strong historical thread runs throughout, as it is a snapshot of our times now. Every chapter covers a specific aspect of the organization represented. For example, how do the engineers who work on the M/S *Mount Washington* maintain its engines when parts are no longer available? Why has the food-judging contest been one of the most popular events at the Deerfield Fair since 1876? How is the Mount Washington Hotel preserving the traditions of another era through its staff today?

In my research, I found many, many instances of New Hampshire at the forefront of a variety of fields. More examples: Story Land is one of the only theme parks in the country that designs and builds its own attractions. The Miss New Hampshire Scholarship Program is eighth in the nation for the amount of money it awards to young women. The Lake Umbagog National Wildlife Refuge serves as a model for establishing refuges nationwide. The New England Marionette Opera was the only one of its kind in the world, outside of the famous Salzburg Marionette Theatre in Austria.

It was a privilege to interview the several hundred people who helped me with this book. They confirmed my sense that this is a state with strong core values. We expect everyone to pull their own weight. We don't just talk about democratic principles—we live them. We know what we believe in and why we believe it. And God forbid if anybody tries to tell us what to do. There is something of all those things in each of us who is from here or has lived here for any length of time. New Hampshire is a place of integrity and we are proud of that.

*Classic New Hampshire*

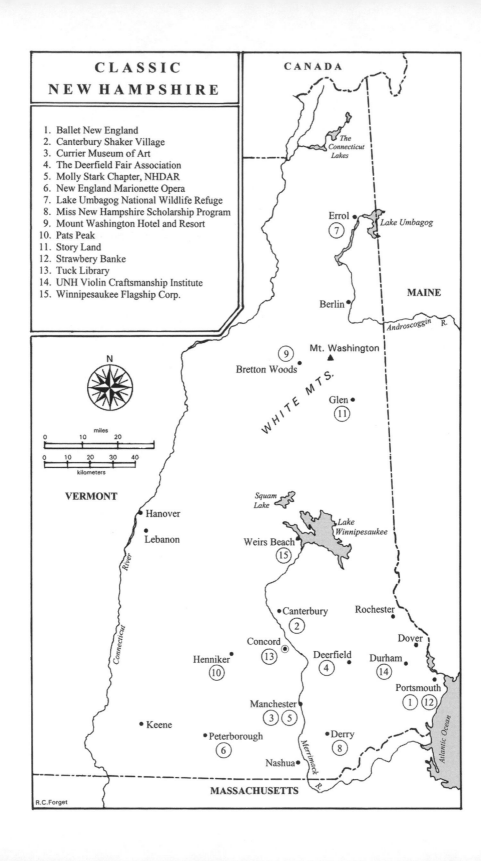

# CLASSIC
# NEW HAMPSHIRE

1. Ballet New England
2. Canterbury Shaker Village
3. Currier Museum of Art
4. The Deerfield Fair Association
5. Molly Stark Chapter, NHDAR
6. New England Marionette Opera
7. Lake Umbagog National Wildlife Refuge
8. Miss New Hampshire Scholarship Program
9. Mount Washington Hotel and Resort
10. Pats Peak
11. Story Land
12. Strawbery Banke
13. Tuck Library
14. UNH Violin Craftsmanship Institute
15. Winnipesaukee Flagship Corp.

CANADA

MAINE

*The Connecticut Lakes*

Errol ● ⑦ *Lake Umbagog*

Berlin ●

*Androscoggin R.*

N

miles
0    10    20

kilometers
0   10   20   30   40

VERMONT

⑨ Mt. Washington ▲
Bretton Woods ●

WHITE MTS.

Glen ●
⑪

*Squam Lake*

*Lake Winnipesaukee*

Hanover ●

Lebanon ●

Weirs Beach ●
⑮

*Connecticut River*

● Canterbury
②

Rochester ●

Concord ◉
Henniker ● ⑬
⑩

Deerfield
④

Dover ●

Durham ●
⑭

Portsmouth
① ⑫

Manchester ●
③  ⑤

● Keene

Peterborough ●
⑥

● Derry
⑧

*Merrimack R.*

Nashua ●

*Atlantic Ocean*

R.C.Forget

**MASSACHUSETTS**

# 1

## Story Land

### "It's Not About the Rides"

On a sweltering Friday morning on the first day of summer, there is already a crowd of kids gathered around Humpty Dumpty, who is sitting casually on a white cement-block wall. He looks just like his pictures, pleasantly plump, blue-eyed, with painted-on green pants and red checked shirt. He's not "real," of course, but the kids at Story Land in Glen are crazy about him. He's the first thing they see when they enter the park.

This is my first visit to Story Land, having only been here during the coldest week of the previous winter to talk with permanent staff. I have no childhood memories of this place, nothing to compare my experience with, and, frankly, I'm not sure what to expect. I'm seeing it fresh, as the kids around Humpty Dumpty are, who, at this moment, are clearly having a ball. "Humpty's been here since day one," says my tour guide, Story Land marketing coordinator Jim Miller. "He used to be flat and two-dimensional, but now he talks and looks like an egg. Originally fairy tales were meant to scare children, but we have the cleaned up, nicer versions here."

Jim is a low-key guy whose own kids love this place. Their friends think he's cool because he works here, but he's certain his near-star status will evaporate in a few years. Story Land, after all, caters to the under-eleven set, as evidenced by the fast-approaching Three Bears' House on our right. Inside, everything is in miniature—the perfect height for kids, but roomy enough for adults. Upstairs, he sits on one of the beds. "This is the papa bear's bed. It's too hard," he says, knocking the wooden mattresses. Tapping and squishing the other two, he demonstrates that, true to the fairy tale, one is too soft, and the last—just right.

Back outside, we stroll by the animated Talking Tree House, created by the Story Land design team in the park's Magic Shop. It has thick, far-reaching branches, an immense butterfly with fluttering wings, a wizened face, and two blue slides protruding from either side. The tree is so wide that staff had to remove the side of the building it was made in to get it out. Right now the entire structure is in motion. From a distance, it is impossible to decipher what is kid and what is tree.

"Children can come here and spend the whole day without ever going on a ride," Jim points out. Indeed, an hour into our tour we haven't yet hit a single one. Instead, we see live goats, pigs, geese, and, yes, three black sheep at Baa Baa Black Sheep—all in clean, shaded pens. There are ball crawls, tunnels, and keyboards that play chimes. Kids—and adults—run in and out of strategically placed misting tents set up to keep everyone cool without soaking them. It's all rather amazing, and I tell Jim that Story Land reminds me of a garden. From wherever we stand, we see trees, turrets, bridges, pagodas, boats, windmills, gazebos, and thousands of flowers in full bloom. Music plays, but not loudly or annoyingly. It's cheerful, matching the primary colors of the rides and attractions.

Climbing a small hill, Jim takes me to a recently refurbished white castle, home of the most popular person at Story Land—Cinderella. Soft music with a regal tone (no harsh trumpets) accompanies us up the walkway. From here, visitors have a perfect view of the gently drifting swan boats, as well as the Pumpkin Coach as it meanders to the front door of the castle. Cinderella, wearing a royal blue taffeta gown, strolls out to meet it. (Jim tells me she is so adored that sometimes little girls wear their own Cinderella gown to Story Land when they visit.) Inside the castle, a throne sits empty at the far end. Kids speak in whispers until they notice the glass slipper on a red velvet cushion encased like a museum exhibit near the door. The younger kids think it's real.

As we walk, Jim leans down to pick up an occasional candy wrapper, but there are surprisingly few. He tells me a dozen employees scour the park with broom and dustpan all day, but that it's part of everyone's job to keep the park clean—as well as keep it safe. When we're watching the Polar Coaster weave by, Jim courteously asks a father to take his child down from a wall where an accident could happen. The parent looks puzzled, but immediately complies. "I wouldn't let my own kids sit up there," Jim says afterward. Outside the Polar Coaster entrance, I notice a couple of kids rolling their backs across a thick white pole that turns out to be solid ice. I ask Jim how it's done, but he won't tell me. "It's magic. Story Land is a magical place," he says, laughing.

Around a corner we happen into a slice of Holland, with a wooden-shoe ride that twirls by a tulip-landscaped pond and a full-size cow with a lifelike plastic udder that streams water. A girl and boy are tugging on it, "milking" the cow, convulsing in giggles as it wildly moos. Story Land has thought of everything, I tell Jim. He grins and points out parking areas for strollers that are big enough to need license plates. At the World Pavilion, the largest food area in the park, there is no pandemonium in the lines. While parents wait, kids are busy spinning a 2,544-pound solid granite ball that sits in a basin of water near the food kiosk. Jim says last year when a child dropped a Lego man in the basin, his parent wrote to Story Land to ask if they could fish it out. At the end of the season when the globe came out, sure enough, there it was. The Lego man was promptly mailed back to the family.

Before ending our tour, Jim says he wants to show me an area that only employees of the park are aware of. It's the staff wardrobe room, where Story Land's three hundred seasonal—mostly adolescent—employees dress for work every day. It looks like a Gap store with neatly stacked rows of pink and blue T-shirts and black pants sorted by size. Jim gestures toward a washer and dryer in the corner, explaining that all uniforms are washed and restocked here every day. A nearby rack holds identical blue Cinderella dresses in a variety of sizes. "The Cinderella role would be too demanding for one person every day," Jim says, when he sees me looking at the dresses. "So we have lots of Cinderellas."

In the break room, ten teen-agers are sitting at tables drinking soda and munching on chips. Employees aren't allowed to break or eat in the park, and those who are playing characters must stay in their role until someone comes to relieve them. For example, Cinderella is told at noontime everyday that Prince Charming requests her company for a picnic. The room is spotless, despite being occupied most of the time by teenagers. On the wall is a hand-lettered sign on bright yellow paper that reads, "You can build the most beautiful facility in the world, but it takes people to make the magic come alive."

It all starts with the annual walk-around. This is when owner Stoney Morrell, operations coordinator Curtis Gordon, maintenance coordinator Chris Marchioni, and several other employees walk the thirty-five-acre park over a full week in mid-September, jotting down everything that strikes them—repairs, ideas for new attractions, operational issues, traffic pattern improvements—anything that will make the park a better place when it opens again the following season. After pruning and prioritizing the list, they assign each item to a department, enter it in a computer, and wait for

This 2000 aerial view of Story Land illustrates the order and planning required to create a colorful, easy-to-navigate children's amusement park. (Courtesy of Story Land.)

the seventy-page printout that serves as the park's winter and spring "to do" list. There are hundreds of items on it—from designing new signs to planting new flower gardens to creating a new hairdo for the schoolmistress in the Little Red Schoolhouse. The list is then separated into binders. All seven departments get one.

This is one reason why Story Land's thirty-five permanent employees think the idea of off-season "downtime" is comical. For five months of the year, they're completely focused on visitors. For the remainder, they're working against the clock to get the park in shape for the next season. If you drove by Story Land's row of houses on Route 16 in the dead of winter, you would never guess that this is what is happening. But when you enter the only house open at that time of year, there is no question you are in Story Land. In the reception, visitors can wait in two pink easy chairs and suck on lollipops from a metal canister. On the wall is a large, framed illustration of a child's fantasy park that looks suspiciously like Story Land.

On this subzero day in February I'm talking with Curtis Gordon about the park's rides: how they're selected, installed, maintained. Like many of the park's permanent employees, Curtis's first job was at Story Land. He was fourteen years old, hired as a parking lot attendant, and he says he liked it because he could ride his bike to work. Now he's operations coordinator, which in other parks would be the same as general manager. Here, though, senior managers are called "coordinators," because Story Land the Business doesn't care much for titles, preferring, instead, to view its managers as coaches.

Curtis always seems to be everywhere at the same time, and his colleagues tease him about it. Indeed, during my week at the park, I bumped into him constantly. In the winter he wears loose sweaters and shares an office above the maintenance shop with maintenance coordinator Chris Marchioni. In the summer he wears shorts and moves his office to the park so that he can be on the scene at a moment's notice. Wherever he is, he blends seamlessly into the background and then, without anyone noticing, is gone again. Year-round he uses a handheld radio, like all employees at Story Land, to communicate with colleagues.

I ask Curtis how rides are different in a child-oriented park like Story Land from those in a larger park that caters to all ages. He tells me the rides can't be exaggerated in any way—not too high, not too fast, not too twisting or turning. In other words, gentle rides for small folk. Those requirements eliminate a great many rides that theme parks generally buy at annual trade shows, but this is not a problem for Story Land. "We don't want the same thing as everyone else," Curtis says. "We want something that's unique to us."

And that is the essence of Story Land. All of the attractions and rides are designed right here, with many being built on-site. In fact, anything that can't be constructed at Story Land is customized for the park by manufacturers who use Story Land's designs to complete the work. There is nothing here that a visitor would find in another theme park, save for a miniature Ferris wheel with oversized cars that staff like because entire families can enjoy the ride together. Otherwise, the park uses its own concepts and people to create all of the light, colors, and sounds that make this park so extraordinary.

To generate ideas, senior staff sometimes go on "creative safaris" to other parks to evaluate if what they are doing could be adapted for use at Story Land. They also visit ride manufacturers directly. For example, a few years ago when the park was planning Oceans of Fun—a kind of park within Story Land—it contacted the Sellner Manufacturing Company, makers of the old-fashioned Tilt-A-Whirl, to find out if the company could build a milder version. Over it's nearly eighty-year history, Sellner had received only a handful of customization requests, but this one captured the company's imagination. Story Land not only wanted to take the whip out of the Tilt-A-Whirl, it wanted the seats in the shape of smiling, green turtles. Working from diagrams created by the park's design team, Sellner quickly built a few scale models. Before long, Story Land's one-of-a-kind Turtle Twirl was a go.

Prepping the location for a new ride can be as simple as pouring a concrete pad or as complex as building troughs and reservoirs for water rides. In the latter case, the work can take eight months or longer to complete. "There's an incredible chunk of concrete underneath some rides that no one sees," Curtis says. Before prep work begins, however, Story Land develops a plan for the area that considers roads, space for emergency vehicles, septic designs, power line and phone cable extensions, and blueprints for buildings. Then the ride normally is shipped by freight and bolted together like an advanced version of any mechanical toy (a professional from the ride manufacturer usually supervises the installation). Finally, Story Land hires a crane to set the ride into its pad, sets up a queue line, landscapes the area, and constructs the support buildings, such as snack bars, rest rooms, and the structure around the ride itself.

Curtis says there is another important consideration along the way— wheelchair accessibility. Not only for the park, but also for the rides. Story Land is in the process of replacing a few older rides with updated versions that can support a wheelchair, but when this isn't possible the park often makes its own modifications. For example, a few years ago, the park designed a train coach alteration that could sink a wheelchair into the coach and thus create a normal sight line. It was an issue because the manufacturer's suggested modifications elevated the wheelchair so high that it towered above the other seats on the train. When the manufacturer came to inspect the change, he was so impressed that he said he wished his company had thought of Story Land's designs first. The park is also adding wheelchair accessibility in a similar way to its one-hundred-year-old carousel.

Most rides at Story Land are powered by electricity and activated by a simple push-button device. Some, though, are fairly high-tech, featuring hydraulic systems, sensors, and logic boards to control timing and ride action. To find out more about the mechanical details, I talk with maintenance coordinator Chris Marchioni, a twenty-two-year veteran of Story Land who oversees ride upkeep, regulations, ride installation and construction, building construction, repairs, and roads. He tells me park rides can last indefinitely, but only if they are tested regularly and maintained well. In season, his crew tests every ride before Story Land opens each day. At the end of the season, the park follows stringent state requirements for testing every ride's critical components on a rotating schedule. "We have very high standards," Chris says. "In some parks operations and maintenance are at odds, and safety is sometimes compromised to keep things going. But that's never an issue here."

Chris takes me down to the maintenance shop, where the bright orange globe of the Pumpkin Coach sits on the floor next to its trailer. His crew is in the process of doing routine repairs on it. Nearby, roller-coaster chassis and axles are laid out on work benches like knees and elbows. "Everything is taken down to its rawest form," Chris says, waving his arm across the scene like a magic wand.

I ask Chris about the towering tent outside his building that looks like a storage area for Hollywood movie props. It's filled to bursting with ships, lighthouses, swans, and other colorful larger-than-life items. "Oh, those are from the park," he replies, comparing the tent to a waiting room. "They'll soon be getting their yearly maintenance check."

In the summer of 1967, Jack Mahany met his wife at Story Land. He was the Pumpkin Coach driver and she was Cinderella. When he first tells me this, I think he's joking, but he assures me he is not. Later I find similar matches throughout the company. It seems to be a kind of Story Land tradition.

Jack says Story Land founder Bob Morrell gave him his first job as a teenager and then taught him to take pride in his work. It's a lesson that followed him as a business owner himself, and now—nearly ten years after returning to Story Land as a senior staffer—continues to structure his work life. "I hadn't realized what I had learned here until later in life," he tells me. "This place has always been run by the Golden Rule. That's how I was 'brought up' here. From the first week after coming back, I knew it was right."

When you first enter Jack's office, you can't help but notice the giant duck head that sits by the door like a greeter (he says it used to be on the

Founder Robert Morrell looks on as his son, Stoney, tests the new antique car ride in 1961. Stoney Morrell now runs the park. (Courtesy of Story Land.)

Story Land Queen swan boat). Out a side window he has a perfect view of Mount Washington. Jack is hairless, lean and athletic in blue jeans. He has no official title but, from the sound of it, I'd guess he's Stoney Morrell's right hand. "I'm like a coach," he explains. "I'm a very positive person." Indeed, the first time I contacted Story Land via e-mail, I received an instant response from Jack. "Certainly!" he responded. "Thanks for asking!"

Story Land doesn't give out visitor statistics, but Jack tells me the park entertains about 75,000 families every year. Between 60 and 75 percent are returning, although he is careful to point out that some visitors return every year, while others might return every decade. Story Land has been around since 1954 and is enjoying what I call the "Fenway Park" effect—a rollover of generations, with parents and grandparents remembering the park as it was in earlier decades. (This can actually be a bit of a problem for Story Land. Returning guests don't like to see anything changed.) "We don't take in a dime between Columbus Day and Memorial Day," Jack says. "The money goes back into the company. That's the only way it's worked. This is a blue-collar business."

One of Story Land's biggest challenges each summer is training its three hundred young employees, or cast members as they're called, to adopt a strong work ethic and esprit de corps. Eighty percent are teenagers, and for many, it's their first job. The weekend before Story Land opens, permanent staff host a high-spirited, two-day orientation designed to get cast members in the right frame of mind for the barrage of young children they'll soon be handling daily. Every year it's based on a different theme and involves a park tour, specific job training, refreshers for the 75 percent of returning employees, quizzes that identify weak spots, and, of course, music and games. "A lot of it is common sense, but the youngest are hardest to train," Jack tells me. "They have no idea yet how to work. So we emphasize body language, common courtesy, empathy"—and, perhaps most important, Story Land's "five S's": safe, smooth, smiling, spotless service. They're so ingrained in employees that they govern everything that happens at Story Land through all ranks.

I ask Jack what he feels the value of a park like Story Land is in an era that sees theme parks getting bigger and faster with every passing year. "Story Land is a safe haven for families with young children," he tells me ardently. "When you're here, the day to deal with reality is tomorrow. Once you get inside the gate it's a total fantasy world. It's a clean atmosphere with beautiful flowers and courteous staff. It takes everyone away from normal life. It's not just about the rides. If people think that, they've missed the point. The people who put this place together and keep it going are passionately obsessed with it. It's a way of life for us."

The creative process at Story Land can best be summed up in one word: collaborative. "There's no one here who's so creative that we only go to them," Stoney Morrell told me. "These are ordinary people who have a good feel for what kids like to do." In fact, the process does often start with the annual walk-around, which not only generates lists of improvements but also drives new projects. Take Story Land's newest attraction, a ride with passenger cars like wooden barrels built around a cuckoo clock theme. The way staff tell it, one year on a walk-around, Stoney and a few employees were considering attractions that might fit a specific spot in the park. Suddenly someone said, "How about a cuckoo clock?" (No one remembers who.) Within twenty minutes they had the whole thing mapped out.

The next thing you knew, Curtis Gordon was flying off to Italy to talk to a ride manufacturer, while Chris Marchioni arranged construction materials and contractors, Jim Miller laid out marketing plans, art department coordinator Donna Howland drew up conceptual sketches, and Magic Shop operator Bob Marquis built models. Before long, the project was advanced enough for Curtis to begin analyzing traffic patterns and for Chris to measure out the land. Then everyone came back to Donna and Bob, who worked together to finalize the design of the end product. Cement was poured, the ride arrived, buildings went up, and there it was—a brand-new Story Land attraction.

This description might be a bit streamlined, but not much more so than reality. Story Land staff know a good idea when they hear one and are so clear, collectively, about what Story Land is and is not that it doesn't take long to—quite literally—gets things moving. Staff followed the same creative process in 1996 when the park built Oceans of Fun, which they call "a big fancy sprinkler." It's a special place in the park built around a yellow submarine topped by a leggy green octopus with thick, blue eyebrows. Inside, there are controls to play with and portholes to look out of that give you the distinct impression you are twenty thousand leagues under the sea. Outside, water mists from everywhere onto a blue nonslip surface. Nearby, the sweet-faced green turtles of the Turtle Twirl slide around in circles.

Everyone readily attributes much of the concept for Oceans of Fun to art department coordinator Donna Howland, but she refuses to take the credit. "Kids love to play with water," she says, brushing aside the subject. "We all brainstormed, and I kept drawing things that worked into troughs that became arms that became an octopus. Eventually the idea made its way into something really fun." In the end, she says, the inspiration came from the staff's own families.

Donna started on the cash registers at Story Land over thirty years ago, after studying fashion design and illustration at the Massachusetts College of Art. She told Story Land founder Bob Morrell she would be happy to help out with signs, and he promptly took her up on it. Now Story Land employs five artists, whose work includes concept development, airbrushing, computer graphics, signs, and costumes.

The day I visit, winter sunlight is pouring through the tall windows of the design studio, which is tucked away in the back of the park. Drafting tables and long work counters fill up most of the space. In the center are rows of miniature white horses, disassembled from Story Land's carousel. Each year Donna's artists repair and repaint twelve of them (out of thirty-six). She leaves it up to the artist to choose the designs, and this year, one of the horses is sporting a star-studded blue saddle with red trim. On the next table over, a sorry-looking pirate is waiting for new pants and a complete paint touch-up. In the corner, a newly airbrushed, lifesize tortoise wears a purple helmet. Donna explains that airbrushing requires detailed work because the artist must create texture effects on the object to give it the illusion of depth.

Keeping the grade school crowd enthralled takes a lot more imagination than creating entertainment for adults, and I ask Donna how she develops designs that appeal to this demanding audience. "You have to be very careful not to make things too scary," she says. For example, to take the edge off the wolf in the Little Red Riding Hood house, they simply removed his big sharp teeth. "We also size things to kids. Even the ticket counters are low so that kids can see over them. And I always use bright, happy colors."

"But safety is something we always think about in our design work," Donna continues. "You have to be careful. If we make a lollipop fence, sure enough some little kid is going to chew on it. If there's a hole in something, kids are going to stick their heads and hands into it. So it has to be too small for that or big enough to get them out. We can't have anything that can pinch little fingers. We once had a rocking horse that was too dangerous for this reason, so we removed it and put something safer in its spot. You've heard about kids who put aside the Christmas gift so they can play with the box? As adults we could get real fancy, but often simplest is best. Kids might just want to play in a sandbox. We might have a brilliant idea, but would a three-year-old think so?"

On Donna's worktable I notice several drawings of cuckoo clocks. Next to them are color printouts of the real thing, which she has downloaded from the Internet. She explains that she is in the process of designing the building that the cuckoo clock ride will loop around in and that Chris Marchioni has recently given her the building dimensions. She shows me a series of drawings she produced on drafting paper that become increasingly animated as we go along. The work is beautiful, with bold colors that highlight the dark brown structure's simple features.

When Donna is finished with the designs, she will give them to Bob Marquis, who will bring them to life in the Magic Shop, a warehouselike building near the design studio. Working alone, it appears that Bob can build just about anything—passenger cars for rides, animated characters, furniture. He even designed and built the rather elegant pastel cabinets that store condiments in the park's food areas. Sometimes he carves foam sculptures and then hard-coats them for use as decorative touches throughout the park. On this day, he is testing the elaborate gear set on a clock he built that eventually will be scaled up in size and function like a real cuckoo clock for the new attraction. To make it look authentic, he bought an old wooden clock for a hundred bucks and is using it as a model for building a prototype.

One of the more distinctive features about Story Land's Magic Shop, besides what Bob actually produces there, is the fact that, according to industry analysts, only the corporate giants have them. Most small to midsize parks prefer instead to invest in frontline features, such as rides, that can provide a quick and measurable return on investment. To make a Magic Shop a reasonable investment, a park must have a well-equipped space, commitment from senior management, and a lot of creative talent on staff. Analysts say it's rare to find all three present in a small park, but Story Land is the exception.

In the early 1990s, Bob Marquis came out of retirement and moved to Glen to set up the Magic Shop. For years he had run an animatronics company in Vermont, working frequently with Disney and Universal Studios as well as with Story Land. Bob Morrell liked the company's work so much that he wanted to replicate its studio at Story Land, but the only person who could do that was, of course, Bob Marquis. "I've learned so much by listening to the people here," Bob tells me. "I've learned that less is sometimes best. I've always worked with people who wanted the most, who wanted things that smoke, walk, fly. But here, the things we build are for everyone. The high-tech things tend to intimidate kids. A simple gopher here will get the same attention as a more complicated thing with a hundred functions that costs $300,000."

Bob's snow-white hair is offset by his black turtleneck, which, at 10:00 A.M., is already covered with a fine layer of dust. Walking from tool to tool, he demonstrates a bending device that twists steel, points out his high-tech lathes, and shows me how the stroke sanders make any surface as smooth as glass. He stops next to a machine the size of two pool tables that resembles a medical scanner with tubes and wires sticking out of it. "This is the router," he says. Pointing to the drills hanging from either side of it, he commands, "Watch this." He sits at a computer and enters dimensions into it, which are transmitted to the router, which cuts the specified forms into a long sheet of plywood. When the router is finished, we have a perfect snowflake-shaped cuckoo clock gear like the ones slowly turning nearby.

He's like a kid in a toy shop. For a while, we crawl around in the loft that surrounds the space—admiring penguins, huge 1960s-style flowers, and lots and lots of butterfly wings. When it's time to go, I, too, am coated in dust.

Robert Stoning Morrell, Jr., was born to Bob and Ruth Morrell in 1956, two years after Story Land opened. There's an old black-and-white photograph of him from a few years later in a Story Land miniature antique car, waving at the camera. His father, who became a New Hampshire legend for his contributions to developing the White Mountains regional economy, is standing behind a porch railing smiling proudly on the scene he created—son and Story Land.

Today "Stoney" Morrell has graying hair that often looks like he just removed a baseball cap. That's because most of the time he wears one. On this day, he is dressed in North Country chic like everyone else at Story Land: plaid flannel shirt and an old blue fleece vest. He has a big, bushy mustache like a lumberjack and wears large, round eyeglasses that define his face. Answering questions, he takes his time to contemplate and then shells out his thoughts one sentence at a time. His staff say he makes decisions the same way.

In much of the literature about Story Land, the story of his parents is told over and over, but there is very little said about Stoney, who, as president of the Morrell Corporation and its most senior coordinator, is responsible for building on his father's dreams. In a small office in the park's winter quarters I ask Stoney what it was like to be a part of Story Land as a child. "Like any family business it was constantly part of our lives," he tells me. "From the time I had consciousness, I was aware of Story Land. But unlike other kids, it was never a place to go and have fun. I could wander around and visit with people, but I was the boss's son. I was in a position to hear about the daily challenges. It was the place I always wanted to be, especially with my father. He bought me a set of tools, and I would go and work with the carpenters. Or I'd help take the small engines apart. I was in a position of privilege because I got to see the inside of this place. The flip side was that I also saw the sometimes agonizing part of operating a small business like this. I saw the total commitment my parents put into this place, and I said to myself, 'There has to be a better way to make a living.'"

So he packed himself off to Dartmouth College in the mid-1970s to study geography, where he slowly realized what an "oddball experience" his childhood had been. Although his parents hoped he would return to Story Land, he instead hopped into his truck after graduation and headed out to Wyoming. Over the next five or so years, he worked alternately as a carpenter and ranch hand, but after a while tired of "so many blue sky days." Eventually he became interested in business and realized there was one waiting for him back home that would allow him to, as he puts it, "celebrate the activity of thinking, creating, and inventing, in countless ways that you don't normally get to do in everyday life." Stoney returned to Story Land in the mid-1980s, his father took on a different role, and he's been running the place ever since.

We talk about the development of Story Land, starting with his father's initial investment of $7,500, which today would be about $50,000. The business has always been run "fiscally conservative, but creatively liberal," Stoney says, "and we've never gone out on a limb that was a make-or-break deal. We've always spent within our means." This wasn't always easy, especially during the years when the park was rapidly filling up its acreage with new attractions. "Now we're enhancing things," he says. "Sometimes the changes are procedural, so you only see them on paper, and sometimes they are structural. My dad saw structures as change, but changes on paper can make just as big of an impact. What is consistent is we are driven by constructive restlessness." He stops to mull over this phrase, which he says came to him only recently and which he likes. "My dad wanted to build things, and that was important then. But we're a mature business now. People come here and expect a consistently great experience."

When Bob Morrell started Story Land, amusement parks had been in existence in this country for over a hundred years (in 1919 there were 1,500 in operation, but only 400 survived the Depression and World War II years). By the early 1950s, Americans had television and other diversions, and were increasingly turning away from amusement parks for other forms of entertainment. Disneyland's opening in 1955 changed that almost overnight by paving the way for a new brand of fantasy parks, which sprouted up all over the country in the 1960s and 1970s. Story Land was a forerunner to Disney, but the park definitely benefited from this boom if only because its visitors had become aware enough of theme parks to seek them out.

To get a theme park off the ground today would require considerably more expense and planning than it did in Bob Morrell's time, and I'm curious what Stoney would do if he were starting one now. "First, you wouldn't do it today in the North Country with a one-hundred-day operating season," he chuckles. "But Story Land works here because this is already a recreational destination. If you're starting from scratch, you work with people who know where to put things. You start with freight in the right place, ample parking, key septic locations. You work with the pattern in the natural landscape that you've been given. And you hire a good park designer who can theme concepts and put it all together in a pleasing manner."

Industry experts estimate it could cost a cool million dollars to start a theme park today if you started out small and planned to grow slowly. The biggest expense is rides. Larger parks often pay a million dollars or more for many of today's most popular thrillers, but prices like that put them completely out of reach for smaller parks. "The bigger parks always have the pressure of bigger rides, but that's not the arena we play in," Stoney explains. "I pay more attention to psychological trends. When we're creating something here, we have a blank canvas and we're going to paint a scene that fits here. If it feels good to us, we trust our instincts that our guests will have the same response. We have our own expectations that drive us, instead of external factors."

"My perceptions of the value of a place like this didn't develop until I had my own kids," he continues. "I realized how rare it can be to experience something together as a family and how hungry families are for this. It's like my dad asked: Are we crucial to society? No. Are we valuable? Yes. When kids leave here I want them to go home and say, 'I danced with a scarecrow' or 'He let me blow the whistle' or 'I'm going to drink my milk out of my Story Land cup every day for the next year.' Not because it's Story Land, but because it was a family experience."

Not surprising, these values sound remarkably similar to those of Stoney's father, who once said, "Story Land conveys a message that fascinates. That does something to most everyone. Cleanliness, courtesy, order, innovation, a sort of changing stability, participation, family communion—[Story Land is] like growing up with one foot in the sandbox." Bob Morrell passed away several years ago, but I am wondering what he was like and how it is for Stoney to be following in the footsteps of someone whose judgment was rarely questioned.

"He was financially very conservative, but he was a pretty liberal thinker. He wasn't locked into the post–World War II thinking of his generation," Stoney tells me. "He was turned on by the most amazing things. He wouldn't always understand the technology, but he understood the emotional response. There's no question he cast a large shadow, which creates a problem for his offspring. But he was respected for the quiet way he did things. There's a part to that of having to measure up to him. He was extraordinary. When I came back to the business, he was very good about slipping into the background. He was always the Big Picture person. I was drawn more to the details, maybe because I saw we needed to get some things in place to keep up with the industry."

"He was compassionately powerful like no one I have ever met," Stoney continues. "He could pat someone on the back and kick him in the butt at the same time. He hadn't always been that way. When he was younger, he was kind of a hothead, always in a hurry. Opinionated. He could be arbitrary. But as he got older, he mellowed into this compassionate power. I was in my teens, looking at this guy who everyone idolized. But I've been able to make my own way, sometimes not very gracefully, and I see myself evolving toward the traits I seek to emulate in him."

## 2

## Miss New Hampshire Scholarship Program

---

"No One Ever Forgets You're a Miss New Hampshire"

"*A*re you here for the pageant?" Dan Tidd asks me in the shaded driveway of his Kingston home on a mild Sunday morning in July. When I explain I'm not a contestant, he looks a little confused. The pageant family is a close-knit one, and he has never seen me before. "Flattery will get you everywhere," I think to myself as I walk up the front steps.

Inside, Dan's wife Elaine appears composed, almost relaxed, despite the fact that she has fourteen grueling hours ahead of her herding twenty-one agitated young women through various stages of the Miss Kingston–Miss Seacoast pageant: morning interviews with judges, afternoon talent rehearsals, and the big event in the evening. "It's not like we haven't done this before," she laughs, when I comment on her cool. This is Elaine's sixteenth crowning as the local pageant director, and it is clear there is little that can rattle her.

By 10:30 A.M. most of the contestants have arrived and are sitting on the wide-cushioned sofas in the living room. Some sport a head full of curlers. One girl with long Goldilocks ringlets shimmers in a glittery pink top. Another wears a T-shirt that says "Rock Star." As they chat, a young woman and her mother walk hesitatingly over to Elaine, who stares good-naturedly at the girl. "In your picture, you're a redhead," she says, smiling. In the girl's picture, she also has short, tight curls. "Oh, this is natural," her mother says, stroking her daughter's now straight, shoulder-length brown hair.

At the last moment, the twenty-first contestant rushes in, her younger brother in tow. He is trying hard to keep her blue satin gown from dragging on the floor, but walking through the sea of femininity has gotten him all flustered. Red-faced, he shoves the dress toward his sister and makes a beeline toward the front door. Now there are only the girls and Elaine, who is dressed in navy blue shorts and a star-spangled shirt. Her soft reddish hair is already set for the evening, stylishly coiffed an inch shy of bouffant. As she stands before them, the only sounds are her mom peeling vegetables over the sink and emcee Dana Rosengard tapping the keys of a turquoise laptop at the kitchen counter. "This is where it all starts," he whispers over to me. "The quintessential path to Miss America."

"I hope you have fun today," Elaine starts. "That's my only goal for the day. If you don't leave here saying you can't wait to do another pageant, we didn't do our job." She pauses, looking around the room. "I like to run a no-fighting, respect-each-other pageant. I don't want anyone touching each other's things and I expect everyone to be nice to each other." At this the girls glance at each other and giggle self-consciously. Then Elaine launches into how the day and evening will proceed. "Can we wear panty hose under our swimsuit?" asks one girl. "Absolutely not," Elaine answers. Concluding, she emphasizes that the pageant experience is about fellowship, not winning. She wants to get across that they are gutsy and special just for trying. "For the new ones who have never done this before, this is like a family," she tells them. "The friendships that will grow from this are incredible. But if you don't win, don't give up. There is always Miss Stratham Fair, Miss Riverfest. . . ." The list goes on.

When Elaine finishes, she directs the girls upstairs to the bedrooms, which she has transformed into dressing areas, to change for their interviews. Soon each will appear before the five judges, who at this moment are sequestered downstairs in Elaine's front parlor. One woman and four men huddle around a large desk waiting for instructions from Elaine, leafing through the contestant information packets she sent them several weeks earlier. In a moment, she sweeps into the room. "The most important thing to remember is that each contestant is competing against herself," Elaine tells them, reading from four pages of notes handwritten on hot pink paper. "You need to be decisive, impartial, and consistent. This isn't a beauty contest, but the girls should be attractive in their own way with a confident and commanding presence. Think of it this way—each girl is applying for the jobs of Miss Kingston and Miss Seacoast."

Scoring these preliminary Miss America contests has become as complex as an Olympic gymnastics event. In each pageant there are four specific "competitions"—interview, talent, physical fitness (swimsuit), and gown. Elaine briefs the judges on each. For interviews, which make up the highest percentage of each contestant's overall score, she tells them to ask "high-gain questions that get the contestants to evaluate and analyze,

Long-time Miss Kingston Pageant emcees Trisha Tidd and Dana Rosengard show a dash of glamour as guests at the 1999 Miss America Pageant, Atlantic City, New Jersey. (Courtesy of Elaine Tidd.)

express feelings, and defend their beliefs." For example, "Would you become a surrogate mom for your sister?" or "What is one of your long-term goals?" She instructs them, after each interview, to ask themselves, "Did the contestant answer the question? Did I discover the real girl?" "Don't fall for the 'victim of hardship' story," Elaine counsels. "You should likewise be aware of the 'halo effect.' And remember, you don't have to agree with each girl's opinion, but they should have stated it well."

Elaine doesn't spend a lot of time on the swimsuit or evening-wear contests. She simply tells the judges to look at posture, confidence, and style, and to record their overall first impression. For the talent contest, it's all about skill, personality, and stage presence. "It's not who has the best vocal range or the highest kicks," Elaine says. "It's showmanship. It's the costume, how they handle themselves onstage. Try not to get carried away by the girl singing your favorite song and forget to notice the skill." She pauses for questions, but the judges don't have any, so she exits, pulling a navy blue cotton curtain across the doorway. From now on, no one except the judges and contestant are allowed in the room.

One by one the girls file down the stairs, most dressed in snappy summer suits and career-girl pumps. An air conditioner blots out most of the sound in the interview room, but from a bench beside the blue curtain I can hear questions. "What are the biggest issues facing families today?" "What determines a person's progress in life?" "What got you interested in pageants?"

In 1987, when Elaine Tidd started the Miss Kingston contest, all she was looking for was a chance to volunteer at the Kingston Fair. One of the fair organizers matched her up with the Miss Deerfield Fair director, who, over the course of one evening, told Elaine everything she needed to know. She's now one of the longest-running directors in the fourteen-contest Miss New Hampshire Scholarship Program. What keeps her coming back, she says, is "watching that seventeen-year-old girl go from knowing nothing about pageants to being twenty-three and becoming Miss New Hampshire." Her own daughter Trisha won three local titles in her pageant days. Her $8,000 of scholarship winnings have helped put her through optometry school.

Among pageant families, Elaine is royalty—not only by the sheer weight of her experience, but also because of her reputation for being levelheaded and fair. Every year she attends the Miss America pageant in Atlantic City, because she says it helps her better coach her local winners. Her contest isn't what insiders call "a big-money pageant," like some that award tens of thousands of dollars. But as all the local contests do, hers puts its winners in the running for the Miss New Hampshire title.

I have never entered a pageant, but, like many Americans, I am fascinated by them. Ever since Miss America became a national icon in 1921, the pageant seems to have changed in tandem with—or perhaps a little behind—how we define "the ideal woman" in American culture. Over nine decades, its emphasis has flipped from beauty to brains, which can best be observed in the scoring. The interview is now worth half of each contestant's overall score in the Miss America pageant, while the swimsuit competition—more of a relic from another era than anything else—has bottomed out at 10 percent. The reason is because most pageant winners on all levels now spend the majority of their time public speaking. Judges feel that if the girls can't express themselves well, they have no business winning a pageant.

Later on, talking with Elaine in her kitchen, I ask her what is different about pageants now than when she first got involved. Fifteen years ago, she tells me, makeup was heavier—so much so that when she took a group of pageant winners out to dinner, everyone in the restaurant turned to stare. Back then, local winners were expected to look like beauty queens, but to act demurely. She says she spent a lot of time teaching her girls how to walk in to the contest interview, sit down, cross their legs and hands in a ladylike manner, and wait for questions. Evening gowns were heavy, beaded numbers in colors like cream and blue that were considered "advantageous" to winning.

Nowadays, however, contestants are expected to look like themselves and to choose simply styled clothing in colors that suit them best. During the interview, they walk around and introduce themselves for thirty seconds before the questions begin. When they are deciding on their platform, which is really a specific vision of how they would like to change the world, they're advised to follow their interests and choose something they feel strongly about. "Now we focus on the basics," Elaine says. "We teach them to care about their *overall* appearance . . . when their personality shines, all girls are more attractive to everyone."

After the pageant, the extent to which the local director becomes involved in the winner's life varies. Some take charge, advising the girl how to dress and act, while others stay on the sidelines, helping out when needed. Elaine takes a strong interest in every year's Miss Kingston and Miss Seacoast, but says she tries not to overdo it. "If the girls have already competed in the state pageant"—because they previously won other local pageants—"there's not much work," Elaine says. "If not, I sit them down here at the kitchen counter and try to get them to think without telling them everything." She coaches them slowly, showing them tapes of previous winners and encouraging them to critique what worked and what didn't. "I try to give them knowledge to grow on," she adds.

Elaine's franchise is part of the state Miss New Hampshire Scholarship Program, which is the largest private provider of scholarships to women in this state. In fact, New Hampshire consistently places in the top ten states nationwide for the scholarship funds it awards through its pageant network. On average, the Miss New Hampshire contest awards about $75,000 each year. Financing comes from business sponsors, as well as a weekly Miss New Hampshire Bingo game in Windham. In addition, fourteen local pageants award about $65,000, bringing the grand total annually awarded to young New Hampshire women to almost $150,000.

It's necessary, though, to give credit where credit is due. In 1947 the Union Leader Corporation rescued the then-defunct Miss New Hampshire

Katherine Pike, Miss Winnipe-saukee 2000, on the night she won the Miss New Hampshire 2001 title, spring 2001. (Courtesy of Katherine Pike.)

organization by assuming primary sponsorship. Only a year earlier William Loeb had acquired the *New Hampshire Morning Union* and *Manchester Evening Leader* newspapers and saw the pageant as a way to further his company's community involvement. The Union Leader Corporation continued its sponsorship of the Miss New Hampshire Scholarship Program, running it from the company's promotions department, until 2001. At that time, the company decided the program had become too time-consuming for Union Leader staff, who in effect were working two full-time, demanding jobs. The company continues to support the Miss New Hampshire program and remains involved, although to a lesser extent than in the previous fifty-five years.

Now the program is run completely by volunteers—over two hundred of them located in most corners of the state. They include a state executive director, five state board members, fourteen local pageant directors, field directors, producers, advisers, chaperones, and many, many organizers. Anyone, in fact, can start a local pageant if they pass a background check and pay a small licensing fee. But staging a pageant is a yearlong endeavor. Besides organizing the event, local directors help raise the scholarship money from business sponsors that will attract contestants to their pageant. Like directors, contestants have few eligibility requirements. Any single young woman between the ages of seventeen and twenty-four who lives, works, or goes to school in New Hampshire and is a U.S. citizen can enter any local pageant she wishes. Unlike pageants outside the Miss America network, there are no application fees. Only winners of local pageants within the state network can compete for the Miss New Hampshire title. In turn, only winners of state pageants, which are part of the Miss America network, are entitled to compete for the national title.

Despite the scholarship awards, there appears to be a stigma around pageants in the northern United States that says, Smart girls don't do them. The reality couldn't be further from the truth. Most contestants are stellar students—typical overachievers who already have proven they have the intelligence, drive, and common sense to make good use of scholarship money if it comes their way. Recruiting girls to compete, however, can sometimes be difficult for local pageant directors in New Hampshire. Elaine, for example, scouts all year. Wherever she goes she doesn't hesitate to approach someone who looks promising. "Say I go to a play and see a talented girl, or I'm in a restaurant," Elaine explains. "I'll ask her, 'Do you have enough money for school? No? Have I got a deal for you!' That's when my husband rolls his eyes and says, 'Here she goes again!'" It works. Every year she ends up with about twenty contestants who vie for two titles in one of the few "double crownings" in the state (the girl with the highest score becomes Miss Kingston; the runner-up is crowned Miss Seacoast.)

In the pageant world, I have heard many refer to girls who have "the complete package"—brains, beauty, talent, and a fit body. No one has it all, of course, but "all" is what they are required to have, especially if they're competing on the national scene. I ask Elaine about this, and she agrees that it's not good enough for a girl only to have a great talent or superb interviewing skills. Most important, though, is attitude. To make it to the next level, contestants must be willing to work on their shortcomings. "I tell my girls that it's not fun to work on those things, but they have to do it," she says.

Like the swimsuit contest? I ask. Elaine looks at me for a second and then laughs. "I tell them, 'You're up there for twenty-four seconds. You can hold your breath that long.'"

The Miss America pageant has had somewhat of a rocky history since its inception in 1921. Originally dreamed up by Atlantic City businessmen to keep tourists in town after Labor Day, the first pageant, which capped a two-day "Fall Frolic" festival, was a beachfront parade of beauties. It had only one rule: all participants must wear swimsuits. When over 100,000 people swarmed the boardwalk to get a glimpse of the girls, some of whom were young teens or otherwise questionable contestants, city officials proclaimed the event a colossal success and quickly made plans to continue it for the rest of the decade. Their reasoning was that as long as there were girls in swimsuits, folks would turn out to see them.

By the late 1920s, however, conservative Americans had begun to take issue with the pageant's attention to the female figure. After women's groups and religious organizations publicly accused pageant organizers of corrupting the nation's morals, the Atlantic City Chamber of Commerce canceled the 1928 pageant. The moratorium held until 1933, when local businessmen revived the pageant by transporting thirty young women to Atlantic City from cities all over the United States aboard a chartered train called the Beauty Express. This time, though, the pageant was a financial disaster. It wasn't until 1935, when organizers hired the legendary Lenora S. Slaughter, that the pageant shaped itself up and evolved into the extravaganza that it is today.

From the start, Ms. Slaughter, who remained executive director of the Miss America organization until 1967, aimed to bring respectability to an event that had gained a reputation over its short history for being somewhat risqué. One of the first things she did was establish eighteen as the minimum age for contestants. Next came the addition of the talent competition in 1938, followed soon after by the gown contest and a personality element. Chaperones were added, as a better class of participant was sought. (According to one source, when a pageant judge once asked Ms. Slaughter what to look for in a winner, she answered, "Honey, just pick me a lady.")

But the real turnaround for the Miss America pageant came in 1945, when the organization added college scholarships to its booty of pageant prizes—one of the first organizations of any type in the nation to award education funds to women. Doing so distinguished—and distanced—the pageant from others that continued to emphasize beauty over a woman's talents, personality, and intellect. For the next fifteen years, the Miss America program skyrocketed in popularity, boosted by its yearly broadcast on television, which started in 1954.

But when the 1960s hit, the pageant didn't seem to notice that the girl next door was attending antiwar rallies while her feminist sisters were downtown burning their bras. By then Miss America had become a kind of national cartoon that seemed completely out of step with changing American values. Resentment of the pageant peaked in 1968, when protesters seeking to mar the event burnt an effigy of longtime emcee Bert Parks outside Atlantic City's Convention Hall. Soon afterward sponsors started pulling out, and television ratings slipped. Something had to change. But it didn't. It was only after the platform was added in 1989, which gave contestants a chance to talk about their commitment to social problems, that the pageant seemed miraculously to have come full circle. For the first time in three decades, girls were identifying with those confident young women onstage talking about issues like AIDS, volunteerism, and older Americans. Suddenly girls all over the country who were gearing up for college were watching the Miss America pageant and saying, "I can do that."

One of them was Katherine Pike, Miss New Hampshire 2001. To her, and to many young women of her generation who have competed in these contests, the goal was never "I want to be Miss America," although that certainly would be nice. Instead, winning was merely a starting point. And perhaps that is what is most different about pageants today than those from even thirty years ago. They are door openers for young women who use them to fund educations and careers they might otherwise never have. After talking to contestants in New Hampshire, I can understand why they don't think twice about strutting across a stage in a swimsuit, learning to walk gracefully in a ball gown, or singing their best rendition of "Colors of the Wind." If the outcome means going to medical school or getting a business degree, they figure it's a small price to pay for a crack at a $25,000 scholarship on the state level—or $50,000 for winning the Miss America title itself.

I've arranged to meet with Katherine Pike late on a weekday afternoon at a café in Manchester. Earlier she called me to tell me she might be late, but she is precisely on time. From the café window, I know it's her right away. She looks as if she has just stepped out of the pages of *Vogue*, but in an understated way. She is petite, dressed in a classic matching beige coat and skirt with white blouse. Her oval chocolate-colored sunglasses are the same tone as her eyes and hair, which is pulled straight back off her face. Despite having spent the day working crowds at public appearances, she is pulled-together and at ease. She is carrying a small wooden case that looks like a treasure box. As she sets it on the table between us, I notice the words "Miss America Pageant" on the lid. Her crown, which she says she carries to all appearances, is inside.

When Katherine won the Miss New Hampshire pageant, the *Union Leader* described her as "speechless." "Life is going to be very difficult for the next year," she told the reporter later on. "I have so much responsibility." That statement probably best sums up Katherine's attitude about her year. "They called my name and I didn't know where to go," she recalls. "I hadn't paid enough attention during the rehearsals. . . . I was sure I wouldn't win. When I was up there, all I could think was, I have to do a really good job—this is really precious. I made up my mind then and there that this would be my priority for the next year."

Originally from Hooksett, Katherine graduated from Wagner College on Staten Island, New York, in 1999 with a degree in theater and speech. She's comfortable in the limelight and a veteran—albeit an unconventional one—of the pageant world. Before winning the Miss Winnipesaukee title in the summer of 2000, she was first runner-up in the same contest, as well as in the Miss Staten Island pageant the year before. She's quick to tell me, however, that she is the last person she ever expected to compete in a pageant. "Women have a stigma they associate with the Miss New Hampshire program if they don't know about it," Katherine tells me. When an acquaintance at the *Union Leader* first suggested that she try it, she says she answered, "I won't walk around in a swimsuit! I'm a feminist!" But when she thought about her tuition bills and the scholarship funds that could pay them, the swimsuit issue didn't seem like such a big deal. "When I first started doing pageants, I could see the professional and personal development I was getting. I was eating healthily, keeping myself fit. I realized, What's antifeminist about that?" she says, shrugging.

After winning the Miss Winnipesaukee title in July 2000, Katherine says she began preparing for the state competition, which would take place the following April. She promoted her child-oriented platform—"extra-curricular activities for a positive social education"—and made local appearances. A few months before the state pageant, she attended the yearly Miss New Hampshire "boot camp," along with the other local pageant winners, where organizers orient the girls about what to expect if they win the state title—mainly that they will spend a lot of time being Miss New

Hampshire. Then the girls receive the pageant rehearsal schedule. With it comes a talk about punctuality, a lack of which could jeopardize their involvement. Rehearsals are held every Sunday in the six weeks prior to the pageant, but they start late enough in the day, Katherine says, "so the girls can go to church."

On the day of the Miss New Hampshire pageant each contestant meets with the panel of five judges, one of which is a former Miss New Hampshire; the rest are judges from other states (state judges are trained through the Miss America organization). Contestants have ten seconds to introduce themselves, ten minutes to answer questions, and ninety seconds to close. "A good interview is ten to fifteen questions," Katherine says. "You have no idea beforehand what the judges are going to ask." On the local level, questions are often about family or school. On the state level, judges want the girls to talk about specific issues related to their career or education goals. "Then you always have the trivia judge," she says. "'Who is the secretary of state?'—that kind of thing."

The morning after the state pageant, a brunch/contract-signing celebration is held for the winner. While the contest is still fresh in her mind, the judges give the new Miss New Hampshire "a very specific critique" to get her ready for the national competition, which lasts about a half hour. During that time she's expected to take notes. "It was rough," Katherine says. The judges told her that her interview went well, but that she would have to stop overusing certain phrases. They told her literally to "jazz up" her song selection (Katherine is a vocalist), add more color to her face, and tone her torso muscles a little tighter. "Then they told me to ditch the high heels I had been told to wear, put on some weight, tone up my legs, and darken my eyebrows. But if one more person tells me about my eyebrows . . . ," she says, laughing.

I ask Katherine why she believes she won the Miss New Hampshire title. Without hesitating, she tells me, "I understood the importance of life experience and I hadn't made pageants my life. I was there to have a good time. . . . I told myself, Just be yourself. It's a role you'll play for a year." But after she won, public appearances started immediately. Soon she found herself grappling with a fundamental issue—staying true to herself. "I could see that I'm a liberal person in a conservative state," she says. "I've tried to find the best in things and to treat everyone with respect. As Miss New Hampshire, you're representing the entire state."

Only four months after winning the state title, Katherine represented New Hampshire at the Miss America pageant in Atlantic City. She had received about $8,000 raised by the annual springtime Miss New Hampshire Ball to buy the extensive wardrobe she needed for the national competition that included everything from "a ton of gowns" to rehearsal clothes to shoes and swimsuits. (Every Miss New Hampshire receives a wardrobe allowance, but the amount varies according to how much is raised by the Miss New Hampshire Ball. Any leftover wardrobe funds are rolled over for the next Miss New Hampshire to use.) Now it was time to pull it all together on the national stage.

Two weeks before the Miss America pageant, Katherine left for Philadelphia, where the contestants would first get to know each other for a few days. Then the group flew to Atlantic City for ten days of posing and rehearsing. Her experience, however, was atypical from that of every other Miss New Hampshire in the pageant's history. That year, the World Trade Center tragedy occurred only a few days before the pageant. The contestants were quarantined for three days while officials decided whether to cancel it. (The contest went on as planned.) Katherine says the girls attended prayer sessions during that time, and didn't do much else.

Pageants have always had a reputation—deserved or not—for being events where prima donnas rule and everyone else tolerates. I ask Katherine what the pageant atmosphere was *really* like in Atlantic City. She says that during daily rehearsals tempers sometimes flared, but that it was generally cooperative. "The night of the pageant you saw the true colors of some people," she says. "Some were completely silent; others broke down when they didn't get into the top twenty. Some were snotty. One, who made the top five, was rude the entire time. Some changed completely after we left Philadelphia for Atlantic City. That was disappointing."

The most difficult thing for Katherine, however, was competing in the talent competition. "It was terrifying," she recalls. "I've never seen so many talented women. I thought most of the contestants would be 'pageant girls,' but they weren't. They were all classic overachievers. We were told we were the most talented group ever. I thought I could compete well. I had done auditions in New York City for years. But it was hard to compete against those women . . . afterward I decided I never wanted to sing in that kind of venue again, in front of eight thousand people and a panel of judges. It took all the fun out of it. Normally I'm nervous before I sing, but it goes away. This time it didn't."

I'm wondering if there was a winner's buzz among the media, as well as the contestants, as the days in Atlantic City ticked by. Katherine explains that there were preliminary competitions every evening with winners announced in each of the four competition categories. The public doesn't see these contests, but the judges do. "The ones who win in the preliminaries tend to make it to the top," Katherine says. "But your self-esteem is on a roller coaster the entire week before the pageant because you're constantly being compared. It's hard not to play mind games with yourself. I was disappointed not to be in the top twenty . . . but the thing that really got me was I wanted to be escorted onstage on national TV with my dad. I did the best I could."

After the Miss America pageant, Katherine came home to continue her whirlwind year that included two hundred public appearances. Every week she was given a list from the state organization office in Derry, which she then coordinated with her part-time job as a marketing specialist. After a while she got used to her chaperone, who accompanied her to every event and helped her manage her time, and to the attention that followed her wherever she went. She got used to wearing panty hose even on the hottest summer days (it's in her contract) and using in public only those products produced by her sponsors. Toward the end of her year, though, as people recognized her more and more, she sometimes found it difficult to be "on" all the time, always to uphold the image of Miss New Hampshire—whether she was going to the grocery store or out to dinner with friends. "I had to remind myself, This is my choice," she says. "But the support I received from people everywhere was amazing. . . . I was so happy to represent this state."

When I ask her what the biggest surprise has been during her role as Miss New Hampshire, she stops for a moment. "I always thought I wanted to be a movie star," she says thoughtfully. "But I realized I just want to be me." She says the experience has taught her to be more tolerant, more patient—that she has learned to "chill out" and accept demands on her time. After all, it's not everyone who gets to sing with the Boston Pops, run with the Olympic Torch, or open a conference for then–New York City mayor Rudy Giuliani, as she has done. "No one ever forgets you're a Miss New Hampshire," she tells me. "There is no better life training, even if you never win a pageant. For poise, confidence, speaking. All those things can only help you in your life."

A few months later, after Katherine had relinquished her crown, I asked her if it had been difficult to give it all up. "It's a weird transition," she said. "My mind was telling me I have to let go." The week before the state pageant, she told me, she had ridden around in her car with her Miss New Hampshire sign in the back window, something she hadn't done all year. "I guess it was my last hurrah," she said, laughing.

. . .

An hour before the Miss Kingston–Miss Seacoast pageant begins, ten well-behaved animal rights activists have gathered in front of the Sad Café in Plaistow. They're protesting that one of the Miss New Hampshire organization's sponsors presents a fur coat to the state pageant winner each year. Near the protesters, a long line has already formed outside the café front door, mostly friends and family of contestants.

Inside, girls are dashing in and out of dressing rooms. Some are still in curlers. From the back of the theater, Dan Tidd, who handles the sound for the show, is testing the system. There's a bit of tension in the air, and I ask emcee Dana Rosengard how it's going. He raises his eyebrows, grins widely, and mouths, "Not well." Taking me aside he says there are so many contestants this year, they've simply run out of time. After each finished her interview, she was fed lunch by Elaine's mom and then transported to the Sad Café for the afternoon rehearsal. But the interviews hadn't finished until 4:00 P.M.

From across the room I wave to Elaine, who has changed into a black ensemble and still—amazingly—appears unruffled, although a little dazed. My husband and I try to stay out of the way. Sitting in the back among a sea of empty folding chairs, we leaf through the program booklet. We recognize some of the girls from previous local pageants we attended in the winter. Overhead, jazz is playing a little too loudly. Girls wearing suits and identical crowns start to gather in a front row. They're local pageant winners, Elaine explained to me earlier, and this is one of the only places they get to wear their crowns. Then my husband starts to chuckle. He points to the "Absolutely No Moshing" signs pinned at various places around the room. He doesn't think it will be a problem.

A few minutes before the pageant starts, the judges file in. Then a glowing Miss Kingston in a red shimmy dress walks with aplomb across the stage waving a final farewell. The girls, looking adult in evening black, crowd onto the tiny stage and introduce themselves one by one, as contestants do in the Miss America contest. Then Dana, who is co-emceeing the show with Elaine's daughter Trisha (she also runs the Miss Riverfest pageant in Manchester), introduces the talent competition. For the next hour, we're treated to a mix of sad-happy love songs, a nicely done hula, a lip-synching number, an expert baton twirler, and quite a few dancers. Despite the bumps during rehearsal, all goes smoothly.

It's a Hollywood moment when, later on, the newly crowned queens, looking more like princesses at this point, pose gracefully side by side as flashes go off all around them. Soon all the girls and their families will head back to Elaine's for a buffet of meatballs, turkey, and Elaine's famous angel food mousse cake. This is when she announces the highest nonfinalist scores, after the winners and runners-up, in the talent and interview competitions. "It gives that little piece of encouragement to those two girls who almost made it to keep trying," she tells me later.

This is also when the judges give Elaine their winners' critique, telling her what each girl did well and what each could do better. It's a process that comes down from the Miss America organization, which allows Elaine to work one-on-one with the judges and then filter the information out slowly to the winners as they prepare for the state competition over the next year. "It helps because the girls might be flying high after they've won," she says. "They need to know they can improve."

A few weeks after the pageant I talk with Dana, who has emceed Elaine's pageant for the last eight years, about the relevance of pageants today and how they still seem to embody the American dream. After all, anyone can become Miss America. Formerly an anchorman and news producer, Dana has been involved in state and local pageant productions as emcee or judge for over fifteen years. For nearly a decade he and Elaine have met for lunch on the same day at the same restaurant in Atlantic City just before the Miss America event. He relishes his involvement in the pageant world. "Working with pageant women is like getting a wonderful subset of the population I have dedicated my professional life to," says Dana, who is now a journalism professor at the University of Memphis in Tennessee. "College-age, responsible, hopeful young people."

Dana has been to the Miss America contest many times, and I ask him about this country's enduring fascination with it as pageantry's grande dame. "The Miss America pageant is a heck of a television show," he answers. "It's good, old-fashioned, clean, American fun. . . . those fifty-one women represent thousands of others who are just as bright, talented, articulate, wide-eyed, fresh-faced, honest . . . and then there remains many a 'beauty queen' in the public view today to remind us of how these pageants can propel women to otherwise unattainable heights." He goes through a short list of prominent professional women who got their start onstage and in television by being in the right place at the right time—in pageants. "The public knows this," he says. "Pageants help make dreams come true."

A few weeks earlier at Elaine's kitchen counter, Dana had begun to talk about "the path to Miss America" starting in living rooms like Elaine's all over the country. I ask him to expound on that. "I think many people think it's all like the Miss America pageant they see on television," he tells me. "Obviously, it's not. What's so great about this program is that it doesn't matter how big the stage is or how many contestants there are; the fact remains that the scholarship dollars are still handed out. Women in New Hampshire are so lucky. Think about it. Your state ranks in the top ten in the entire country for scholarship dollars awarded."

"Elaine, through her program, is all about the girls," he continues. "There's nothing fancy about her living room or about the Sad Café, nothing extravagant about her production or her postpageant party. It's done from her heart. Volunteers like myself help her do it from our hearts. . . . Elaine represents the best in volunteerism and she's making a great contribution to our potential future leaders. People like her help make the Miss America program happen, which hands out money, which pays for education, which allows young women to be whatever they dream of being. As a man, I can tell you I'm jealous as hell."

# 3

## UNH Violin Craftsmanship Institute

## "Stringed Instruments Are Like Our Own Vocal Cords"

*I*n a classroom in Putnam Hall at the University of New Hampshire, two long rows of workbenches stretch across the floor. Twelve desk lamps mark the workplaces of students, who on this warm midsummer morning are huddled around instructor Karl Roy. Sitting at one of the benches he asks, in accented English, "Why should you not do this?" pointing to the top piece of a violin. No one says a word. As he demonstrates what went wrong, some students take photos with digital cameras. When he's done, he goes to the next workplace and then the next, critiquing and demonstrating like a physician on morning rounds with a pack of residents.

It's the same scene every weekday morning while the one-month UNH Violin Craftsmanship Institute, run by the Division of Continuing Education, is in session. Every summer since 1973 students from all over the country, as well as the world, have traveled to New Hampshire to learn the sixteenth-century craft of violin making from the institute's instructors, who are widely regarded as the best in their fields. German master violin maker Karl Roy, former director of the 150-year-old Bavarian State School of Violin Making—the oldest and most acclaimed in the world—is one of the institute's masters.

In 1973, a UNH continuing education director visited Karl's school in Germany hoping to recruit faculty for a summer violin repair workshop. At that time, there was no place at UNH for music students to take their stringed instruments for repair, and the university thought it made sense to establish a program for that purpose. Karl didn't have any faculty to lend, but he offered to teach a course for music students on violin repair himself. The university eagerly took him up on the offer, and gradually the program grew into what it is now—a month of intensive one-week classes taught by three instructors and two teaching assistants covering violin and bow making, as well as repair. Classes function like workshops, with instructors roving from student to student, tutoring each at their own skill level.

Many of the 150 students who attend the program annually are professionals in the violin and bow crafts, who come to UNH to sharpen their skills. The rest are often from precision-oriented day jobs in fields like medicine, aviation, computers, and engineering, who are gradually learning violin or bow making with the hope of one day opening their own shops. What makes the Violin Craftsmanship Institute unique is that it's the only place in the country—and many say the world—where professionals, as well as career changers, can learn and practice their craft without having to attend a year-round, full-time program or sacrifice quality of instruction. Many return year after year, but Karl is clear with his students that it takes a long time to develop proficiency. "It's hard to convince students that violin making can't be done the American way," he tells me when he's through with the morning critique. "You can't just read a book about it and be done with it. It takes many years of practice to build a satisfying instrument."

Karl is in his early seventies, fit and trim in a powder blue polo shirt tucked tightly into freshly laundered jeans. He's a polite man with old-world manners who first learned violin making in his late teens from his father-in-law in Mittenwald, Germany, where he grew up and still lives. The town has the special distinction of being called the "Village of a Thousand Violins," because it continues to carry out a 350-year tradition of violin making. The story goes that in the mid–seventeenth century, Mittenwald was on the brink of economic collapse when an international trade route moved away. During the crisis, a local farmer sent his son to Italy to learn violin making from the men who called Antonio Stradivari, that most famous of violin makers, a colleague. The young man eventually returned and taught the skill to townspeople, who took to it so readily that within a short time half the town was making violins. This wasn't completely by accident, however. The types of wood needed to make violins—spruce and maple—grew in abundance nearby.

In Germany, a violin maker's training, like all other crafts, is regulated by law. You start out as an apprentice in a school for three or so years, take a state exam, then work for four or five additional years under a master. You can then take an additional state exam to earn a master's diploma, which, if you pass, permits you to open a shop and use the title of master violin maker. To Americans, where no certification is needed to make stringed instruments, this may seem restrictive, but Karl assures me it is not. The system ensures that high standards dominate—both in violin-making shops as well as in schools. For example, besides learning technique, students at the Mittenwald school study music theory and history, instrument repair, business, bow making, and how to play the instruments themselves. With such extensive training, it's no wonder that German violin makers are considered the best in the world.

When I ask Karl, who has taught at the UNH Violin Craftsmanship Institute every summer since 1974, how he continues to perfect his craft, he is puzzled. "Perfect?" he asks, as though the idea were preposterous. "I continue to learn by doing, by teaching," he says. "I tell my students that 50 percent of violin making is training the eyes. They first learn to recognize what is nice and what is not nice. First, it must be in the head. Then the hands will follow and know what to do." Karl uses a teaching method based on repetition, requiring students to practice over and over until they are proficient enough to replicate results consistently. In between, he peppers his classes with history and theory, which students say they enjoy as much as his demonstrations of technique.

This is easy to understand. The history of the violin is a story of evolution that begins centuries before Christ and eventually ends with the emergence of the instrument in sixteenth-century Italy. It was in the northern cities of Cremona, Brescia, and Venice that the violin appears to have evolved from several stringed instruments from the folk tradition, which had already been around for hundreds of years. "You have to understand that violin makers didn't one day sit down and say, 'Today I will make a violin,'" Karl explains. "There were many predecessors to the violin, such as the lira da gamba. Today's violin developed from the early fiddles from medieval times. The outline was like an egg. Then the center got narrower to make room for the bow."

"But the setup of violins made in the early sixteenth century was different from what you see today because the musical requirements at that time were lower," he continues. "Violins were originally made for chamber music, but as soon as the public got access to public concerts and opera houses in the early 1800s the instruments had to fill bigger halls. The audience requested a louder sound, but please remember that louder doesn't always mean better." Violin makers found they could accommodate these new requirements by modifying the neck angle and using different types of strings. Karl says this is what brought the violin closer to its appearance today.

In the well-established world of violin making, you'll find no academicians studying how to build a better violin. It's a mature craft that draws from time-tested methods slowly refined into those used today. Constructing a violin starts with a design for the instrument, which considers not only how it will look but also how it will sound. Karl creates his own violin patterns, as do most good makers, which he bases on older molds. He is careful to point out, however, that not everything old is good. "You have to be experienced enough not to hang onto half of a millimeter, to know what to do and not do. We are not slavish to conventional designs." When it comes down to it, he says, "musicians are just looking for a good-sounding instrument. They know little about workmanship. There is no such thing as a certain type of violin that is most popular."

In the United States there are four full-time programs in violin making, but only a handful of American makers who have earned international recognition for their work. Karl often judges at prestigious violin-making competitions around the world, and through them he has had the opportunity to examine his craft from many cultural angles. I ask him if there is a difference between the way American and German violin makers build their instruments. Yes, he says, Americans use more power tools and rely less on their own hands to shape and develop the instrument. In Germany, where more violins are produced than anywhere else in the world, makers sit at a small workbench and use only a modest-size electric tool, such as a band saw, and a few hand tools. I suggest the discrepancy may be due partly to the fact that the old-world methods of the German makers haven't always been transferred to makers in the United States. "Modern masters know what they are doing, but it is not written down anywhere," Karl agrees.

In the days of the Italian masters, all violins were handcrafted, but that is not so today. Experts say that five to six thousand better-than-average-quality instruments are turned out by hand each year, costing anywhere between $8,000 and $20,000. If you compare that to the one million "cookie-cutter" violins produced annually by manufacturers at an average price of $600, you'll understand why the commercial variety is especially popular in school programs. The difference in quality, however, is like the difference between a sculpture and a trinket made from a mold. "We are not interested in violin manufacturers," Karl says, scowling. "Before the Communists, there was a place in Saxony"—an area formerly part of East Germany—"that produced—and I say 'produced,' not made—so many violins for export to the United States that they had their own U.S. consulate." Nowadays, it's the Asian countries that have stepped up demand by buying commercially made violins for educational programs almost as quickly as manufacturers can produce them.

Karl and I are interrupted by a student with a question. Squinting through his spectacles, Karl inspects the thin metal template she hands to him and points to a section of it. "Try to see it please," he tells her, and explains what he wants her to change. Then he asks her to repeat his explanation, which she does, although somewhat hesitatingly. "I would open the curve a little more," he continues. "Otherwise it becomes visually longer, and that becomes a lack of elegance. It's a training of the eyes." She nods, but still looks puzzled. Handing the template back to her, he says, "In other words, move it a little this way."

When you think about it, it makes sense that the Violin Craftsmanship Institute is located in New Hampshire. This state has a long history of appreciation for wood quality through furniture making and other crafts. Germans have always nurtured a similar appreciation, which they have channeled into one of the strongest traditions of wood craftsmanship in the world. In violin making, the quality of the wood dictates the quality of the instrument. It affects the entire instrument—from the way it vibrates to the actual sound it produces.

Over the past four hundred years, makers have figured out that the ideal wood combination for a violin is spruce for the top and maple for the other parts. Together, these woods possess the strength, elasticity, endurance, beauty, and weight needed to produce a superior sound. But if you ask a violin maker about the relationship between the wood and the acoustical results of his work, he will probably respond in one of two ways: passionately because he knows how to play the instrument, or blankly because he does not. Karl is in the former category and explains that, as a violin maker, if you don't know how a violin should sound, it would be fairly difficult to make a good one. Aesthetics are important, he acknowledges, but if you can't play the instrument, you may as well hang it on a wall.

I ask Karl to talk to me about wood and acoustics, expecting a sermon on the science of sound. He has, after all, authored two books that deal specifically with this topic. "Why can a beautiful old, expensive violin be copied in form to the finest detail, yet not sound like the original? The wood factor cannot be denied," he writes in *Violin Woods: A New Look* (Karl researched the book with a forest resources professor at UNH). Instead, he tells me that "acoustics is a simple thing. The people who research acoustics only study what is happening in the air, not what is happening on the ground. This is wrong." In the seventeenth century, he explains, the Austrian violin maker Jacobus Stainer achieved a higher quality of sound with his instruments than the Mittenwald makers had

Master Violin Maker Horst Kloss adjusts the cello of a client in his Needham, Massachusetts, workshop. (Courtesy of Horst Kloss.)

ever reached. To the eye, however, the materials used by Stainer were precisely the same.

To determine the difference, Karl and his colleagues studied various cuts and types of wood under a micro-microscope. The conclusion? "Stainer had no secrets," says Karl, who subsequently published the results. "The German makers cut their trees in the winter, when the trees were low in sap, but Stainer's wood, which was also cut in winter, was floated to him down the river Inn. When we looked at what happened to the wood when it floated, we found that it became light and could vibrate like the wing of an aircraft. Our wood, on the other hand, became strong and stiff like concrete after it was cut. It could never be softened again, because the cell pits harden within a few weeks of cutting the trees."

The Italians of Cremona, who created what are now the most highly valued violins in the world, also received their materials from floated woods. "And that was the answer," Karl continues. "You can hear the difference." Today in Mittenwald, makers follow Stainer's process for seasoning wood. They still cut their trees in winter when sap is low, but then they float the logs for a few weeks in the river Isar, cut them into pieces, and stack them away from the sun and wind, which can crack the wood, to allow them to season for a few months. After this, the wood can be used for up to a year.

Karl says he doesn't have time to make violins today, but his two sons are both master makers. When I ask him how many instruments they might make in a year, he scolds me. "There you are asking for statistics again," he says. "A maker finishes one, then starts the next. It's steady work. It's impossible to say how long it takes to make a violin. No one in Mittenwald makes violins on a production line." But is the skill more of an art or a craft? I prod him. Pausing, he answers, "I never thought of it that way. I think it's a little of both." He is, in fact, correct. The German word for art — *kunst* — is derived from the word *kunnen* — to do.

To illustrate the point, he tells me a violin makers' joke. "There was a musician who took his violin to a maker and said, 'It doesn't sound very good. Can you do something?' So the maker adjusted the sound post slightly." Karl adjusts a phantom sound post and continues. "The musician played and said, 'Yes, this is good,' and went home. The next day he returned. 'We are almost there,' he told the maker. 'But can you adjust it a little more?' This time the maker held his hand over the bridge and turned his back, pretending to make a change. 'Oh, this is perfect!' the musician exclaimed, but the following day he returned again. 'I really think there is something wrong, because it doesn't sound right,' and he handed the violin to the maker. 'Come back in two weeks, but not before,' the maker told him seriously. 'I will need a lot of time to test it and adjust it.' The maker put the violin in his closet and didn't touch it again. Two weeks later, the musician returned and played his violin. 'Oh, now you've got it exactly!' he told the maker." Karl's eyes twinkle. "And then, of course, the musician was presented with a very high bill."

Several of Karl's students are now standing behind him, enjoying their instructor's antics, but also waiting for answers. I'm sure that we are finished, but he leads me to a corner of the classroom and opens a large black instrument case standing about four feet tall. Gently he lifts out a soft brown, curvaceous instrument. It has sloping shoulders, a thick neck, and two complete sets of strings, one more or less on top of the other. He tells me it's in the Renaissance-era viola da gamba family, which is more of a cousin to the violin than a direct descendant (translated from Italian it means "leg viol," because, similar to a cello, it is played while seated with the instrument held in place by the knees). This one has an intricately carved gargoyle-like head at the end of the neck. Karl says he made the instrument thirty years ago and sculpted the end piece by hand.

The instrument causes a firestorm in the classroom. Half the students rush over to take photographs, while the other half stand back admiring the piece. It is so beautiful that, for me, the line between art and craft instantly blurs. Posing with the instrument, Karl encourages his students. "You see, if you can build a violin, you must be able to make all types of stringed instruments."

In the classroom next door, a thin man with stick-straight posture is conducting a lesson on restoring and repairing violins. Also a native of Mittenwald, and a graduate of the same school Karl Roy directed for years, Horst Kloss manages his classroom like a laboratory. "I treat everyone as a full professional," he tells me. "I push them hard in a constructive way." Indeed, when he enters the room, students fall silent. "I think they breathe a sigh of relief when I'm out of earshot," he chuckles. "But they all need to walk away with the knowledge and know-how. When they go home, they know what to do."

Like Karl, Horst emphasizes process over spot problem-solving. He started teaching with the Violin Craftsmanship Institute in the mid-1990s out of concern that the lack of standards for violin making in the United States was creating an excess of inferior instruments. As a master in his profession, he felt a kind of duty to step in and ensure that at least the students at UNH would learn his craft as it should be taught. Respect is a key word with him: respect for his students, respect for the instruments, respect for the instructor. "I have twelve students and there are twelve different approaches," he says.

Since he was fourteen, Horst has been studying violin making and restoration. When he was growing up, he says, there were so many violin shops in his town—fifty to sixty in a town of only eight thousand people—that he would hear violins playing on any street he walked down. "Violins were not pieces that you hung over a mantle," he tells me. "The purpose was so much greater. Being exposed to this environment I thought, I would like to do that." In 1964, when he was twenty, he came to the United States to continue his violin-making studies at a well-known shop in Chicago, eventually receiving his master's diploma with high honors from the Mittenwald school. Now nearly sixty, he has cared for many important historic stringed-instrument collections, including those of the Boston Museum of Fine Arts, and restored all types of stringed instruments dating from the sixteenth century. He works with musicians from many countries, both well known and not so, who come to him because he is the only one they feel they can trust with instruments that are sometimes valued at several hundred thousand dollars.

Later I visit Horst at his workshop, a small building behind his home in Needham, Massachusetts, where he works alone and runs his business. At the top of a narrow staircase we enter a medium-size, perfectly square room grounded by a well-worn red Oriental carpet and strung along three sides with wire. At first I don't take it in, but hanging from the wire is an astonishing array of over a hundred violins in many shades of reddish brown. There is life in this room, a definite energy that emanates from the instruments themselves. Under a window, Horst has fashioned a work area where he has neatly lined up his tools, all within reach. A violin stripped of its accessories lies naked on the bench. Without using too much imagination, I envision that this is what a violin maker's workshop probably looked like two hundred years ago.

For most of my life I have found the violin enigmatic, and judging by movies like *The Red Violin,* which tells the story of ownership behind a mysterious, centuries-old violin, so have many others. I have never studied the instrument, but my mother attempted it years ago and lamented its difficulty. Superstar violinist Itzhak Perlman has compared the complexity of playing the piano to that of the violin, concluding, "There is no comparison . . . the problem is the difficulty of playing the violin."

Horst is formally trained to play the violin, bass, and cello, but views the roles of the player and maker as interwoven. The two work together to coax the most pleasing sounds out of instruments that are best described as demanding. "Anyone who owns or works on a violin is only its caretaker. You are part of that instrument's life for a short time," he explains. "In my own work as a maker and restorer—there is so much to it. I listen to the player's concerns and then use this information to adjust the instrument acoustically so that it excites the musician. When the player plays, the instrument should sing, allowing the player to focus on the music. In the end, a successful player pleases the audience, and the triangle is complete—restorer, player, audience."

Many of Horst's clients are violinists with well-known orchestras who own several violins—some costing as much as a million dollars—that they use for different purposes. For example, one may be for teaching, another for outdoor concerts, and still another for playing in the orchestra. At this level, all are irreplaceable. When musicians bring their instruments to Horst, he says it is his responsibility to determine the maximum sound potential of each instrument and to draw it out. The point is neither to add anything nor to take anything away, but to work with what is there in the best interest of the instrument. To do otherwise could lead to tonal changes that could alter the instrument's character and, some might even say, its very soul.

"There's much more to it than the bow touching the strings," Horst says, explaining how sound is created in a violin. "With wind instruments the sound is created by manipulating the valves for air movement. On a classical bowed, stringed instrument the process of producing sound is more lengthy. The coarseness of the bow hair and stickiness of the rosin sets the strings in motion. This vibrating motion sets the bridge"—the raised part on the front that keeps the strings separated—"into a rocking motion, which involves the bass bar and sound post in the interior of the instrument. In the end the top and back create a back-and-forth movement of air. The sound is a result of acoustical manipulation."

Keeping an expensive violin that is used frequently in good condition requires the same kind of routine care as maintaining, for example, a car. Similar to a car, whose problems are often diagnosed by listening to the sound of its engine, a violin undergoes frequent adjustments that are, in fact, often created by the weather. In the North, where a violin's wood contracts in winter and expands in summer, there is always a danger of cracking, so twice a year, for many of his clients, Horst changes the sound post as well as the bridge. "In the winter, the instrument doesn't ring," Horst explains. "The upper strings scream. The vibration pattern isn't at the maximum. The sound is uneven. It doesn't speak as easily. And all that has ramifications for the player."

Beyond routine repairs and adjustments, Horst also restores violins, which can take anywhere from a few weeks to several months depending on the extent of damage. For example, if an accident has occurred Horst works with the musician to re-create the event mentally so that he can visualize exactly how the wood splintered. Then he travels backward through the accident to "figure out the system" and establish a plan for restoring the instrument to its original condition. When he understands what happened, he'll carefully take the instrument apart. A violin's wood is so thin and fragile, however, that it can be unstable to work with unless he creates a mold for the instrument's top. This allows him to do two things: he can rebuild and reglue the edges without damaging them, and he can completely reshape a deformed top. In the latter case, the top is moistened, placed on the mold, and held there by small sandbags for several weeks, allowing it gradually to take the shape of the mold. When the top is completely dry, Horst removes it and can then complete the repairs without causing further damage.

As we talk, it's clear that the materials Horst uses are important. First there's the glue. The issue here is that it has to be strong enough to hold the instrument together, but pliant enough to allow the restorer to open the instrument with a fine knife. The glue also must have the correct acidity so that it doesn't discolor over time. Most restorers today use a hide glue similar to what has been used for hundreds of years, which they apply thinly around the edges of the violin. Varnish is another factor. The most transparent varnishes are best, but Horst says they also must have an elasticity that is in harmony with the elasticity of the wood. "If the varnish is too hard and brittle, the sound won't be rich," he says. "If it is too heavy, thick, or dense, it won't let the instrument open up and breathe. You have to know what you need to make the instrument do what it has to do."

When violin makers complete a new instrument, they expect it to last long into the future. I'm curious, though, about the differences between new and antique violins. With the five hundred or so remaining Stradivari violins often fetching stratospheric prices, I ask Horst if it's because the quality is better than modern ones. The more a violin is played, he tells me, the better the sound quality, which is why the older ones are so valued by musicians. A mature violin has "learned" what vibrations are natural from different parts of itself, but with new violins, he explains, "the wood doesn't yet know what to do. There's a breaking-in period, and after that the sound becomes smoother and smoother. The whole violin begins to work together to produce harmonious sounds."

I ask Horst what it feels like to hear a musician play an instrument he has created. "It's exhilarating," he tells me. "You become like a parent watching them make discoveries and you are happy for them." And if he were buying a violin today, how would he choose it? "I would ask, What are my needs?" he says. "Am I a soloist, a chamber player, a symphony player? Then I'd have a choice between an antique, which is more expensive, and a modern violin. After that, I'd ask a lot of questions."

Walking over to the side of the room, he brings back two violins and holds them by the neck in front of me. "Which is the better instrument?"

he asks. The one in his left hand is reddish and slighter thicker in the belly than the other. It looks a bit full of itself, sassy even. The one in his right hand is a rich chestnut brown, its wood finely marbled. It appears to have settled into itself, as if it no longer needs to impress. I pick that one, although I have no idea of its quality or age. "I don't need to say anything to you and you can see which is the better instrument," he answers, obviously pleased.

It was built in 1730.

If Lynn Hannings and Horst Kloss compared the atmosphere of their classrooms at the Violin Craftsmanship Institute, they would probably joke that one follows a natural flow (the bow makers) and the other follows a natural order (the restorers). But like Horst, Lynn, who has been teaching bow making here for almost twenty years, doesn't want her students to imagine they can learn it all in one summer. "That would create a great network of underdeveloped bow makers," she says. "It would be irresponsible for me to do that. The people who come back year after year have a really clear love of bow making."

Lynn's teaching emphasis is helping her students to make a connection to the wood, and she says the way she advises each student is different. "Confidence is a big factor in this," she tells me. "They need to believe there's a place for them whatever level they are at. They need to feel comfortable with the fact that it takes time to learn. . . . to see a student struggle with what we call 'a bowlike object' that by the end of the class makes music—it's the most profound thing to watch their pride. I'm honored to be part of that tradition."

Most of the year Lynn creates bows in her workshop, which is located in a Maine village about an hour's drive from Portland. She's a native New Yorker, but moved to Maine close to thirty-five years ago to become a bassist in the Portland Symphony Orchestra and is still a member. When I tell her I couldn't imagine trying to discuss the violin without also covering the bow, she concurs. "After all," she says, smiling, "unless you have a bow, it's a banjo!"

Similar to working with violins, bow making requires the same kind of patience, precision, and attention to detail. It takes two to three weeks to make one bow, and Lynn is able to make only about twenty-five of them each year. But I'm curious how someone would come to this specialized profession, so I ask her, "Why bows?" In high school, she explains, when she began studying to become a professional bassist, she was already interested in bows. When she moved to Maine she found herself spending an inordinate amount of time traveling back and forth to a bow maker in Boston for adjustments and decided she would learn the craft herself. "From the moment I started doing this, I knew it was the right thing," she says.

We talk for a while about the sound of stringed instruments and the differences between them: the bass and cello being smooth, mellow, sometimes full of longing. The violin, though, can be tense, sharp, urgent—or warm and inviting. "Stringed instruments are like our own vocal cords," Lynn says. "There is something very human about them. With other instruments, you have to start and then stop to breathe. The music is constantly being chopped up. But with stringed instruments, the sound is sustained, similar to our vocal chords." Orchestras, she says, stagger the sound of the stringed instruments so that there is no interruption. "It's very powerful to be able to hold that sound."

Just as the Italians refined violin making, it was the French who refined the bow-making process in eighteenth-century Mirecourt, France. "Surprisingly, bows have changed very little since then," says Lynn, who once studied the French bow-making tradition in Paris on a Fulbright scholarship. "All the things we think of as modern changes occurred around 1750." It was around that time that bow makers started using the reddish wood of the rare pernambuco, a tree that now grows only within a fifty-square-mile area in a mountainous region of Brazil. Bow makers today still use pernambuco, which is highly valued for its exceptional density and flexibility, but with so little available and constant demand, depletion is an ongoing threat. Lynn tells me bow makers worldwide are acutely aware of the issue and have formed the International Pernambuco Conservation Initiative, in which she is heavily involved, to promote the sustainability of this tree well into the future. "In my mind, the cells of our body connect to the cells of the wood," she tells me. "We need to be very responsible in how we use these materials."

Besides the wood, another essential component of a bow is the horsehair that produces the familiar squealing sound when rubbed across a violin's strings. The number of hairs strung on a bow depends on a complicated balance of length and weight between the violin and the bow, although the average number is 150. "Less than that and the sound gets a little skimpy," Lynn says. "More than that and the sound can be muted." In the 1970s, bow makers used horsehair from Siberian horse tails because the strands were three feet long, strong, and resilient. But by the time an order of the hair made its way to Lynn's doorstep, it had more than doubled in price to about $1,000 a pound. Now, Lynn says, because trade relations with China have improved, she can get the same kind of hair for about $400 a pound.

Each bow a bow maker constructs is individually crafted and possesses characteristics unique unto itself, according to many factors. These include the acoustic properties and strength of the piece of wood used to make the bow, the weight of the bow, and the degree of camber—or bend—in the stick. "You can take six bows that look exactly alike, and each will produce a different sound," Lynn says. Another bow maker I spoke to explained the phenomenon this way: one bow might bring out the sound of the violin, resonating with the vibrations of the instrument, while another might absorb the vibrations, and thus reduce the clarity and volume of sound.

For this reason, the bow a musician chooses to use depends to a great extent on the type of music that will be played with it. Most professionals normally work with two to four bows and would likely choose, for example, a lighter-weight bow to play baroque music because it would be more responsive when playing the faster sections of music. The sound the musician would be aiming for would be smooth and sweet. Bows used to play modern music, which often requires a more aggressive approach as well as a greater physical effort by the musician, are often heavier and stiffer thus creating a greater volume of sound. In general, Lynn explains, "the bow has to be like a diving board. It has to spring back. There can't be any bumps along the way. The curvature of the bow has to be right. It can look right, but unless the curvature is uniform, it will affect the playing of the bow."

Several years ago, Lynn returned to school to study occupational therapy because she wanted to better understand the physiological factors around musicians' injuries. She had suffered from tendinitis in her shoulders for years, but assumed the problem was her. It had never occurred to her that the culprit was her bow. She now designs ergonomically correct bows that work with a musician's body. "Musicians hurt all the time," Lynn says. "I'd say up to 85 percent of them play in constant pain. But they're quiet about it because it can threaten their place in the orchestra. Musicians would hate it that I'm talking about this at all."

If a bow isn't balanced properly, it can put undue stress on the smaller bones and muscles in the hands and wrists, creating a similar imbalance inside the body. "It can be a fight every day for the musician to use their bow, and it shouldn't be that way," Lynn explains. "Changing the weight of the bow by only one gram—that's about four paper clips—can totally change the musician's approach to the instrument and can dramatically influence the musician's health." Interestingly, the music world draws from the sports medicine field to catch injuries early—or prevent them altogether—so that professional musicians, who hold their instruments in the same position and use repetitive movements for hours every day, can overcome injuries and play longer into their careers. "The musician is most important, not the bow," Lynn says. "It's fitting the bow to the musician."

Back in the classroom, Lynn says she spends a lot of time on ergonomics, but also teaches students that focusing on technical strides—or even the skill of bow making—is not enough. "You can make a beautiful bow that's a thing like a table or a chair," she says. "But I would rather have a bow made with inferior materials that has soul, than a work of art that doesn't." Like Karl and Horst, she says she's been fortunate in her career to have studied with people who have helped her develop her skill, as well as a keen appreciation for carrying on the tradition of instrument making. "I've had passionate teachers who committed their lives to this art and brought such joy to it," she tells me. "They've inspired me with the attitude to pass that on. It's my responsibility. I'm the next generation."

# 4

## Winnipesaukee Flagship Corp.

### "If It's Tuesday, Turn Right"

*A*t 10:55 on a Friday morning, postal clerk Lesley Watson is busy in the front of the mail boat sorting packages. Skipper Leo O'Connell stands near the entryway greeting passengers, joking with them as they board the *Sophie C.* Stringy white clouds stretch overhead in a sky that's as blue as July, though it's a dry, eighty-degree day in mid-September. The crowds of summer are gone, and today Lake Winnipesaukee is quiet.

The *Sophie C.* can seat 125 people, but this morning there are only about 60, a die-hard bunch who came out for the mail boat's last run of the season. At 11:00 A.M. sharp, the skipper gives the horn five quick toots. The sharp smell of diesel permeates the wheelhouse, the command center at the front of the boat, as we slowly pull away from the dock at Weirs Beach.

For the next two hours, we'll meander along a southerly route, dropping off and picking up mail at eleven island stops. In midseason, when the summer camps are active, Lesley sorts 500 envelopes and packages a day on board, and picks up 500 more. In an average season, she tells me, she sorts and delivers 40,000 pieces of mail. This number sounds astronomical to me, but I notice that today the postal meter reads 39,720.

The *Sophie C.* is the only floating post office on an inland body of water in the United States. She's also the smallest post office in the United States and has become something of a tourist attraction in her own right in recent years. Last year, for example, passenger numbers were up by 25 percent. Crew members are continually surprised by visitors from as far away as California who show them stories about the mail boat clipped from local newspapers. While there is limited seating inside the boat, most people scramble to the blue plastic seats on top to enjoy panoramic views of

(Courtesy New Hampshire Historical Society.)

the seventy-two-square-mile lake and, on a clear day, the gently rolling foothills of the White Mountains in the distance.

The Winnipesaukee Flagship Corp., whose three-boat fleet also includes the M/S *Mount Washington* and the *Sophie C.*'s sister ship, the *Doris E.*, picked up the mail route as a contractor to the U.S. Postal Service in 1969. (Back then, it cost just six cents to mail a letter.) The contract wasn't new, though. A floating post office of one type or another has been in service on the lake since 1892. The *Sophie C.* is only the sixth vessel since then to continue the venerable tradition of delivering mail seasonally to island residents.

Built in 1945 by Boston General Ship & Engine Works, *Sophie C.*'s first assignment was shuttling passengers between Wolfeboro and Weirs Beach—a job she did well for almost twenty-five years before being recruited for mail service. She's a workhorse of a boat, seventy-six feet long with an iron and steel, fully fireproof hull. When she plies through the water at full tilt, drafting six feet and creating a wide wake behind her, she feels solid and smooth. A new 365-horsepower engine was installed in 1988, and she can now cruise along at speeds of up to seventeen miles per hour.

U.S. Postal Service signs are posted prominently on her white hull, as well as inside. There is no question about *Sophie C.*'s mission.

This is Lesley's first year as the mail boat's postal clerk, and now, at the end of summer, she is deeply tanned below her knees and elbows. Smiling into the sun, she says she likes the job just fine. From a nook on the right side of the wheelhouse that's barely large enough for her to stand in, she humorously shows me how she daily sorts five three-foot sacks of mail. It's difficult to hear her above the noise of the engine and the skipper's running tour of the islands over the boat's speaker. "People love the postmark," she yells, holding up an envelope displaying the "Laconia, NH, U.S. Mail Boat Sophie C." cancellation. "Last week I marked a hundred wedding invitations."

From another, even smaller nook, she weighs packages and large envelopes on an old, slightly rusted postal scale, last calibrated on June 16, the first day of this season. Stashed on either side of the scale are the tools of her trade: postal rate cards, tape, postcards, and a cardboard box neatly displaying a wide assortment of black-handled postal stamps. "It's a whole lot of work to get and sort the mail every day. Then it's like eleven social events when we make each stop," Lesley says, tucking a loose tuft of glossy black hair under her bright blue sun visor.

We're approaching our first stop, Bear Island, the second largest of Lake Winnipesaukee's estimated 244 islands (the precise number is hotly debated among lake dwellers). Twenty people are waiting on the dock for the boat's arrival, but Lesley tells me it's triple that in the middle of summer. That's when it's like a festival every day, she says, with kids holding tag sales on card tables and dogs following her around, begging for the biscuits she keeps in the front pockets of her navy blue shorts. It might be busier in the summer, but the folks who are still on the islands after Labor Day are what many in the region call "the true islanders."

Lesley ties the boat to the dock and walks purposefully with her overloaded mail crate toward a wall of sixty-four somewhat battered mailboxes. Some display names, others are numbered, but quite a few don't have any markings at all. When I ask Lesley how she knows which boxes belong to whom, she just smiles. Working quickly, she returns to a small crowd of Bear Islanders waiting for her. They've come on board to buy postal supplies, water, chips, or ice cream. A few gather in front of the soft-drink machine, where a friendly, handwritten sign reminds them: "This machine chokes if you use wet bills—please use dry money."

After ten minutes, the boat is ready to move on to the next stop, but behind us is a strange sight. Next to each of the eight or so posts attached to the dock are boys and girls perched to dive. As the boat pulls away, they jump with great fanfare into the boat's wake while everyone—on the boat and off—cheers loudly. "The kids come early to stake a claim to a post and then jump," Lesley explains, laughing. "It's a tradition that's been going on for years. No one can remember when, or why, it started."

Skipper O'Connell grins widely as he revs the motor gently for effect. At the helm, he cuts an impressive figure in aviator glasses and an all-white uniform with three gold bars on each shoulder. He isn't particularly tall, but his posture is impeccable. Few people know the lake as well as the skipper. He spent most of his boyhood summers at his grandparents' camp on the northwestern edge of the lake, an area defined by thin fingers of land that present navigational challenges to even the most capable sailors. He says he became so intrigued with navigation that, one summer, he took out a map of the lake, alphabetized each square inch, and memorized every single angle and feature on it. "I'm addicted to this lake," he tells me, as he looks out on the water. To this day, he knows precisely where he is only by look-ing at the islands and shoreline around him.

"There are over a thousand navigational markers on this lake and you have to know where all of them are. But you also have to be able to navigate without markers because they can move, like the one over there," he says, pointing to one nearby that's a smidgen to the right of the clearly visible rock below it. "Navigating at night on this lake is like figuring out different shades of black." Experienced Winnipesaukee sailors will recognize that as an understatement. With so many small islands, depth changes ranging up to 213 feet, and a crowded boating landscape, some call Lake Winnipesaukee one of the most difficult lakes to navigate anywhere—day or night.

The final stops on the route are simple handoffs, where Lesley tosses a mailbag to someone on a private dock. Precisely two hours after we left it, Weirs Beach looms ahead. When the boat lightly bumps the dock, Lesley jumps out and ties the boat against it. Leo stands again at the door of the wheelhouse, well positioned to thank each passenger as they file out. An older man pats him gently on the back. "Lucky for you I was on board to help you along today," he says. Leo laughs heartily. He knows the routine. Down the plank, Lesley hands everyone a postcard, each stamped with the coveted *Sophie C.* cancellation.

Jim Morash's office is cramped but neat, hidden behind the also cramped but neat bustling ticket office of the Winnipesaukee Flagship Corp. Fortyish, he's a tall man with a trim mustache that defies his boyish looks. Today he is dressed in Navy-style whites—white chinos, white polo shirt, immaculately clean white sneakers. "I'm originally from Vermont, so I call myself a fourth generation tourist. My heritage on this lake goes back a hundred years," he tells me. Coming from the general manager of the company that operates the M/S *Mount Washington,* that statement carries weight. Up here, it doesn't matter if you're a native of the lake, just as long as it's in your blood.

Like Leo O'Connell, Jim spent his childhood summers at a family camp on Lake Winnipesaukee. During college summers he worked as a deckhand on the M/S *Mount Washington,* studying business and history the rest of the year. He likes working with kids and says he briefly considered a career as a history teacher. But in the end it was the business of history that called to him the loudest. Over the next twenty years, he steadfastly worked his way up the ranks of the Winnipesaukee Flagship Corp. doing a variety of jobs—from marketing to learning to pilot the fleet. He is immensely proud of the fact that he is the only former deckhand ever to make it to general manager, which he was promoted to in 1999. He is also one of only three captains who operate "the *Mount,*" as the M/S *Mount Washington* is affectionately called by everyone around here.

Jim uses one word to describe the 130-year-old company he manages: "mature." But it's sometimes been hard for the company to stay current in a state where everybody knows its name. "We've really had to be attentive to changing with the times," says Jim, who still skippers the *Mount* thirty hours each week during the summer. "In the 1970s, we added the dinner cruises, which are still extremely popular today. In the 1980s, we extended the *Mount Washington* by twenty-four feet to add more capacity. In the 1990s, we hit a huge milestone by celebrating our one hundred twenty-fifth anniversary. And in 2000, we nabbed the port of Meredith, which has turned into one of the prettiest waterfronts on the lake."

As we talk about the history of the company, Jim pulls out scrapbooks. Here's the *Sophie C.* on August 14, 1945, being hauled via truck from Boston through the streets of Laconia. And here's the enormous iron-encased "barn door" rudder attached to the hull of the *Mount Washington*. An entire scrapbook is devoted to the addition of a twenty-four-foot section to the *Mount* in 1982.

But it's not only the boats that make this company so tradition-laden, Jim points out. Most of the company's fourteen permanent employees have worked together for over fifteen years. When they say they feel like an extended family, they mean it. (Author and historian Bruce Heald has served as purser every summer for almost forty years and has written several popular books about the lake, its boats, and its inhabitants.) Of the 110 seasonal employees hired every summer to handle everything from serving food to selling tickets, Jim says, 60 percent return year after year. Many are, in fact, related. Working for the Winnipesaukee Flagship Corp. has become a rite of passage among many families around the lake.

Out of all the company's employees, however, it's the three captains who hold the highest esteem as the undisputed masters of the legendary M/S *Mount Washington*. All employees wear some type of epaulet on their uniform: silver bars if they work in service, gold if they work in operations, and one, two, or three bars depending on the employee's level of experience. But it's only the captains who have earned the rarely awarded four gold bars, which command the kind of respect usually reserved for heroes and heads of state.

Not everyone gets there. You're a pilot before you're a captain, and the company requires that you first train on the two smaller vessels in the fleet before taking on the sturdy but capricious *Mount Washington* (seasoned pilots say it's like driving a tractor-trailer on a highway full of small cars). At that level, you can spend years piloting the *Mount* before moving up to captain if you're promoted at all.

"Being promoted to captain depends on how you handle the crew, ship, emergencies, passengers. We just know it when it's time for someone to move up," Jim says, adding, "It took me a decade before I was promoted to captain." I ask him what it is about captains that causes awe among even the most jaded of passengers. "Generally people are just glad to know someone is in charge," he says. "As a younger captain, though, your height is important when you're in uniform. It helps you command respect. I'm six feet two. If there's a problem and I walk over, people calm right down. Older captains also command a lot of respect. With the older captains, people melt."

A few years ago, the company was embroiled in a fracas regarding its docks, and I ask Jim to tell me what happened. "A lot of the problems go back to the late 1800s when the B & M Railroad owned the docks," he tells me. "B & M turned the docks over to the towns, but they were never deeded." Consequently, over the years the company has had to renegotiate the terms on all of the docks it uses. Currently it owns the docks at Weirs Beach, Alton Bay, and Center Harbor, and leases the ones in Meredith and Wolfeboro from those towns. Today, it would cost at least $100,000 to build a new dock at any one of these locations, which is why Jim spends a large part of his maintenance budget every year on keeping the all-wood constructions in top condition. A few years ago the company even paid for scuba-diving certification for three employees, who can now handle all underwater dock maintenance throughout the year.

Such versatility is typical for this small company, whose employees wear many hats and often refer to their job as "a calling." Many spend their summer days off cruising on the *Mount* because they know that no day is ever the same on the lake, whose lovely Indian name means "Smile of the Great Spirit." While company loyalty is important, it's the lake and its traditions that make them long to be here, wherever else they are.

As testimony, Jim reaches to the wall behind his desk and pulls down a framed two-dollar bill with a postmark on it. He tells me he got it in February 1976 to mark the bicentennial. Instead of taking it to his local post office for a cancellation mark, as was common to do that year, he waited. He knew he would be on board the *Sophie C.* on July 4, 1976, when it would be the only post office in the United States open on that day.

On the pier at Weirs Beach, I can see Leo O'Connell rushing down the plank past a thin line of one hundred waiting passengers to bring me aboard the M/S *Mount Washington*. He's got one eye out for a couple who called earlier requesting a marriage ceremony. In addition to being a pilot and scuba diver, Leo is a justice of the peace and performs about seventy-five onboard marriages every year. But this couple hasn't shown up. A minute later, we're climbing up a narrow staircase to the wheelhouse near the top of the ship, where the captain is giving orders to the crew.

"There's a lot of tradition associated with this room," Leo tells me, as we step through the entryway. "Just to get here means you've really had to prove yourself." The *Mount*'s wheelhouse is roomy enough for two big men to move around each other and cluttered enough for them to feel comfortable. It has tall windows, giving a clear view of everything on three sides of the boat. From the front, a four-foot-high wooden wheel, built for an oceangoing tug, dominates. Above it a small handwritten sign says, "Tuesday, Thursday, Saturday, Sunday, Turn Right." ("It's a joke," Leo assures me.)

Originally from Massachusetts, Leo shoots squarely from the hip and doesn't hesitate to tell it as he sees it. He's the kind of person you'd trust to pick up your kids from school because you know that not only would he be there on time, he'd probably be there early. A respectful person, he is likewise respected by colleagues for his sense of humor and ability to handle people well. For the last decade he's worked for the Winnipesaukee Flagship Corp., but spent years before that as a marine patrolman on this lake for the state of New Hampshire.

As the first sound of the engines reaches us, Leo watches their revolutions per minute (rpms) on the console behind the wheel. Like all operators of the *Mount,* he handles the ship gently, keeping the engines spinning at 200 rpms during the warm-up and a mellow 400 rpms, or fifteen miles per hour, during the cruise. The ship's two 1946 diesel engines, each as powerful as thirty-two Chevrolet V-8s, are low revolution by design (compared to today's 10,000-plus rpm machines) and remarkably fuel-efficient. Per passenger mile, the *Mount* is one of the most efficient vessels on the lake, using only forty-five to fifty gallons of fuel per hour. Her nine-thousand-gallon tanks are large enough that she only needs refueling every ten days.

"Looking good," comes up through the speaker from the engine room. As pilot, Leo is responsible for launching and docking the boat, while the captain stands outside the wheelhouse and guides him and the crew. Standing at the helm, Leo tells me that the *Mount* is actually quite simple to operate. The boat is either moving forward, stopped, or moving in reverse. But simple doesn't mean easy. Wind—how strong and from which direction— determines how the boat is handled, and it's different for each cruise every day. "It's always a judgment call," Leo says. "Because of the way this boat is built, it's like a big enclosed sailboat. It can move as quickly sideways as it can forward in a strong gust of wind."

Technologically, however, the *Mount* is as state-of-the-art as they come. At the console, a global positioning system, installed two years ago, is connected to the ship's radar and compass, which, together, can indicate the ship's location on the lake within six feet. Prior to 1976, when radar was installed, the captain's rule of thumb was that if he couldn't see nearby Eagle Island, the *Mount* stayed put. With today's technology, visibility isn't needed, and weather-related cancellations are all but nonexistent.

The console also includes a wide variety of engine gauges, a radio that transmits lake reports from the ship to WSAR in Wolfeboro, a ship-to-shore radio connecting the boat to the ticket office on the pier, and a direct speaker to the engine room. If they needed to, Leo and the captain could communicate with any crew member on the boat through the thirteen lines and twenty-two phones that connect the wheelhouse to all areas of the vessel.

Standing near Leo is an old-fashioned-looking brass instrument resembling a clock on a four-foot stand. He says it's a telegraph, installed with the engines in 1946 and similar to the one on the *Titanic.* The telegraph is linked to the same instrument in the engine room and once served as the main communication system between these two key parts of the vessel. That was in the days when the engines could be controlled only from the engine room. If the captain wanted the engineer to cut the power to two-thirds, for example, he would manually turn the gauge on the telegraph to the "2/3" mark, which would rotate the telegraph gauge in the engine room to the same mark. Now, though, the captain and pilot control the engines directly and communicate with the engine room through a speaker system. In the unlikely event that either of these systems fails, the telegraph is in working order and can serve as a backup.

This mix of old and new isn't unusual for a vessel that has been around for as long as the *Mount,* although she isn't the first in her class. The original *Mount Washington,* launched in 1872, was completely destroyed by fire in December 1939 after sixty-seven years of service. The boat's captain, Leander Lavallee, quickly regrouped. Only a few weeks after the fire, he bought the hull of the S.S. *Chateaugay,* which was being used as a clubhouse by the Burlington (Vermont) Yacht Club, and had it refitted with a boiler, propellers, and engines. Less than eight months later, the *Laconia Evening Citizen* reported that over twenty thousand people turned out on August 12, 1940, for the afternoon launching of the *Mount Washington II.* In 1942, however, the ship's engines were removed by the U.S. government to aid the war effort. She didn't sail again until 1946.

Since then, the M/S *Mount Washington* has become a rather cherished symbol of summer in New Hampshire, attracting 100,000 passengers each season who enjoy sailing on a vessel that, outwardly at least, hasn't changed much in over fifty years. Leo says people are so used to seeing the *Mount* at the same time every day that the company receives tongue-in-cheek complaint letters if the boat ever goes a little off schedule. As we talk, we notice motorboats on all sides of us slowing down to get a better look. On a lake of cabin cruisers and Jet Skis, the *Mount* stands out.

With the boat safely launched, Leo and I leave the wheelhouse to tour the ship. I ask him how in the world the *Mount* is able to carry 1,250 passengers without everyone feeling cramped. That's easy, he says. The 230-foot vessel is so compartmentalized that thinning the crowd isn't a problem. The *Mount* has five bars, four decks, and three dance floors. With music available on three decks for the evening dinner-dance cruises, and food available on all decks for all cruises, he says, the ship just never feels crowded.

Every cruise on the *Mount* is staffed by fifteen to twenty-five crew members, which always include a captain, who is responsible overall for the ship, crew, and passengers' safety; a pilot; two engineers, who work in the engine room; a purser, who handles the ship's money; a deck officer, who is like a "head concierge" and is responsible for passenger control and comfort; three deckhands, who keep the ship clean; a galley supervisor, who manages the kitchen crew; and a bartender. Jim Morash handles most of the crew scheduling, which often includes late night and early morning shifts.

The passengers' experience with the crew is considered so important to the company, Leo says, that employees are hired primarily for their personality and ability to work well with the public. The senior, year-round employees then conduct specialized training as needed. "I've relieved seasonal crew members a few times who were having a bad night, rather than risk a passenger having a bad experience with someone," he tells me. "It doesn't happen often, because we train employees in customer service before they're allowed to work on board. Around here there's no such thing as saying 'It's not my job.' You'll see the captain vacuuming or taking out the trash. We all have to pitch in to turn the ship around quickly for the next cruise."

Problems with passengers are infrequent, but if the crew can't resolve them, the deck officer steps in. Deck officer experience is sought after by pilots, Leo says, because it's regarded within the company as essential training for pilots who wish to become captains. "As a deck officer, if you never hear from the captain, you're doing your job. That's an old saying in the ranks," he says. "If it goes past you to the captain, you know you have a hornet's nest. That's when the captain uses his deckhand experience. The problem has to be resolved immediately and well."

Leo stops momentarily in the Steamboat Lounge, a function room located below deck that isn't open to the public. In here, you can supposedly see the seams where the ship was cut in half in 1982 for the twenty-four-foot extension, but the only evidence I notice is a small step down to the lounge where Leo says there once was none.

Back on deck, we immediately descend again, this time down a steep metal staircase to the small windowless galley. Here two young women are shredding lettuce for the fresh salad that's part of the ongoing buffet upstairs. Two huge Blodgett ovens stand next to each other. There is a walk-in freezer nearby. All the ship's dishes are washed down here, which can raise the temperature to uncomfortable levels in the summer. It can get so hot that the galley crew must rotate regularly between upstairs and down to accommodate everyone's comfort level.

Not too far from here another door leads to an even more uncomfortable spot on the ship—the engine room. Before descending into it, we pause on the landing to don protective ear guards. Even from the top of the staircase, the rhythmic pulsing of the engines is so loud that it's physical. An engineer meets us at the bottom of the stairs. He's used to the racket and simply swoops his arm to indicate where the two vast engines—each about four feet high and twelve feet long—sit side by side, working. Hanging on the wall behind the engines are series of tools so large that, stacked on top of each other, they look like silver dinosaur bones.

Two engineers are always aboard every cruise on the *Mount,* but they too must rotate out of this closed space every half hour or so to escape the heat and noise (it reaches 120 degrees down here in the summer). The only exception is during launching and docking, when both engineers are present. During the cruise, they check the emergency and other systems, do preparatory work for oil and water circulation in the engines, prepare backup systems if storms are approaching, get the generators up and running for refrigeration, and do all minor repairs to the ship, such as fixing the lighting or plumbing. Everything the engineers do is recorded into the ship's logbooks, which create a maintenance history and reference point if anything should ever go wrong. The logs are also available to fire marshals and other officials during spot inspections.

All of these measures are part of the company's general safety policy to anticipate problems before they happen. Each year inspectors from the New Hampshire Department of Safety check everything on the *Mount*— from the number of life jackets on board to the air tanks that start the engines. Although the ship is required by law to carry only three fire extinguishers, it carries forty. Leo says there is always either a paramedic or other medically certified employee on board to respond to minor emergencies. If a major problem occurs, the *Mount* can communicate directly with Belknap County and Carroll County dispatchers. At all times, Leo says, the captain and pilot know precisely how many people are on board the *Mount*.

Back in the wheelhouse, Leo starts to slow the engines. About a quarter of a mile from Weirs dock, he stops them altogether. The *Mount* has no clutches, he says, and needs at least a quarter mile to coast to a standstill. When we're nearly at the dock, he restarts the engines and carefully maneuvers the vessel into its berth.

As the engines quiet down, I ask Leo how difficult the *Mount* is to operate. "The best advice I ever got about handling this vessel was from a veteran captain who told me to 'take the best points from other captains, throw away what you don't need, and develop your own personality for handling the *Mount*,'" he tells me. "This boat is an institution. It's like driving the Old Man in the Mountains around the lake."

Weeks later, I'm driving toward Center Harbor on Route 25 East, when the road suddenly bends to the right and, unexpectedly, there is the *Mount*. She looks smaller, nestled into a single dock—like she's hibernating. A white canopy covers her shady side, shrink-wrapping her against the heavy ice and snow expected in the months ahead.

This is the winter headquarters of the Winnipesaukee Flagship Corp., where the fleet is worked on through the off-season in the company's boatyard. It's on the water, housed in a brick red, barnlike building, but it's easy to miss unless you know it's there. As I get out of my car, a man in dirty overalls and a yellow Pennzoil cap walks across the parking lot. He waves, but at first I don't recognize Leo O'Connell out of uniform.

We walk inside the red building together, where most of the permanent crew of about ten guys is sitting around a long wooden table drinking coffee. They're taking a midmorning break from the welding they're doing on the *Sophie C.* The workshop looks like any area where there are engines close by, except it's remarkably tidy. Several round white life preservers from the *Mount* hang on the walls. To the left over the rest room I notice a 1960s-era sandwich board listing a variety of meat grinders for $1.45.

During winter, the company's onboard hierarchy melts away. This is when engineers and pilots work together with captains to get the fleet into top condition for the next season. After a hectic five-month cruising season, the atmosphere in the boatyard is collegial and relaxed. From now through April, the crew will work through a long list that includes repairs, painting, and a thorough cleaning of all three vessels. Every year the crew also tackles one major project. A few years ago they added an ice cream bar and new ladders to the *Mount*. This year they're rebuilding the Meredith dock.

While the captains rule in summer, fleet engineer Darryl Watson is in command of the vessels the rest of the year. Darryl is originally from Maine and came to the company part-time in 1978 on his way to somewhere else. Over the years he's earned the same measure of deference in his shop as any captain on board the *Mount*. He's a bear of a man with slicked-back hair, whose wife is postal clerk Lesley Watson. As we sit chatting in the cool air, he is interrupted several times by crew, double-checking instructions or updating him on status. They call him "Doc," because he can quickly and precisely diagnose any problem in any engine just by listening to it. He says it's luck, but Jim Morash says Darryl is the number one reason why the company practically never experiences any downtime in the fleet due to engine trouble.

I ask Darryl how his guys are able to keep these old boats in top condition year after year. It's not easy, he tells me, laughing. Engine parts, especially for the antique engines on the *Mount,* are hard to come by, mainly because they're no longer manufactured. "We have to anticipate problems a year in advance because it can take months to locate a part," Darryl says. "Mechanics today don't even know what the parts are, never mind be able to help us find them."

A few years ago, the company was fortunate to find and buy an old engine, like the ones in the *Mount,* that Darryl and his crew now use only for parts. While this has bought them fifteen to twenty years before they have to think about replacing the *Mount's* engines, it hasn't solved all their problems. For example, if the crankshaft goes (the part that turns the propellers), it can't be replaced. That means it probably would have to be manufactured separately—a very expensive endeavor. In the meantime, Darryl's engineers keep the *Mount's* engines in such fine condition that passengers sometimes ask why there aren't any diesel fumes.

In the winter of 1982, the company undertook a project that Darryl can still describe in such detail that it might have happened last month. In order to accommodate a larger number of passengers, the company cut the *Mount Washington* in half and added a twenty-four-foot extension to its middle. An aerial photo from the time clearly shows the boat in two pieces at the center, like a dissection in a biology class.

Before planning the project, Darryl says the company obtained quotes for the work from a number of shipyards. The prognosis across the board was that it would take at least thirty-five people and a minimum of twelve months to complete. But the idea of putting the *Mount*—the lifeblood of the company—out of commission for a year was out of the question. So the company decided to do the work itself. For two years, the engineering team planned the project, even calling a former owner, then in his eighties, out of retirement for guidance.

When it was finally time to start, the crew was so prepared that there were no surprises. Even the weather cooperated, allowing them to get most of the outside tasks completed before heavy snows arrived in January. Although delicate and time-consuming, Darryl explains, the work was remarkably straightforward. Basically, they sawed the boat in half, set the new twenty-four-foot section in between the two pieces with a crane, maneuvered it in place, trimmed it, and welded the ship back together. Then they reconnected all the plumbing, lighting, and electrical systems in the boat to accommodate the new section. It took fourteen men only six months, with no overtime and no injuries, to complete the work, Darryl says proudly. The result was an extension that lengthened the *Mount* to 230 feet and increased its weight by 100 tons to 750 tons.

Interestingly, the extension made the *Mount* more fuel-efficient by improving its length-to-beam (width) ratio. But it also made the boat so buoyant that it took thirty tons of ballast to stabilize the vessel. The *Mount* now drafts only nine feet of water, and Darryl says it moves better and faster than ever before. "When after all the hours of planning and work, there were no leaks in all the miles of welding, we got a good amount of satisfaction from that," Darryl says, sitting back in his chair.

A few moments later, Leo appears to take me over to the *Mount* for a last look around. He tells me that when they brought the boat over to Center Harbor in late October, they removed most of the movable equipment to store it ashore for the winter. As we walk up the plank, this is evident. The only items noticeable are neatly stacked chairs and tables. Four snowblowers, lined up symmetrically on deck, are ready for work.

In four months, the crew will begin to spruce up the *Mount* with new coats of paint. Then they'll initiate a bevy of safety inspections so that by early May she'll be completely ready for the Shakedown Cruise—the first of the year, when she's awarded her safety certifications with great ceremony by state officials. It's the same every year.

Right now, though, that day seems far away. Outside, the water is black. A hard white sun struggles to break through a mask of clouds. The empty boat feels cold and hollow, bouncing back sound off its floors and ceilings. But as we look around, I see a good sign. None of the boat's clocks were set back at the end of daylight savings time. Winter may be closing in, but on the *Mount,* at least, it could still be summer.

# 5

## Ballet New England

## "Ballet Is Very Mathematical"

*I*n the second-floor dance studio of a Daniel Street building in downtown Portsmouth, James Franklin sits alone, motionless, his legs propped up on a brown utility table, clipboard in lap. On a blistering day in late summer he is waiting. In five minutes, two dozen teenagers will pour into the room hoping to catch his eye during auditions for Ballet New England's annual *Nutcracker* production. Dressed entirely in black, he wiggles his toes through gray leather dance shoes.

Downstairs, the *Waltz of the Flowers* is spilling out of a borrowed CD player into a hive of children registering for the auditions. Most are wearing pink tights and black leotards, hair pulled back tight into tiny cinnamon buns at the top of their heads. Parents hover around a makeshift outlet snapping up Ballet New England T-shirts and tote bags. Outside, tourists stroll by, fanning themselves in the heat, oblivious to the commotion inside.

Almost every year since its founding in 1980, Ballet New England has staged a traditional Christmastime production of the *Nutcracker,* involving most of the organization's expansive Center for Dance Education. New Hampshire has many such dance schools, but Ballet New England is different. With a number of nationally recognized faculty members, it has attracted regional attention for its technical excellence as well as its commitment to what it calls "the whole student," not merely the dancer in each. Some preprofessional students who have studied both with Ballet New England and large, big-city companies say the classes here are better. They appreciate the emphasis on technical training they say is preparing them well for the real world of dance.

The school's classes are held in three wood-floored studios of the Connie Bean Community Center, a charming 1916 building near Portsmouth's waterfront that Ballet New England has occupied for most of its existence and is quickly outgrowing. In the last few years, the school has more than doubled to three hundred students, requiring that it hire a director for the jazz and other nonballet programs. This has allowed codirector Angela Carter, who coordinates the ballet programs, and artistic director James Franklin to concentrate on creating a first-rate *Nutcracker* production, which is staged at The Music Hall every year.

James is actually nearing the end of his last season with Ballet New England, and he has graciously permitted me to attend his *Nutcracker* auditions—something not even parents are allowed to do. For the next four months I'll be visiting Ballet New England frequently to record how the organization stages this large, unwieldy production that casts over one hundred children in forty roles in two separate casts. Nearly as many volunteers help bring the show to life, along with a small professional staff.

At precisely 1:00 P.M., James opens the door to the studio. Twenty-six adolescents—twenty-five girls and one boy—walk as confidently as they can manage into the room. Suddenly pink legs are everywhere, stretching, flexing, hopping. James claps his hands, and the students scurry (gracefully of course) to find a place along the barre that lines three sides of the rectangular room. Ballet slippers and water bottles litter the sides. When James turns on a floor fan, the breeze ruffles the number pinned to each student's back.

Although James is well into his sixties, his body is muscular and pliant. Youthful even. A single gold hoop dangles from his right ear. Calling out ten numbers, he politely asks everyone else to wait outside the studio door until he calls them back in. He isn't a big man, but his voice makes up for it. Just then, Angela Carter slips into the room. Her presence is familiar, and relief briefly crosses the faces of the girls standing awkwardly in the middle of the room. As the audition starts, they look to her constantly. She is their guiding light, but James is the harbor. Today they have to make it to him.

"You have one chance. Be happy to get my attention!" James bellows, as he paces before them. There is no music, so he creates a beat by singing silly rhymes or counting out the steps. Occasionally, he demonstrates. Sometimes he purposely throws them off. Now he is asking them to start on their left foot, rarely done in ballet. "Your other left foot, my dear," he says kindly to a girl who instinctively starts with her right. (Later, he tells me he does this to prepare them for handling unexpected situations onstage.) A cell phone rings for an eternity from deep inside a bag against the wall. Everyone ignores it. In an hour the audition is over. Following ballet etiquette, James claps for the students as they leave the room.

And so it goes for two days, through the tiniest of students to what James calls his "tall teens." Although he and Angela have taught many of the older students for more than five years, the auditions let them see how the kids do on their own without the structure of a classroom, where they are constantly told what to do. After each audition, the two confer over their clipboards. A few days later, they pin the results and rehearsal schedule on the second-floor bulletin board where Ballet New England posts all its news. This year there were enough spots for everyone. The competition, as it turned out, was over who would get the best roles.

At James Franklin's second retirement party a few years ago, he had recently finished a complete restaging of Ballet New England's *Nutcracker*— something that has happened every few years throughout the organization's history. But his hips were acting up and he felt ready for a less demanding phase in his career. After being bid a fond farewell by his colleagues, he went home to his wife and stewed. Within a few months he was back. The *Nutcracker* was keeping him up nights, he told everyone. He wasn't satisfied and he wanted the chance to do it again.

James describes himself with somewhat false modesty as an Indiana farm boy who came late to dance. In fact, he didn't don a pair of dance shoes until he was nineteen and a sophomore in college. "My first problem was wearing tights. There seemed to be a lot sticking out in front and in back," he laughs. After two days he got over it. It did not occur to him, despite starting his dance career when many were ending theirs, that he would not be a success.

Sitting in the sunroom of his home on the Exeter River, his eyes sparkle a bit as he reflects on a distinguished career that includes dancing at Radio City Music Hall and in off-Broadway productions, teaching at the acclaimed Houston Ballet, running his own studio in Florida, directing the Fort Wayne (Indiana) Ballet, and a long stint as a lead dancer in Las Vegas. He's danced with them all—Peggy Lee, Jimmy Durante, Andy Williams. "The names are endless," he says, waving his hand. But there is one issue that's still a sticking point. Auditions. He's always hated them. "I didn't have the ego for it," he tells me. "Most roles I got because people knew me." To this day he wonders if he could have gone further if he had just. . . .

In 1994, James and his wife scouted out the Portsmouth area as a potential place to live and run a studio. He came across a Ballet New England poster "with a chubby Asian girl on it. I thought I would like this place because the student in the poster looked healthy," he says, referring to the anorexic look of students at many ballet schools. He eventually ended up directing the artistic arm of Ballet New England, where one of his greatest joys is working with his teaching staff. "There is no difference between the way our school and schools of professional ballet companies are run," he observes. "The teaching staff must be exceptional, not merely good. Any of my staff could teach at the Boston Ballet."

I ask James how staging a ballet comprised mostly of children is different from staging one with adult dancers in companies like, for example, the Houston or New York City Ballets. Before he answers the question, he explains how his own role would be different. As artistic director in a professional company, he says, he wouldn't deal directly with the children. Someone else would teach them the steps, and then a ballet mistress would perfect the dance through rehearsals. At Ballet New England, he's involved in the dance education of each student, as well as every aspect of the *Nutcracker*—from developing the choreography to finding the professional guest artists who play the adult leads in the production.

Working with children in a large production is tricky, he says, because the experience has to be both educational and fun. "This isn't playtime, I tell them. It's a responsible production. I want them to understand that they aren't like the kids in the audience." To establish the order essential for managing two complete casts that must learn the music, steps, and stage directions in only a few months' time, he works closely with a small team. While the prop and costume ladies get busy behind the scenes, it's Angela Carter, as the *Nutcracker*'s ballet mistress, who rehearses the students until the only sound in their heads is the *Dance of the Sugar Plum Fairy*.

I have always wondered how choreographers create the sequence of steps that make up the whole, and I ask James about his own methods. "In an ensemble of dancers, you always have to go with your weakest dancer and keep it simple," he explains. "With your principals, you try to challenge them." To do that, he works out the choreography for each piece of the ballet during rehearsals with his dancers. "Some choreographers have it all prepared beforehand. I can't do that. I have to listen to the music." Then he watches how the dancers respond to it naturally before drawing a blueprint of the ballet in his mind. This is the process he followed in the previous year, when he created a new *Nutcracker* from scratch.

But how does he remember the thousands of steps across so many roles in a two-hour ballet like the *Nutcracker*? Up until the 1970s, he says, the dance world used labanotation, a written system of recording dance movements on musical scores using a series of squiggles to denote head, arm, and foot movements. Dance companies worked directly from these sheets

Angela Sears Carter, Co-School Director, intently watches her students at Ballet New England's studios in Portsmouth, New Hampshire. (Photograph by Ralph Morang /newenglandphoto.com.)

to teach themselves the choreography of any dance they wished to learn. Nowadays, companies wheel a VCR into the studio, pop in a video, and take it from there. In this, Ballet New England is no different. The production works from a professionally made video of the previous year's performance, which James tweaks—or changes outright—during rehearsals. "The kids get the steps very quickly," he says. "Especially the ones who have been in the *Nutcracker* before."

It takes James and Angela two to three weeks to "set" the choreography, after which he directs run-throughs of the entire production several times a week right up to opening night. At this moment, though, he has two big headaches: finding three guest artists from professional companies to play the principal, adult roles in the production and scheduling enough rehearsal time for the rest of the cast. "Rehearsing enough is really my biggest anxiety," he says. "The kids have to be rehearsed every week so that they don't forget the steps."

In a professional company, where dancers work together every day, this isn't an issue. But Ballet New England's students attend school during the week. That means no weeknight rehearsals and tough competition for the students' time on weekends. James knows he's asking a lot. Before rehearsals start every year, he gets all cast members and their parents together to explain why attending every rehearsal is important. He tells them that being in the *Nutcracker* is a commitment. That it's not fair to the cast members who do show up when others don't. For the most part, James says, everyone complies.

One afternoon, midway through the *Nutcracker* rehearsal schedule, I walk into a Ballet New England studio to find James seething. "I had a tantrum at rehearsal last night," he tells me, eyes flashing. "They just weren't dancing." Already late in October, rehearsals could be going better. It's not that the students don't know the steps. Angela has been rehearsing them for weeks. When I watch them, the difficulty is apparent. During the most important ensemble pieces, a delayed reaction is rippling through the lines so that while one girl is stepping, another is already leaping.

An hour into the rehearsal, things start to smooth out. James calls out orders, paces back and forth, counts out the beats on the armrests of his chair. But then we have an incident. One of the lead dancers slips and falls thunderously to the studio floor. More embarrassed than hurt, she flees to a side room alone. Unnerved, two more girls slip. Several others miss whole sequences of steps. Music playing, James tells them to continue and calmly walks off to find the girl who fell. In a few moments, she emerges on his arm, wiping away tears. James cracks a smile and says, "It was a beautiful fall. Very nicely done."

She starts to laugh, and so does everyone else. "You know, my daughter fell during an important audition once," he tells them, "and she cried all the way home. But when she saw the video of herself, she couldn't stop laughing." He says falling is something that happens to every dancer. You simply get back up and keep dancing. The fallen dancer gives James a grateful glance, taking her place back in line. As this somewhat awkward gaggle of sensitive teenagers prepares once again to take it from the top, I think to myself, "And very nicely done to you, Mr. Franklin."

At the end of the rehearsal, James still has something on his mind. He tells the students to sit on the floor before him as he paces for a moment, collecting his thoughts. "We are not displeased with rehearsal today," he finally says, pausing again. "But you know, if you're mad at yourself, we see that. So you make a mistake. Is it going to stop the show? You can't take whatever happens to you out on your audience or your instructors. This is what dancing is all about. Doing it over and over until your bunions fall off." He motions them to get up. They quietly exit as the next group enters the room.

While rehearsals resume, volunteers are working all over the building—sorting through costumes and props, supervising groups of very young students, figuring out who will do what on opening night. With a full-time staff of only four, plus seven part-time instructors, Ballet New England relies heavily on its volunteers throughout the year. "A lot of these volunteer jobs are paid positions in professional companies," says Joyce Tucker, who has been a volunteer in many capacities for the organization since her daughter first attended classes here in 1989. For the last decade Joyce has coordinated all backstage activity for the *Nutcracker* production, which covers hair, makeup, and costumes. "Our job is to make sure the kids go out in one piece," she continues. "The changes are fast. For example, Clara has twenty-four seconds to go from her nightdress into her party dress. It takes two volunteers to do this. It's very stressful for both the volunteers and the dancers. The audience has no idea that all this is going on backstage."

Another longtime volunteer, Ellen Patton, coordinates the front of the house—ticket sales, boutique operations, and ushers. In addition, volunteers chaperone the youngest dancers in the production, who are five or six years old, sell raffle tickets, distribute flyers and posters, sew costumes, and make props. In all, twenty are needed to effectively stage each of the *Nutcracker*'s eight annual performances. "Like most organizations, there's a core of volunteers here," Ellen says. "Some are here all the time. Before the volunteers were organized by Patsy, fewer people took on more responsibilities. Finding leaders is always hard. We have more experienced parents now, but we tend to see the same people year after year."

Ellen is referring to Patsy Lorentzen, who took over as Ballet New England's executive director in 2000. One of the first things she did was devise a volunteer structure. "The need for this was immediately evident to me," Patsy tells me later. "Too few people were spread too thin without much recognition and, although things did eventually get done, it was not without cost to these wonderful volunteers. . . . Organization is my middle name, and having worked successfully with many boards and their volunteer structures, I knew exactly what to do. I just needed to make sure I presented this idea so that all would want to participate, and not run from it."

Patsy is the kind of manager who understands that in order to work well with people, you must solicit their input—and their buy-in—before making changes. When she talks, her words are measured and thoughtful. She is a warm person, soft-spoken, but not shy. I had heard about some turbulent times in Ballet New England's past, and she doesn't hesitate to give me an abbreviated version of what happened. Suffice it to say the internal struggles that plagued the organization from the late 1980s well into the 1990s were fairly typical of many cultural groups at that time, when harried artistic directors were also expected to run day-to-day operations. Organizations have gotten away from this by hiring professional administrators, like Patsy, who handle all business functions, including fund-raising, public relations, and financial management.

Interestingly, when Patsy was hired by Ballet New England's board, she knew nothing about dance, except as a member of the audience. In that way she was different from any of the organization's previous executive directors. Prior to taking the job, she had founded a successful consortium of engineering societies, running the nonprofit out of a building on Beacon Hill in Boston that the consortium purchased through heavy-duty fund-raising. The Ballet New England board liked her entrepreneurial spirit so much that they promptly commissioned her with reining in the company, finding new quarters for the school, and turning the *Nutcracker* into the solid moneymaker it needed to be.

From the start, Patsy hasn't been interested in bad blood. "I truly believe that creating partnerships is the best way," she tells me. "I'm always searching for ways we can all work together to be more successful." This isn't just talk. When she sees something that needs fixing, she fixes it. For example, in her first summer with Ballet New England, she noticed that the hardwood floors in the school's studios were badly worn from years of dance classes. She knew there was no money in her budget to get them resurfaced, so she called four volunteers, told them to bring their families, and organized two weekends when the group stripped and resealed the floors in all three studios. She got the equipment and materials donated by local companies. Likewise, she had heard that many patrons thought the costumes worn by the lead dancers in the *Nutcracker* no longer looked fresh. One day, when she was leafing through *Dance* magazine, her eye caught on an ad for costume rentals, and on a whim she called the Boston Ballet to ask if it did such a thing. Sure enough, it did. Patsy contracted to rent nearly new costumes, which had been used in Boston Ballet productions, for only $75 each.

This year's *Nutcracker* is costing $125,000 to produce—about a third of Ballet New England's annual budget—most of which will return to the organization through ticket sales. Ballet New England contracts with The Music Hall for the space and all related items such as lighting, sound, sets, special effects, stage management, house management, crews, cleaners, and ticket sales—which means that if the *Nutcracker* doesn't at least break even, paying for it can eat into operational funds. To make sure that doesn't happen, Patsy spends a lot of her time applying for grants, seeking out potential sponsors, and otherwise promoting the production. But it can be difficult to get and keep people's attention, she says, when theatergoers have several competing *Nutcracker* productions in the area to choose from.

From that angle, Patsy feels strongly that it's the Ballet New England school that will lead the organization into a new era. Growing the school, she says, will attract the best teachers and artistic directors, which can only have positive repercussions for the school's *Nutcracker* production. And with a strong educational base, Patsy is certain the company may, sooner than later, realize its long-term goal of developing into an important regional dance company that stages several other productions each year, in addition to the *Nutcracker*. "It's my responsibility to make the dollars work," she tells me. "But to build the school, it's also important for us to build relationships with parents. From a business perspective, they're our clients. They pay the bills, but their kids are here for very different reasons. Our teachers need to develop relationships not only with their students but with the parents."

Because Patsy is not from the dance world, I ask her what she's found toughest about producing the *Nutcracker* in the last few years. She says it's been the learning process, but when she sees possibilities for partnerships—whether it's inside or outside Ballet New England—she doesn't hesitate to make a contact. "This is our best," Patsy tells me earnestly. "I want the community to say, 'We're lucky to have this production. It was incredible.' You can try to control every aspect, but that's not what this is about. It's about doing the best we can. And that means getting the best performers, the best costumes, finding the best way to fill the house, making sure the props are where they should be, making sure the lights go on and off at the right times, getting local hotels to donate rooms for our guest artists. It also means making sure parents feel good and that our students feel good—that they value this experience as something special in their lives. It all has to work for it to be your very best."

To watch Angela Carter dance, you would not guess she is on the cusp of forty, but you would certainly believe that she has been dancing since the age of three. As a former professional with the well-regarded Milwaukee Ballet, Angela has spent hours on stage in a wide variety of roles. Tall and slender, she has long, flame-red hair and carries herself with a dancer's grace. Her students adore her. She is both role model and ingenue.

Angela has been directing Ballet New England's ballet program since 1998, channeling some 250 ballet students into twelve levels of classes each year and staying on top of their progress (she also directs the adult ballet program). Her expectations are high, but she says she knows intuitively when to pull back and when to push forward. "Otherwise, kids stay in their comfort zone."

Traditional ballet schools like Ballet New England tend to emphasize technical training over artistry, the idea being that artistry is a skill students can grow into as they progress. Technique, on the other hand, must be taught from a student's first class. Bad habits learned early are almost impossible to root out as a dancer develops. "Not all students are good in both technique and artistry, so I help them focus on what they need to work on in each of those areas," Angela explains. "For example, some kids take drama classes so that they can do better playing roles. Others take voice lessons to help them move better with the music and rhythm."

Angela's students say that one of her main teaching points is adhering strictly to the rituals of ballet etiquette. Angela describes this simply as "manners in the classroom," but her brand of etiquette goes right to the heart of ballet. No longer practiced uniformly in the dance world, it's a civilized mode of behavior that's been handed down from teacher to student for several hundred years. It requires such traditions as curtsying to the instructor at the beginning and end of every class, respecting the teacher by remaining absolutely quiet in class, moving in an orderly fashion around the classroom, and standing stock straight at the barre at all times. The reason for this is simple. Ballet teachers know that if students are focused and disciplined, they'll work harder, get more out of the class, and become better dancers in the long run.

"I tell my students that ballet is very mathematical," Angela says. "We're creating patterns to rhythm. All the elements must be learned and trained." When she's rehearsing her students to perform in the *Nutcracker,* she takes this thought a step further. "I tell them to think of it this way: a series of steps make up a combination, combinations make up variations, and variations make up the ballet. Choreographing a ballet is like writing a novel that makes words into sentences into paragraphs into chapters."

Ashleigh Tucker is a longtime student of Angela's and, at eighteen, on the fast track to a professional dance career. At five feet nine inches, she's unusually tall for a ballet dancer. She has catlike eyes, and her blond hair is normally swept straight back into a bun. Onstage, she is imposing. Sitting in a small room off the rehearsal studio, she's taking a break from practicing the several leading roles she's playing in this season's *Nutcracker*. Her mother, Joyce, hands her tangerine slices and, between mouthfuls, Ashleigh tells me she's always loved the *Nutcracker*. When she was young, an uncle taped it for her and every Christmas she would dance to it, sometimes all day.

Over the last decade, the time she has spent in ballet classes has gradually increased, from one class a week to three to nearly every day. This is her typical weekday schedule: school from 8:00 A.M. to 2:30 P.M.; ballet from 3:00 P.M. to 9:00 P.M. On Saturdays she helps teach classes and attends rehearsals. Sundays she works in a bagel shop. "We made her get a job so that she can see what hard work is like outside of ballet school," Joyce says.

"I've never been involved in school activities," Ashleigh chimes in. "I've never played a sport or joined a club."

"Her peers are here," Joyce explains. "There are close to fifty academic schools from the area represented at Ballet New England, and these kids don't get recognition in their schools for what they do here. They give up parties, sports, and lots of other activities in order to dance. No one in this school would ever say 'You're not a part of our clique.' Ashleigh is accepted here. That's extremely comforting to a parent."

Joyce describes her daughter's bedroom as "overflowing"—mostly with photos, posters, statues, and sayings all related to ballet. But when I ask Ashleigh what draws her to dance, she isn't sure how to answer. This is the only world she has ever known. "It's the sense of achieving something," she tells me, squirming a bit. "I love just being in the theater—the lights, costumes, makeup. I love the whole atmosphere. Sometimes I have to work at bringing out my emotions when I dance, because my foot hurts or I'm tired. But when I'm onstage, I feel the audience is watching me, like I'm alone out there and I'd better make the best of it for the audience."

"This is hard for these dancers," Joyce points out. "They have to want to do this. It has to come from them. No one could ever make someone do this."

Joyce has been involved in Ashleigh's dance education from the start and credits the teachers here with developing her daughter's skills, carefully guiding her toward a dance career through the school's preprofessional program. Ashleigh says her teachers taught her discipline and never to give up. "The standards are higher here than in other ballet schools," she tells me. "Angela's classes are what dance classes should be. They're packed with so much that they feel like four hours. Angela is very strict." In the physically demanding ballet world, where discipline is sometimes the only thing that gets a dancer through the day, "strict" is the highest form of compliment.

As a former Ballet New England board member, Joyce has had a hand in guiding the organization's school toward these very standards her daughter now benefits from. "I've always considered this the best center for dance education in the region," she says. "The preprofessional program was set up several years ago and soon got the label of being competitive. But we didn't want that label. We wanted Ballet New England to be available to anyone. When we started our hip-hop classes, that helped open things up because we started getting guys, cheerleaders—kids you don't always find in a dance school. We want to be known as the best school for dance, and the absolute best school for ballet. . . . James has really made a difference here. He's been an incredible force. He loves these kids and he's extremely generous with them. When our choreographer left in November 1997, James just took over. He had a vision and didn't want to leave until it was completed. He runs rehearsals well. No one's ever unhappy."

One sure sign of a flourishing ballet school is the number of its preprofessional students accepted into four-week summer dance programs hosted by major dance companies around the country each year. Highly competitive, serious ballet students between the ages of thirteen and eighteen audition for them in droves and wear their acceptances like a badge of honor. Not only do these programs allow students to observe how they measure up against students of similar skill from other schools; they also can serve as an early indicator of how far students might go in their careers. This is especially true if they are accepted into particularly competitive or demanding programs.

Joyce tells me that in the previous year all ten of the Ballet New England students who auditioned for summer programs were accepted, including Ashleigh, who attended the Boston Ballet program, which selects only three hundred students out of two thousand. "Auditioning is so important for them because they learn about disappointment," Joyce says. "For example, in California a few years ago, Ashleigh studied with one of her idols. But this person turned out to be undisciplined and flighty." Pausing to look at her daughter, Joyce continues. "Ashleigh's the queen of this little world, but when she goes to summer school her height becomes an issue. She realizes the dance world is a competitive place. She's not your quintessential petite ballet dancer."

Keeping Ashleigh in ballet classes year-round requires financial sacrifice. First, there's the $3,000 for dance classes during the school year. Then there's the $4,000 for the four-week summer program. And don't get Joyce started about the $1,000 spent annually on dance shoes, which retail for

$60 a pop, and other dance accessories. "It's not easy," Joyce says. "My husband and I are only middle-class people. We both work." (Their other daughter, an eleven-year old, is a competitive swimmer.)

It's obvious that Joyce respects her daughter's drive and commitment, but I'm not sure she entirely understands it. When she tells me that she and her husband, who has also served as a Ballet New England volunteer, are both former "jocks," I wonder what it's like to be part of this rarefied world if your natural orientation is somewhere else. "In school I would take detention rather than attend a dance class," she laughs. "Although the dance world is not our own, the interest is in spending more time with our daughter. My husband and I say she has to follow her dream even though we worry about her. We're encouraging her to go to college, although she would rather join a dance company next year when she graduates from high school. We're trying not to interfere, but instead to give her alternatives. She's a self-assured kid, but she's been isolated. We have always told her, 'We want you to be a smart dancer.'"

When I agreed to help out backstage at a performance of the *Nutcracker,* Joyce Tucker asked me to dress in head-to-toe black. "That way the audience won't be able to see you," she told me. And now on a Saturday afternoon at The Music Hall, it's so quiet that you would never guess it's only an hour before the curtain goes up. I had expected to see kids running around, excited, but the cast is on a staggered schedule, allowing the hair, costume, and makeup volunteers to work on one small group at a time.

In the back room behind the stage, racks of elaborate costumes take up most of the space. Joyce and her crew have been here for hours, pressed tightly into the far corner. It's like an assembly line. When Joyce is finished with makeup, the hairstylist takes over. Then there's a final primp by the costume mistress. They don't need me. There are plenty of parents on hand to assist. So I wander around backstage in the dark looking at the props. Next to me is a four-foot papier-mâché ice cream sundae, a similarly made gigantic wedding-style cake decorated with gold grapes, and a small bowl of walnuts. Music Hall technicians are starting to test sound and light. Strains of the familiar music waft through the building.

Everyone, including Patsy Lorentzen—who seems at once in the front of the house and backstage—is completely calm. Even the youngest kids are sitting quietly in one place, enjoying the dark, cool atmosphere of a theater in waiting. It occurs to me that while most kids' lives revolve around summer vacation, many of these kids live for their annual stint in the *Nutcracker*.

At 1:40 the theater starts to fill. James walks by quickly, black cape flowing behind him, his eyes accented dramatically with dark lines. Besides directing the production, he is also playing the fearsome, but kindly, Herr Drosselmeyer—Clara's uncle, who comes on stage at the beginning of the ballet and presents her with the nutcracker. A stagehand appears out of nowhere and announces "ten minutes," which ripples like an echo through the ranks. Angela is onstage practicing lifts with her partner. As effortless as this looks to the audience, from here I can see it is not.

We can hear the audience now. The backstage area is flooded with the excited dancers who will appear onstage first. There is a strict protocol about this. With so little space in the side wings, and almost total darkness, no one is allowed back here unless they are in the next act, chaperoning, or looking after props. I'm obviously in the way wherever I stand, but a tall gentleman suddenly rescues me, wordlessly shuffling me to an empty spot at the base of a metal staircase leading over the stage.

"Ready?" someone asks. "Places everyone." The lights go off, and it's completely dark until the curtain rises on the dot of 2:00 P.M. Small voices whisper, "Good luck." The teens, wearing heavy stage makeup, now look like professional members of a corps de ballet. One of them asks Joyce, "How are my eyebrows? Do you think they're thick enough?" Joyce nods and waves her back in line. "They're still kids," she whispers to me.

Throughout the performance, James stands alone in the wings, still wearing his cape, watching with rapt attention. A small girl starts to approach him but is grabbed by one of the teens. Shaking her head, the older one whispers, "It's not a good time." Later, when it is over and they've taken several bows to enthusiastic applause, the entire cast flies off the stage, exuberant. They danced well. It was a good audience.

A few weeks later I call James for a final wrap. I hadn't been able to attend the dress rehearsal, held a few days before opening night, and I ask him how it had gone. He sighs audibly. "Dress rehearsal. It was just *terrible*," he says, drawing out the syllables. "The kids were nervous, it was a mess. I'm not a noticeable drinker, but that night I went home and poured myself a stiff one. I was deeply disturbed. You question yourself. You wonder what you could have done to produce a different outcome. But on opening night it all came together and I was a hero. It was thrilling. There's a saying in the business, 'Bad dress rehearsal, good show.'"

I mention several humorous touches that I had never seen in a *Nut-cracker* production. One was a character who returns to an empty stage, looks around like he's missed the party, and walks off again in disappointment. Another happens when an athletic dancer whips off his hat at the end to reveal a lovely girl with flowing hair, much to the audience's amusement and surprise. Still another requires a small girl to return to the stage, pick up a flower left behind, sniff it, and exit with attitude. All these flourishes—elegant, understated, and executed with perfect timing—clearly delighted the audience.

"Oh you got them all!" James exclaims gleefully. "I call these 'Franklin flourishes.' They're really just a part of my personality. Ballet is sometimes so terribly inward-focused and narrow. So focused on 'you did this wrong, you did that wrong.' Humor is very important."

So after weeks of tweaking and revising, was he at long last satisfied with the outcome? Yes, but it never really was about him, he replies. "What's most important is the final appearance of the *Nutcracker*. If it's done well, or it's done poorly, the audience will know. I'm not big on negative energy. We want our kids to be fabulous—they're out there with professional dancers holding their own. Not all students should be in the front row, but they all need the experience of being in a ballet."

After I hung up, I thought about something Angela had said a few weeks earlier, when I had asked her what the *Nutcracker* experience means to her students. "Everyone who works in this production learns about working as a team," she told me. "They're learning from other kids and it makes them say, 'Wow, I want to be like that.' They can also see how what they learn in the classroom is directly applied to dancing onstage, and it gives them experience working with different types of people. Being in the *Nutcracker* is an education in itself. Even if they never dance again after they leave Ballet New England, I hope it stays in their memory as a very special experience, and maybe helps give them the confidence to try other things in their lives."

# 6

## Deerfield Fair

### "Judges Can't Afford to Be Wishy-Washy"

*E*arly on the morning before the Deerfield Fair opens, a small city is in the making. You don't see many people, but evidence of human activity is everywhere—from the sound of country music blaring to the constant beeping of trucks backing out. On either side of the fairground's avenues, booths are going up. Piles of cardboard boxes sit next to a long row of gleaming, green John Deere tractors. Tomorrow at this time, the near-empty parking lot will be filling nicely and the smell of fried dough will be everywhere. For now, though, there is no rush. Slow and steady is the rule.

By the time I enter the white rectangular exhibits building near the center of the fairground, I feel a bit of a stranger in this land of horses and big machines. But I'm welcomed by Household Superintendent Carol Tordoff, who is supervising the food-judging contests taking place here today. They're always held the day before the fair opens to give the judges time and space to get through the hundreds of entries from all over the state. The Deerfield Fair is only one of many agricultural fairs in New Hampshire, but winning a blue ribbon here puts you squarely in the category of best of the best.

As we stroll down the length of the building, Carol points to the large glass cases on our right containing a wide assortment of baked goods and fanciful cakes. They'll be judged tomorrow. Farther down almost twenty dozen jars of canned foods are stacked in four rows along the wall looking a bit like a stained glass window. Two tables covered with white paper display jars of honey and maple syrup. In all, there are close to four hundred entries in Carol's department this year, over half of which are in the canning categories, although numbers are down slightly over the year before.

Carol, dressed comfortably in jeans and sneakers, has been the household superintendent for over a decade, and was the assistant in this department the decade before that. Like many of the people who run this fair, her roots here run deep. Yesterday, she and her assistant Michele Bauer, who produced the 2000 *Deerfield Fair Cookbook,* were here for hours methodically registering entries and assigning the exhibitor numbers that allow fair administrators easily to track winners. The system is computerized now, but not that long ago all tabulating and tracking was done by hand.

Every year the Deerfield Fair prints a general premium list, almost one hundred pages long, that specifies the categories, rules, and regulations for every contest. For example, if you wanted to enter the poultry contest, you would learn that there are 36 categories in the Poultry Department, including best light goose and best feather-legged bantam. In the Household Department, you'd find 220 categories—more than any other department in the fair—covering everything from carrots to pickles to apple pie. "Every year I look through the list to see if I want to change anything, but I usually don't," Carol tells me. "One year we talked about taking out the succotash and lard because no one ever enters those contests anymore, but we've always had all these categories as far back as I can remember."

Winning a ribbon for your apple pie is still as big a deal as ever, but no one enters this fair's food contests for the money. Prizes in the Household Department range from three dollars for first place to one dollar for third. The Deerfield Fair uses the Danish system of judging, which measures each entry on its own merit against a recognized standard. This means the judges award as many first-, second-, and third-place awards as merited. In contrast, the American system ranks entries against one another and awards only one first-, second-, and third-place prize.

I ask Carol if using the Danish system results in an abundance of blue ribbons, rendering them somewhat meaningless, but she says that usually doesn't happen. She chooses her judges for their knowledge and professionalism and expects them to do their job. "I have two judges for the preserved foods and one judge each for the honey and maple syrup," Carol says. "I used to have two judges for the baked goods, but they'd get sick after the judging, so now I have four." Occasionally the judges are lenient, she admits, but most years they aren't.

Waiting for us at the wall of jars is Claudia Boozer-Blasco, a University of New Hampshire (UNH) Cooperative Extension Service educator. Claudia, also dressed in jeans and sneakers, has been judging the canned food contests at the Deerfield Fair for the last few years. She's all business as she confirms the judging criteria and procedures with Carol before she and another judge turn eagerly toward the pickles. With the air of an expert, she selects a jar, holds it up to the light, turns it upside down, unscrews the lid without breaking the seal, and marks the scorecard that accompanies each entry. Although she spends only a minute or so on each entry, she is focused, methodical, and unhurried, giving each jar equal attention.

Standards for canned foods are different than for other categories in the Household Department. For one thing, the food isn't tasted. Instead, entries are judged entirely by appearance. When Claudia peers into the samples, she is looking at the liquid content (it should cover the food), head space (the area between the food and the lid that determines air content), how tight the seal is, the uniformity of color, texture, and cut of the food, and special considerations for each category. With jellies, for example, clarity is key. Pickles, however, shouldn't be packed too tightly, and the color must be true to the vegetable inside (no brown tomatoes). What Claudia is really doing, however, is hunting down clues—clues that expose unsafe food preservation methods.

"When Carol first asked me to be a judge," Claudia tells me, "I said I'd do it because I saw it as a good way to encourage the food safety aspect as a high priority in deciding who wins prizes. I always encourage people to enter only U.S. Department of Agriculture–approved recipes. That would be any recipe printed in a commercial cookbook. The ones printed after the late 1980s are best because government standards became stricter for canning." On the issue of creativity, Claudia is equally circumspect. "In general, I don't encourage original recipes, although we have no way of checking this. It's one of the biggest issues in food judging."

Carol reminds the judges to be encouraging in their comments on each scorecard so that folks will want to try again next year. Claudia picks up a jar of uniformly cut sage-green pickles speckled evenly throughout with pimiento and gingerly turns it upside down. "Isn't this lovely?" she comments to the other judge. After a moment's hesitation, she writes on the scorecard, "Nice presentation, but not enough head space," and moves on. As she nears the end of the first row, two women begin recording winning entries and tag each with a red, white, or blue ribbon.

Nearby, a young woman wearing a burgundy and blue–striped T-shirt is testing the fifteen maple syrup entries lined up before her. From one of the quart-size jars, Janis Conner, an inspector with the New Hampshire Department of Agriculture, Markets, and Food, pours a sample into a tall glass cylinder and checks it for clarity. Holding it up to the light, she gazes intently at the amber fluid inside and says, "See those tiny particles floating here? That's sugar sand. It was caused by a chemical reaction when the sap was boiled." She picks up another jar. "See those thin dark threads?" I don't. "That's from the filter used by the producer. It was probably made of wool or felt."

The maple syrup contest uses the American system of judging. For each sample, Janis enters a mark on a scorecard, for a total of one hundred points in four categories: clarity, density, packaging, and taste. When she's finished checking the entries for clarity, she inserts a glass hydrometer into the liquid. As it floats, it measures the density—or sugar content—of the syrup and, like a thermometer, displays a numbered reading. Giving me a simplified explanation, Janis says density is important because it determines whether the sample is legally syrup. If the density is too high, it could crystallize. If it's not dense enough, it could ferment.

The entries range in color from a honey gold to a deep molasses brown, and I'm wondering what the color difference signifies. Janis tells me the lighter the color, the earlier in the season the syrup was produced and the more delicate the flavor. Likewise, the later the trees are tapped, the darker and more strongly flavored the syrup will be. "At the Deerfield Fair, though, color doesn't matter, so long as it's Grade A syrup," Janis says. She's referring to the federal regulations that grade maple syrup according to color and flavor. Grade A syrup is either Light, Medium, or Dark Amber. It's the best table syrup you can buy. Grade B, sometimes called "cooking syrup," is darker than Grade A Dark Amber, but because it's so robustly flavored, it's normally used for cooking and flavoring.

Interestingly, New Hampshire's grading laws are stricter than the federal regulations, which makes the syrup produced in this state thicker than required. Vermont and Canada are equally strict, but some states, like Massachusetts, have no grading laws at all, although they, like all states, do follow federal standards. Janis says if a producer from that state, or any other, wants to sell maple products here, they must meet New Hampshire's regulations—and that's where Janis comes in as a state inspector. "You can't have inferior products out there," she says. "It damages the reputation of the maple syrup industry in the state as a whole. Part of my job is to ensure that consumers are getting a good maple product."

Janis is getting ready for the final and most significant part of the judging—the tasting. From under the table she pulls a Tupperware container of pretzels and a quart-size bottle of water out of a bag and sets them next to the row of entries. "That's to cut the sweetness," she says. Pouring a sample from one of the jars into a small glass cup, she dips a plastic spoon into the liquid and sips delicately. After noting the score, she eats a pretzel, rinses the spoon in a bucket of water next to the table, and dips into the next sample.

"Flavor has a lot to do with when, during the sugaring season, the syrup is produced and how long it's cooked," Janis explains. "Too long produces a caramel flavor like a lollipop. Also there's something the industry calls "buddiness," which can be a distinct characteristic of syrup produced from sap that's collected later in the season as the buds are starting to swell on the trees. It can taste kind of like a stick."

I ask Janis why she sniffs at each sample before tasting it. With maple syrup, she tells me, the judge's sense of smell is just as important as taste. To show me why, she holds one of the dark samples up to my nose. It's sour, like vinegar. One year, she says, she was working with an entry that had fermented, as this one has, but she had forgotten that its density was light and had tasted the sample. The flavor was so unpleasant that she's never gotten it out of her head. She's more careful now to taste only those samples that are at the correct density. She sets this one aside, noting on the scorecard why the producer earned no points for taste so that he can correct it next year.

Meanwhile, at the table next to Janis, honey judge Alden Marshall has just arranged twenty-one jars of honey into five neat rows, four or so jars deep. He's a slim man with a precise manner who retired a decade ago after a career as an electrical engineer. He now runs B-Line Apiaries out of Hudson, producing ten thousand pounds of honey a year. He is so well known on the honey-judging circuit—at fairs in both New Hampshire and Massachusetts—that I have to nudge him a bit to find out about his own record as a contestant. "Oh, I've won first place enough times," he tells me modestly. "You can do only so much with the product. The bees do the rest."

The entries in front of Alden are similar in tone to the lighter maple syrup entries, except the darkest honey is reddish like fresh apple cider. Alden tells me that the federal grading system for honey is based on color, which is why he has arranged the jars from lightest to darkest. But there's a lot more to honey than hue. Most important, honey has five judging categories: extracted, which is the clear liquid you buy in your supermarket; cream, a finely crystallized honey (this isn't the same as whipped, which is extracted honey with air in it); chunk, when the comb is cut to fit the jar that also contains liquid honey; comb, when the comb is uncut in its jar, without liquid; and cut comb, when the comb is cut to fit the jar, also

Ruth Stimson (center), honored in 1992 by the Deerfield Fair Association for fifty years of service as a judge at the Deerfield Fair. (Left to right) Peggy King, Priscilla Watts, Ruth Sanborn (in back), Ruth Stimson, Delores O'Neal, and fair president Bud Rollins. (Courtesy of Deerfield Fair Association.)

without liquid. Most entries in the Deerfield Fair are extracted honey, and each entrant must register three samples. This demonstrates to the judges that the entrant can produce consistent results.

On the table, Alden has placed a black wooden box that contains a low-watt bulb and two tinted glass panels, giving the judging area the appearance of a laboratory. He and another judge place one sample at a time between the glass panels and closely inspect the honey for crystals, which become iridescent in the light and easy to spot. Alden doesn't talk much, but when he detects crystals, he swiftly pulls the jar out of the box and replaces it with another.

The honey contest uses a point system similar to that used for maple syrup, but the judging criteria are somewhat different. The scorecard lists density, absence of crystals, cleanliness (of the liquid), flavor, and packaging. For honeycomb entries, uniformity of the comb as well as the thickness of the chunks are also considered. Overall in the world of honey, cleanliness, followed by flavor and density, rule.

After a half hour, Alden has checked all the entries for crystals. Density is next. He takes a small black tool from its protective case that he calls a re-fractometer. It looks like the instrument eye doctors use when they tell you to look into the light. Next he picks up a toothpick, dips it into a honey sample, smears the honey on the inside panel of the tool, closes it, and stares into it. The reading must equal the exact density—or moisture content—of honey when it's in the hive. "Honey has to have a low mois-ture content or it ferments," Alden says, as he hands the instrument to me. It's like looking through a kaleidoscope, only with numbers along the side.

I ask Alden why there is such a wide range of gold tones in the honey en-tries and how this relates to the bees. His explanation shows how closely bound the production of honey is to yearly changes in nature. "Color vari-ations are a function of the flower, weather, and soil conditions. There are a lot of factors involved," he tells me. "Weather affects the amount of nectar produced by the flowers, but spring and early summer are generally the most productive times of year. When you see pussy willows and dandelions come out, it's the beginning of high season, although bees start pollinating before that with plants that bloom earlier." With so many variables in na-ture, Alden continues, "a particular plant might produce slightly different shades of honey from year to year."

In New Hampshire, our plant life is so diverse and our open spaces so small that bees produce what the industry calls "mixed honey." This means bees in this state have such a busy spring schedule that producers can't guarantee the pollen comes from a particular type of plant. Producers in larger states, however, can specialize in a specific type of honey because there are more open tracts of land, relative to New Hampshire, with fewer types of plants growing on them. For example, clover honey often comes from the Midwest, citrus honey is produced in Florida, and cranberry honey is usually made on Cape Cod.

Alden is examining the samples for cleanliness now, checking for dirt, lint, wax, or foam in the liquid. He calls the other judge and the two huddle over three jars of a red-toned honey. Alden thinks he's detected "something foreign" in one of them, down near the middle of the jar, but I don't see a thing. The foreign substance, however, is as clear to them as though a moose were floating in it. They compare the samples a bit longer and conclude that the substance is a particle of dirt, which Alden notes on the scorecard.

Taste, however, is somewhat easier to judge. Alden tells me honey should never have a smoky flavor, which can happen if the beekeeper uses a smoker to drive the bees from the colonies to collect the honey. Likewise, it should never taste scorched—something that occurs if the beekeeper heats the honey too high to reduce its moisture content. I ask Alden about his own taste standards, expecting a complicated answer similar, perhaps, to tasting wines. But he shrugs off the question. "It just has to taste like honey," he says.

If you went to the first Deerfield Fair on September 28, 1876, you wouldn't have visited the expansive fairground of today. The one-day event, organized in celebration of the country's Centennial, was held in Deerfield Center in and around the town hall, with cattle tie-ups arranged in nearby open spaces. The horse sheds of local churches were also put to good use as additional pens and stalls for animals.

In the late 1800s, Deerfield was still primarily a farming community, and the fair was a splendid way for the town's citizens to show off their good work. Fair-goers watched oxen pulling and horse competitions, listened to their favorite bands at the bandstand erected in front of town hall, and cheered for premium winners as their names were announced. Horses, cattle, sheep, swine, and poultry all were judged for excellence.

If fair-goers wanted to see the exhibits—and most, it appears, did—they paid twenty cents to enter the town hall, where the displays completely took up the building's two floors. These were no ordinary displays, however. The emphasis was on variety and what we'd today call the "wow factor," instead of on perfection. On the first floor, giant four-foot cucumbers sat next to thirty-two types of pears. Cages of rare pigeon, turkey, duck, and chicken specimens cluttered the floor. Upstairs were the needlework, flowers, baked goods, canned items, and a small exhibit of crafts.

It's not clear why, but many people expected the first Deerfield Fair to be a disappointment, including the *Exeter Newsletter,* which reported that "a good many staid [*sic*] away thinking it would prove a failure." It's true that the first fair in Deerfield wasn't a financial success (it could pay only half the premiums it awarded). But there was something in the air that day, a celebration of community spirit that went well beyond New Hampshire's patriotic mood that Centennial year.

So when the fair was over, and despite no initial plans to do so, the enthusiastic volunteers who staged the first Deerfield Fair began making plans for the second. And then the third. Within a few years, the fair was established as a local tradition. Farmers from communities all around Deerfield looked forward to the good-natured competitions, while their wives entered their best products in the food contests.

In fact, the food contests had quickly become a fair favorite with everyone, so much so that organizers decided to expand them. A notice posted in the weeks before the September 25, 1878, Deerfield Fair urged participants to "enter preserves and canned fruits, pickles, etc. as it is our purpose to make this a prominent feature of the exhibition."

Former Deerfield Fair food judge Ruth Stimson isn't surprised about that. Food preservation has always been a big part of New England food traditions, she tells me. "It was especially important during both world wars when the government was encouraging self-sufficiency." Ruth worked as an educator for the UNH Cooperative Extension Service until 1982, when she retired after forty years. Although she has judged everything from rugs to dairy products, it was always part of her job to judge food contests at fairs. (After she retired, she continued to judge flowers. In 1992, to her great surprise, she was escorted to the middle of the horse show ring at the Deerfield Fair and honored for fifty years of service.)

Ruth is approaching her mid-eighties and is the kind of person my grandmother would have called a "hot ticket"—sharp, confident, her own woman. Back in the 1940s, when many women were less independent than today, she had her own car and a master's degree. Once, in the 1950s, she drove a "big, black Pontiac" owned by UNH to a national conference in Washington, D.C., because few of her colleagues had a driver's license. Ruth is telling me these stories in her comfortable Hampton home, where we're surrounded by boxes of historical material she's collected over the years. She compiled a yearbook for each of her forty years in public service; they are so rich in detail that the UNH Library has expressed interest in adding them to its special collections.

Despite her age, Ruth still gives talks about the history of food preservation and challenges me to tell her how the canning process was developed. When I falter, she exclaims, "It was Napoleon!" It turns out that the French government offered twelve thousand francs to anyone who could figure out a way to preserve food so that Napoleon's armies could bring it with them "on the road," so to speak. Nicolas Appert, a French confectioner, won the prize in the early 1800s (after fifteen years of experimenting) by taking food-filled glass jars, corking them, and submerging them in boiling water, thus sterilizing the contents. But when Napoleon's men transported the glass containers of meat, fruit, and even milk, the result was a lot of broken glass. In 1810, an Englishman patented a similar method to preserve food in airtight tin-plated cans.

The canning process was refined quickly so that by the late 1800s, when the first Deerfield Fair took place, it had become an integral part of food preservation in most homes in the United States. (Although it's always been referred to as canning, the process itself is called preservation and normally carried out in the home using glass jars.) It was this very experience with food preservation, Ruth says, that kept the nation strong during the lean times of both world wars.

"We had a saying back in the 1940s: 'food will win the war and write the peace,'" she recalls. "The reasoning behind this was that if everyone, the troops and the folks back home, were fed well and kept strong, then everyone could fight better—whatever their effort in the war. The government encouraged everyone to grow their own food. Community gardens were available in cities throughout New Hampshire for anyone without land. At that time, whatever Uncle Sam wanted, we tried to do it."

As an Extension educator for a government-sponsored program, Ruth's job during the war was to promote self-sufficiency by teaching people about food preservation methods. The information was considered so vital that Extension workers all over the country adopted a system that allowed them to work with designated neighborhood leaders who acted as their agents—disseminating information about nutrition, gardening, and food preservation door-to-door. In Rockingham County alone, there were 126 canning leaders.

Ruth says fairs were also very helpful for disseminating information to large numbers of people. When she judged her first food contest at the Deerfield Fair in 1942, she had been in her new job for only a few weeks. But she wasted no time. When she was finished judging, she spent the remainder of the fair talking to homemakers about food preservation methods. She also made sure people knew about the government-sponsored canning centers, where anyone who didn't own canning equipment could bring fresh produce and meats and get them preserved safely by experienced Extension leaders. There were thirteen such centers in New Hampshire. Ruth circulated among those in Rockingham County to enforce safety standards.

In 1943, at the height of World War II, there was no Deerfield Fair due to the nationwide gasoline shortage. By that time, there was also a glass jar shortage in New England, and Ruth helped operate a jar exchange for those who needed jars or had extras to give away. She then spent much of her time teaching people how to safely preserve many kinds of foods using different types of jars. "If we had to do that again today, I have a basement full of glass jars," she says, laughing.

After the war, Ruth says preserving became less popular as women began working outside the home and as frozen and processed foods became more widely available. "People had become more consumers than producers," she observes. "They'd come home from work and want to see their family, not learn how to can corn." She's noticed that horticulture and crafts have slowly replaced canning and preserving as popular interests at fairs and says that flowers are now everybody's favorite. Still, most years she judged the food contests at the Deerfield Fair it was not unusual to work with five hundred to six hundred entries.

In fact, food contest entries peaked at the Deerfield Fair in 1973, when there were over a thousand entries in the food preservation categories alone. She says it took over twelve hours to complete the judging that year. "Let's see what could have caused the peak," she says, digging in one of her boxes for her 1973 yearbook. Opening it to a specific page, she nods. It happened during the energy crisis, when home gardening was big and recycling had just taken off. She recalls another peak—1992—when there were just over six hundred canning entries. That, too, was a recession year.

I ask Ruth if she has noticed much change in the Deerfield Fair premium list over the years, or in the types of foods entered. At her fingertips happens to be a recent list. She thumbs through it slowly and then tells me the categories really haven't changed much at all. "There are fewer canned meats, maybe, but jellies and marmalades are no different today than fifty years ago. Pickles and relishes, they're all the same."

But as she pauses, I get the feeling this isn't such a good thing. "You know, it's not up to the Extension workers to suggest changes, but I don't think they need all this," she says, tapping her hand on the booklet. "I'm counting eleven types of quick breads. Muffins—they have plenty. It's up to fair management to take out items that no one enters anymore. Just because a category was on last year's list doesn't mean it has to be there year after year."

Ultimately, though, it's the judges who call the shots. Drawing from her fifty years of experience, Ruth has definite ideas about what makes a good judge. "I have six factors," she says, holding up her fingers to count them off. "A knowledge of the subject; patience in answering questions from the public even if it delays the judging; the ability to make decisions—judges can't afford to be wishy-washy; a systematic attention to details like following the premium list categories class by class; common sense; and a feeling of optimism for the process." Optimism for the process? "You want to feel that people have tried and some can learn to do better," she concludes.

. . .

Only an hour into the first day of the Deerfield Fair, hundreds of cars, many with Florida plates, are already parked outside the main gate. There is no rush, no chaos or pandemonium, despite the eighty thousand people per day, on average, who attend this fair during the four days it's open each year. Everyone knows they'll get their turn—to park, to enter, to see the sights. It occurs to me that if the world worked the way the Deerfield Fair does, it would be an orderly place indeed.

The horse show is in full swing, and there are long lines at the doughnut booths. Every stand is an address along these avenues—fried dough, apple crisp, fried dough, drinks, hot dogs, french fries, more fried dough. As I enter the exhibits building, I notice the maple syrup and honey entries have been placed inside a glass case, the winners displaying fancy rosette ribbons. The four baked goods judges, who do their judging on the first day of the fair (much to the enjoyment of visitors), are sitting behind the cases, wrist-deep in plates of muffins, cakes, and pie.

The two judges on the left are handling breads and cookies, while the other two are tasting the sweet breads and pastries. Assistant Household Superintendent Michele Bauer is in charge today. She explains that the judges begin with the less sweet baked items and work their way slowly into the very sweet. As she talks, she cuts slices of quick breads into small pieces for the judges to taste. When they finish, she transfers the leftovers to another plate and places it on the counter for visitors to try. Several people take samples and call over to the judges, "Hard job you guys have today—eating all those sweets!" The judges laugh, but they know how they will feel in a few hours, and they're in no hurry to get there.

Later on, I talk at length to the lead judge in the cookie and bread categories, Raymond Buzzell, who has judged at the Deerfield Fair for over a decade. Raymond is a retired UNH baker, and he tells me he was always at his job at Stillings Hall every day by 4:00 A.M. In thirty-four years, he was late only once, when he couldn't get through a blizzard.

When Raymond judges, he looks like he's enjoying a delicious snack with a friend, sipping coffee, taking his time to savor each small bite. But looks are deceiving. Raymond is a professional and he is identifying the undertones of every item he samples. For example, last year he judged twenty-four entries of chocolate chip cookies. For every one, he says he looked for something distinctive, a special quality that set the cookie apart from all the others. "I always think, What made the baker make it this way?" Raymond explains. "Then I try to analyze the ingredients against my own standard. In the end, it still has to be excellent to win a prize, no matter how creative it is."

There are no scorecards in baked goods judging. Instead, Raymond judges on eye appeal, texture, and—definitively—flavor. He says when he tastes something, he can usually tell precisely what the cook can do to improve it. "Many people don't realize that adding vanilla to a chocolate recipe will bring out the full flavor of the chocolate. Sometimes that's all that's needed," he says.

Even with this kind of clarity, Raymond says he still finds it hard to choose winners. People cook according to their own preferences. Some like gooey chocolate chip cookies, others like them crispy. I ask Raymond how much a judge's personal preferences enter the mix. "You have to ignore your own likes and dislikes while judging," he says. "Just because you don't like something flavored with mint, for example, doesn't mean it's not a good cookie. If I don't like something because of a personal preference, but the other judge loves it and thinks it deserves a prize, I'll go with their decision."

To keep his palate fresh, Raymond sips coffee while he judges, although many judges, he says, stick with water. "The key is not to eat too much of each sample and to take short breaks." When he's finished, he simply feels full. "I'm a sweet freak," he tells me, smiling a bit guiltily. "So eating a lot of them isn't a problem for me. When my wife and I go out to dinner, I sometimes have a small main course, and two or three desserts. It drives her crazy."

•  •  •

It's been a long day, but before I leave the fair, Michele Bauer gives me a copy of the latest Deerfield Fair cookbook, the 2000 edition. She produced this edition and says she collected hundreds of winning recipes for ten years before finally culling the lot down to 188. I'm aware of the Deerfield Fair cookbooks, and my impression is that they have been printed every decade or so, but Michele tells me that's incorrect. Only six have been produced in the entire history of the fair: 1911, 1923, 1930, 1935, 1988, and 2000.

When I get home, I contact Deerfield Fair historian Joanne Wasson to find out if a complete set of the cookbooks exists. It does, she tells me, and I'm rather amazed at my luck that she happens to have the only known set. A few days later, I drive back to Deerfield to spend a morning at Joanne's kitchen table poring over the books, the older of which were used by her mother. Joanne is a retired Latin teacher and has been the official Deerfield Fair historian since the 1980s. A few years ago, she published a popular history of the fair in honor of its 125th anniversary.

We spread the cookbooks out across the table. The four older ones are yellowed and spattered with food stains, with pencil notes written in the margins of many of the pages. Joanne tells me there's a difference in how the older and newer editions were produced. The 1911, 1923, 1930, and 1935 Deerfield Fair cookbooks are traditional and include a wide variety of recipes submitted by local residents. The 1988 and 2000 editions feature only Deerfield Fair prizewinning recipes. What they have in common, however, is that they were all produced by the Deerfield Fair Household Department and they are all heavy in the baked goods categories.

What's particularly interesting about these cookbooks are the differences that accumulated in the four editions between 1911 and 1935. You can chart a history of the early modern United States through their pages. The 1911 cookbook has forty pages of recipes, and it was the only edition handed out free with admission. The fair covered printing costs through the eight additional pages of advertising. "It was a tremendous success," Joanne says, carefully turning the fragile pages. "All the women had one, and they used them. As you can see, the older books were used so much, they eventually fell apart."

The table of contents in the 1911 cookbook is similar to the contents in any general cookbook of today, including pickling, preserving and canning, breads, soups, meat, fish, and a wide variety of dessert categories. But I notice many ingredients you no longer see in recipes: sweet milk, lard, bolted meal. Most recipes have only a few standard ingredients, such as flour, milk, eggs, or meat, and are simple to make. Directions are few. There were only a few ways to prepare food back then, compared with today, and the recipe writer assumed you would just know what to do.

Given what a nation of chocoholics we've become, recipes including chocolate are glaringly absent from the 1911 edition. (It wasn't until just after World War I that chocolate became readily available in small packages in this country.) Instead, I see popovers, oatmeal bread, pancakes, molasses cookies, jelly roll, angel cake, and Indian pudding—still New England staples. I'm curious how these recipes compare with today's versions, so later on I take out my Betty Crocker cookbook and compare a few of them. I've always had the impression that people used more butter and eggs back then, but I find the recipes from the older cookbook, overall, lower in fat. For example, the sugar cookie recipe calls for one cup of butter, while Betty Crocker calls for one and a quarter cups in an otherwise identical recipe.

The 1911 cookbook is filled with charming proverbs, folksy sayings, and quotes from Shakespeare—mostly related to food. "To make a perfect salad, there should be a miser for oil, a spendthrift for vinegar, a wise man for salt, and a madcap to stir the ingredients up, and mix them well together," quotes a Spanish proverb. Under the pumpkin pie recipe, which instructs cooks to stew a pumpkin for an entire day before making the pie, is this from Henry Wadsworth Longfellow: "You'll dare deny the truth, there is poetry in pie," reminding cooks that their hard work will, indeed, pay off.

The 1923 Deerfield Fair Cookbook, which cost thirty-five cents, indicates a slight advancement in kitchen technology. Ice cream is a new category. In the 1930 edition, all types of fritters were big. It's the 120-page 1935 cookbook, however, that shows the entrance of processed foods. Probably produced by the daughters of the women who created the 1911 edition, many recipes now call for peanut butter, packaged cream cheese, cans of soup, marshmallows, cheese, and shortening. Sandwiches are now a category. Cake recipes, with gas or electric ovens in most American homes by the mid-1930s, take up almost a quarter of the book.

There are also many more recipes with an international bent than in previous editions, as a generation of immigrants settled down and started contributing to this country's culinary history. I see Chinese pie, Spanish meat, Swedish meatballs, Welsh rarebit, soufflés. And with more modern kitchens, it's clear that cooks were getting creative. For example, a tomato soup cake makes me wonder, What was she thinking? But with a few pounds of cream cheese as its base, it was probably delicious.

The basics are here, too, and many of these recipes have become American classics: oatmeal cookies, macaroni and cheese, meat loaf, chicken pot pie, waffles, scalloped potatoes, applesauce cake, brownies, and lemon pie. But there are no chocolate chip cookie recipes until the 2000 Deerfield Fair Cookbook. Here there are page after page of them—by far the most popular recipe in the book.

I think it's safe to say that all six of the Deerfield Fair cookbooks have become classics in their own right, although it's a shame that a whole generation of local culinary tradition was passed over between the 1935 and 1988 editions. Still, Joanne tells me that many people have held on to the older cookbooks as family keepsakes. Over several generations, they've served as constant reminders to cooks to keep baking their favorite pie and try once again for that elusive blue ribbon at the Deerfield Fair.

# Chapter 7

## Strawbery Banke Museum Dunaway Store

### "Timbers Never Tell Their Age"

**W**hen Strawbery Banke director Kathy Stiso Mullins first learned that I wanted to write about the museum's Dunaway Store, she was surprised. "It's the most 'non-original' thing at Strawbery Banke," she wrote in an e-mail. "We're supposed to be about preserving history and buildings, and this doesn't fit the bill in either case. The architectural design is not even appropriate for what would have been found in this region." Kathy is absolutely right.

Officially opened on June 10, 1967, by then–first lady Lady Bird Johnson, Dunaway Store's main purpose was to generate significant income for restoring historic properties at Strawbery Banke well into the future. Since it opened, however, the store has endured a kind of stepchild relationship with the institution that built it. I don't say "restored" because, as Kathy pointed out, the Dunaway Store was never part of Strawbery Banke's preservation and restoration plans. Instead, it was constructed from the timbers of an old barn in Dover donated to the museum in 1965. As such, it is the only nonoriginal building on the ten-acre, forty-plus-building compound.

This isn't readily apparent, however. The store sits back on an odd lot, front turned away from the street, but with left lateral vision of Prescott Park and Portsmouth's waterfront. It's not easy to see that there is a store here, or even that this is the entrance to Strawbery Banke—one of New England's premiere historical museums. Instead, you notice a pleasant-looking, two-story wood structure wrapped in gray blue siding that resembles a house more than a place of commerce. Dunaway simply melts into a row of historic buildings on a narrow lane that stretches into the museum's land away from Marcy Street.

But on an early Thursday morning in late October, it's so foggy that you can barely see the waterfront from the store's parking lot. Store manager Nancy Gulley meets me outside and hustles me through the front door before I have a chance to shiver. Inside, the gas fireplace is lit, and its warmth hits us the moment we enter. The only thing missing is hot cider, but the room is fragrant with the essence of cinnamon emanating from a display of earth-toned mugs and spice mix near the hearth.

I have not been inside the Dunaway Store since the late 1960s, when, growing up in Portsmouth, I would ride my bicycle here on hot summer days. With a handful of nickels I could buy a good-size bag of penny candy—licorice, chocolate cubes, fireballs. Then I'd sit on the store's front porch and eat it, watching the world go by. Over these thirty-five years, the store does not strike me as greatly changed. It's still an appealing place, with cream-colored walls and exposed wood beams across the ceiling. The big jars of penny candy are gone, but kids can buy similar sweets set out in small baskets. The difference is that each item now costs a quarter.

Nancy tells me she and her staff put up the Christmas decorations the night before. Although it's not yet Halloween, they seem appropriate here. Dunaway is a building that looks best dressed for Christmas. Looping through the condensed aisles, she points out the changes she has made since taking over as manager a few years ago. First, staff removed four ten-foot shelves and several huge cases to open up the space and create more room for displays. At the same time, the store got a thorough cleaning and paint job—something Nancy doesn't believe had happened since the 1960s. Finally, she had the museum ticket booth moved to a kiosk outside the store to relieve congestion, and then sold off the inventory that hadn't been touched in years. "These right here are the most popular items in the store," she says, stopping at an enormous pool of marbles in all colors and sizes. "Lots of schools have marble courts these days, so they're extremely popular with kids. For others, it's a walk down memory lane. We sell marbles every day."

From here, we walk past the stamp counter (the Dunaway Store is also a post office) and ascend a back staircase to Nancy's compact office, where neat rows of memos are hanging from her walls like decorations. She tells me that, personally, she doesn't like to shop but that business is another story. On this day a twelve-inch pile of catalogs sits on her desk, each containing multitudes of yellow sticky tabs marking the items she'll buy for the store's winter season.

Originally from Chicago, Nancy is a vivacious person with a quick wit and a genial midwestern personality. She's been the store manager and director of merchandising at Strawbery Banke since 2000. But after several decades of working with many types of companies, Nancy has found her job at Strawbery Banke different from anything else she's ever done. "In the profit-making world, you're told to go out and make money, but here in the non-profit world you have to learn to work within the museum's mission," she explains. "That means the merchandise has to complement the work of the museum." If it doesn't, museums face paying unrelated business income taxes on any profits they make from their stores. Simply put, a museum's mission and merchandise must match.

Nancy is a businesswoman working in a nonbusiness environment, and I ask her how this affects her ability to run the store as a profitable enterprise. She hesitates. "We don't capture more than 50 percent of the people visiting the museum and that's not a good statistic for us," she says. "But we're outside the museum walls, and that makes it more difficult for us to draw people in. We don't want to be in competition with Portsmouth businesses. That's not our role. But on the other hand, this *is* a business. We want people to come here for things they can't find anywhere else—like hand-painted furniture, historical patterns, or needlepoint kits."

Nancy tells me she just spent three days working with a museum store consultant who is helping her and her staff get sales back on track after a disappointing couple of years. Annual sales amount to about $350,000, but this is somewhat low for a store with 1,500 square feet of floor space. It takes two full-time and seven part-time staff, plus a handful of seasonal volunteers, to keep the store open throughout most of the year, but salaries can be a drain when store sales are down.

To maximize sales, Nancy buys specifically for each customer wave throughout the year, which means more gift items for tourists in summer, more educational toys for the three hundred to five hundred kids who descend daily on the store in spring, and more big-ticket and artsy items for the international customers who visit in the fall. Throughout the year, though, the store is packed almost to the point of overflow with everything from history-related books to handcrafted coffee mugs. With four centuries to pull from, it can feature almost any item with an historical bent and still sit well with tax collectors. This is an issue, though, because without a narrower scope, the store's identity can get all mixed up.

The trick, as always for a museum, is in tying the commercial with the educational, an issue managers of Dunaway Store have been grappling with for almost forty years. To help visitors make that correlation, Nancy and her staff are currently putting up signs around the store that explain various items' connection to the Strawbery Banke Museum. "Maybe a visitor saw a pot in one of the houses that they like," Nancy says. "Now they can buy that same pattern here that's ovenproof and microwavable. That's part of our job. We should be able to tell visitors about each item in the store and how it relates to the museum."

I ask Nancy what she notices when she visits other museum shops. Is she looking at the items? The prices? The presentation? "When I visit other museum shops, I always look around and ask myself, What do they believe in?" she replies. "To have a successful museum store, you have to believe in something, display it well, and offer it in mass quantities as tastefully as you can. Because what you're saying through your store is, This is what we're about. These are the things that we, as the institution as a whole, believe in."

In 1957, Portsmouth librarian Dorothy Vaughn got angry. For several years, she had watched the demolition of some of Portsmouth's most important old buildings, but the razing of the Jacob Treadwell House—a near twin to the nationally significant Moffatt-Ladd House—was the last straw. When her brother asked her to address the local Rotary Club on any topic she wished, Dorothy barely needed notes. She spoke passionately about the city's loss of so many historic buildings, listing them one by one. Then she called attention to a neglected, or "blighted" as it was called then, ten-acre tract near the waterfront that the city had singled out as a potential large-scale urban renewal project. At that time, the area was filled with tenement houses and scrap metal yards. But what bothered Dorothy was that it also contained many houses that were once part of Portsmouth's original Puddle Dock settlement—one of British America's busiest eighteenth-century seaports and the only part of Portsmouth that was not destroyed in the Great Fire of 1813. If the houses in this area were razed, she reasoned, there would be few remaining traces of Portsmouth's earliest beginnings.

It wasn't the first time the city's waterfront was getting attention. In 1935, the Works Progress Administration and National Park Service (NPS), working with local historians, conducted an analysis that identified the former Puddle Dock area as—unquestionably—historically significant. In its subsequent report to the U.S. Interior Department, the NPS recommended that Puddle Dock be fully restored, commenting that only a handful of southern capitals could compare with Portsmouth in historical richness. It's not clear whether the Portsmouth Housing Authority was aware of that report when, in 1954, it conducted its own preliminary studies of the area that earmarked the "Marcy–Washington Street Project" as its first for urban renewal consideration. Further studies a few years later by the housing authority suggested the land would be ideal for use as a waterfront garden apartment district.

Dorothy knew about the city's plans, and she didn't mince words. If someone didn't act soon, she told the Rotary Club, the city would lose an area of such historic importance that it would have national ramifications. Her words finally struck a nerve. By the end of the evening, a small group formed to explore the issue further. Within six months, the group, which now included many influential people in the seacoast area, had generated so much local interest that plans for creating a "Colonial Village" modeled after the work at Colonial Williamsburg in Virginia were in full swing. The time was right. Momentum for the project quickly built. The following year on November 12, 1958, Strawbery Banke, Inc., filed for official tax status as a nonprofit organization.

Between 1959 and the early 1960s, the organization worked steadfastly, with Dorothy Vaughn at the helm, to clear a number of obstacles in its path. First, it would have to convince federal authorities to revise urban renewal plans for the area, something authorities previously had shown no interest in doing in other states. Next, it would have to change a New Hampshire state law that required demolishing every building in an urban renewal project regardless of its value. And third, the group would have to raise enough funds to begin the actual restoration of the houses.

With the clock ticking quite literally just ahead of the wrecking ball, the organization persuaded a state senator from New Castle to introduce a bill that would change the state urban renewal law and pave the way for preservation of historic houses all over New Hampshire. The group's cause was, by now, so well known that there was nary a comment by the legislators, and the bill was quickly written into law. Soon afterward, federal officials agreed to scratch plans for the garden apartment district. As long as the area was being developed to obliterate blight, they said, it still fit into the urban renewal formula.

A bit taken aback by its success, the organization was further surprised when initial fund-raising efforts proved easier than expected. In August 1959, five prominent local women each pooled ten dollars for materials to make strawberry corsages and boutonnieres. The plan was to sell the items for ten dollars each at a September 1 Strawbery Banke fund-raiser the women had organized at the Colonial Theater in Portsmouth—a showing of a documentary film about John Paul Jones. The ladies sold dozens of the items at the event, and in fact completely sold out long before the evening ended. It was a propitious start. A few years later, these same women would found the Guild of Strawbery Banke whose only purpose would be to raise funds for the young institution and, in so doing, would eventually operate three successful stores.

By the early 1960s, work was well underway at Strawbery Banke to evaluate which structures should be saved in the ten-acre compound, as well as whether endangered historic buildings might be moved there from other parts of the city. Using a detailed 1813 map of Portsmouth, preservationists went from building to building in the Strawbery Banke compound, following one basic rule: they would select buildings for restoration whose "footprints" appeared on the 1813 map, and would relinquish buildings that did not. Eventually, preservationists decided that no building in the Strawbery Banke compound would date from after 1830.

New Hampshire State Architectural Historian James L. Garvin was Strawbery Banke's second employee and, later, its first curator. During the summer of 1963, he worked at Strawbery Banke as an administrative assistant and wrote this about the work of the institution's early preservationists for the November 1998 *Strawbery Banke Newsletter:* "The tools that preservationists routinely relied upon today were as yet unthought of. Federal policy was focused on slum clearance and rebuilding, not on preservation. There was no National Register of Historic Places. There were no State Historic Preservation Offices. There were no federal standards or publications offering help in the treatment of historic structures. The fledgling Strawbery Banke was entirely on its own as it struggled to develop an approach to the preservation of Portsmouth's architectural heritage."

Interestingly, if Strawbery Banke were established today, it's unlikely that any of the houses on its compound would be razed. But as Mr. Garvin pointed out, the preservation movement in the United States was young in the early 1960s, and its purpose was still being debated in many institutions throughout the country, including at Strawbery Banke. And not everyone in Portsmouth thought Strawbery Banke was a brilliant idea. "Strawbery Banke had not yet attained credibility with the people of Portsmouth," Mr. Garvin wrote in the same article. "Because Strawbery Banke had been named the redeveloper for an urban renewal project, many people blamed the museum for evicting Puddle Dock residents from their homes. Because many of the founders of Strawbery Banke were well-to-do, Portsmouth natives often stigmatized the museum as a plaything for the rich, an institution that seized the homes of the poor in order to create a 'cultural attraction' for tourists from far away."

The entrance to Strawbery Banke's Dunaway Store Museum Shop, Portsmouth, New Hampshire. (Courtesy of Strawbery Banke.)

Despite the controversy, the institution continued to analyze buildings, eventually recognizing that it would be better to save as many houses within the Puddle Dock neighborhood as possible, rather than make room for buildings that might be moved there from other neighborhoods of Portsmouth. "In the end," Mr. Garvin reports, "Strawbery Banke was allowed to purchase a site with 25 old houses left standing. On September 24, 1964, Strawbery Banke, Inc. handed officials of the Portsmouth Housing Authority a check for the balance due on a purchase price of $28,686, and became the owner of the heart of the old Puddle Dock neighborhood."

When Strawbery Banke finally opened to visitors on May 29, 1965, it had been eight years since Dorothy Vaughn first spoke to the Portsmouth

Rotary Club. Now, preservationists were celebrating the institution as a national model. Significantly, Strawbery Banke was the first urban renewal project in the United States whose goal was to preserve an historic area, rather than demolish it for redevelopment. It had taken extraordinary and unprecedented cooperation among federal, state, and local urban renewal authorities, civic groups, and private enterprises to establish Strawbery Banke. Its impact rippled through the preservation movement like a sound wave, transforming the institution from one librarian's vision into a symbol of the movement for the remainder of the 1960s.

On October 4, 1965, the *Manchester Union Leader* ran a three-inch blurb about the 1964–65 New York World's Fair held during those years in Queens, New York. In the previous weekend, the newspaper reported, over sixty thousand people had visited the New England Pavilion, registering its highest attendance so far. The pavilion was a popular six-state exhibit of all things New England, but its biggest attraction was a bona fide replica of a traditional New England country store. Sponsored by the Dunfey family, who owned a chain of hotel and motor inns in the Northeast, the store was packed with over 250 items, including skates, sleigh bells, tools, gunpowder, and barrels of corn.

New England's country store was really an exception to what most exhibits offered at that World's Fair, which billed itself as a showcase for future technological advancements. Through 140 pavilions on 646 acres, visitors were dazzled by exhibits on everything from computers and the race to the moon to lasers and Formica. But perhaps this brave new world proved a bit overwhelming for many of the fair's 51 million visitors. Amazingly, amid the nuclear power and telephone technology exhibits, the New England Pavilion with its brimming country store was a hit.

Soon after the fair ended in mid-October 1965, the New England–based Dunfey family approached the Strawbery Banke board of directors with an unsolicited offer. Did they wish to take advantage of the great interest shown in the country store by purchasing it intact for $20,000? By this time, the board had hired retired naval officer Captain Carl A. Johnson to handle the daily operations of Strawbery Banke. The captain, who once ran the Portsmouth Naval Shipyard and had a fondness for fancy titles (he asked for and was given the title of executive vice president, which today would translate most closely into general manager), immediately jumped at the Dunfey offer. He knew he was going to need money—a lot of it—to build Strawbery Banke into an institution on a par with Colonial Williamsburg, and a store could be just the vehicle to help him do that.

Although the institution didn't have the funds to accept the Dunfey offer, Captain Johnson told his board he liked the idea of establishing a country store at Strawbery Banke and planned to pursue it. Only two weeks after turning the Dunfey offer down, he contacted Dean, Perry, Hepburn & Stewart, a Boston architectural firm well known for its extensive work at Colonial Williamsburg. In a memo to the firm dated early November 1965, Captain Johnson outlined what he saw as the most viable options for establishing the store. They could modify an existing Strawbery Banke building, acquire another building from Portsmouth or its environs, or construct a completely new building as a replica. Saying that he favored acquiring or constructing another building, the captain concluded by asking the architects to "please consider this a matter of urgency."

With an architect secured, the captain's next step was to find an affordable building. If he wanted to ride the momentum of country store popularity generated by the World's Fair, he knew he had to act quickly. But after a month-long, New England–wide search, he came up short. The institution simply didn't have the funds to transport structures from other states. Turning back to Strawbery Banke, he then investigated other unrestored houses within the compound, but concluded that none were "arranged, within, in such a manner as to provide reasonably adequate unobstructed floor space for a store," he reported to his board.

Finally, in early December Strawbery Banke received a new offer that would require little investment of funds. Paul McQuaid, an automobile dealer in Dover who had heard of the institution's plight, offered to donate a 42-by-60-foot building he owned on Portland Avenue in that city, which was known as the Guppy Barn. No one at the time knew exactly how old it was, but the barn's hand-hewn beams and wooden pegs for nails suggested it might have been built in the late 1700s. This time, with little hesitation, the board accepted the offer.

An agreement was drafted several days later, stating that the barn would be disassembled, all usable timbers and wide boards would be saved, all nails would be removed, and all lumber would be transported to a designated location on the property of Strawbery Banke. The institution would then use these materials to construct a completely new building to be used as a country store. Disassembling of the old barn started immediately, on December 10, 1965.

Meanwhile, the board debated the store's location. The most obvious site was a lot on the corner of Marcy and Charles Streets, where an "historically insignificant house," as Captain Johnson called it, was being considered for demolition. Known as the Edward Ayres House after a former owner, it was probably built after 1850, although its foundation appeared to be much older. In a January 1966 memo to his board, the captain proposed that the Ayres House be demolished and that a new structure, comprised of the Guppy Barn timbers, be erected in its place. He told his board that if they at least kept the foundation, "it would provide a connection, admittedly tenuous, with the historic past." By late February, the Ayres House was gone.

On March 2, 1966, Captain Johnson authorized Philip W. Baker, Inc., of Antrim, a company that specialized in restoring New England properties, to begin building the Strawbery Banke country store. After an extensive evaluation, Baker agreed to build a full cellar, install heat and wiring, build the frame, chimneys, and fireplace, stain finish the inside and outside of the building, install toilet facilities, and construct office and storage space.

At about the same time, the board secured funding through the S. Judson Dunaway Charitable Foundation of Dover for the entire cost of the project, which came to about $71,000 ($400,000 in today's dollars), including the builder's and architect's fees. S. Judson Dunaway, founder of the Expello Corporation of Dover, makers of various household products, had taken a personal interest in the project because, as a young boy in Standardsville, Virginia, he had worked in his father's country store. His sole request of the board was that the Dunaway General Store, as it would be called, resemble his father's original store in Virginia as closely as possible. (This explains why the architectural design of the store is dissimilar to the eighteenth-century New England-style buildings of Strawbery Banke.)

With funding secured, the architectural firm got to work and quickly created a design that included a welcoming front porch, exposed beams from the ceiling, and, of course, a large fireplace. Now the final, and perhaps most difficult, step was to define how the store would fit with Strawbery Banke's educational mission. Grace Casey, an antiques dealer in Gilmanton Iron Works who was helping the board set initial standards for the store, drafted a memo that summed up the board's ideas this way:

"The purpose of the Dunaway General Store, like that of the Strawbery Banke project, is to evoke the entire era of American life over the long period during which this nation was created. A general store is an essential part of any such reconstruction of the American past for it was . . . an American original created by the necessities of living. . . . Without a vivid presentation of the economic ethos any historical restoration on the scale of Strawbery Banke would be hollow; it would be a house without a kitchen.

"Fulfilling such a function in the Strawbery Banke theme, the Dunaway General Store should serve an educational purpose, illuminating the retail life of America by displaying artifacts from a variety of periods and by being reconstructed in such a way as to show the evolution of the institution itself." And while the store should provide direct financial support to Strawbery Banke, she continued, "it should serve as one of the major educational and artistic attractions . . . a microcosm reflecting in its diversity and tradition the whole concept of Strawbery Banke."

Fifteen months after work started, Dunaway General Store opened to the public with an initial inventory worth $5,000 and a small exhibit of objects relating to the museum's growing collection of artifacts. Then–first lady Lady Bird Johnson presided over the half-hour, midmorning ceremony on Saturday, June 10, 1967, after which she inaugurated the Dunaway Store Post Office and bought two nineteenth-century children's books, along with spools of red and beige thread. When the event was over, press photos taken that day show a beaming Lady Bird striding purposefully over a row of shrubs with a puzzled-looking entourage of Secret Service men in tow.

With such a promising start, I would like to report that the store immediately fulfilled its goals, but that is not what happened. Despite the board's commitment to Dunaway, all did not go well in its first years of operation. First, Dunaway lost money. Second, as the preservation movement matured, the store was singled out by detractors as an aberration from Strawbery Banke's overall educational mission. By the late 1960s, the institution's board of overseers, which was comprised of prominent historians and museum professionals from around the country, had begun to view Dunaway as the most visible example of what was wrong with Strawbery Banke at that time.

According to archival documents, overseer Dr. Richard Rowland, a Smithsonian Institution scholar, summed up his peers' views in a reproach delivered before the Strawbery Banke board in April 1968. Bluntly ticking off his objections to the store, he told the board that Portsmouth, in the eighteenth century, never had a store such as this and that he wondered why they had taken this course when "there were already commercial buildings available for this purpose." Most definitely, "the building, architecturally, is a mistake." And besides that, he sniffed, "the merchandise is unworthy."

By 1971, the Dunaway General Store still hadn't turned a profit and was starting to draw funds away from the very projects it had been created to support. In an effort to reverse this, the board decided to hand over daily operation of Dunaway to the highly successful fund-raisers of the Guild of Strawbery Banke, Inc. The Guild embraced the task—as it did all its various pursuits—with such vigor that within a few years, Dunaway was already on its way to solid profitability.

Based on this, you might think that the connection between Strawbery Banke and the Guild was strong, if only because of the symbiotic nature of the relationship. Archival records, however, show that Strawbery Banke and the Guild perpetuated a rivalrous association for years that eventually led the institution to accuse the Guild of being concerned only with its own survival. The discord dated back to 1962, when Guild leadership approached the Strawbery Banke board and asked it to consider making the Guild an official part of the institution. The proposal made sense. The only reason the Guild existed was to raise funds for Strawbery Banke's restoration work. But then something unexpected happened. After much debate, the board voted not to support or sponsor the Guild. Ironically, the decision was purely financial. Board members were concerned that by extending the institution to include a fund-raising mechanism, Strawbery Banke's tax-exempt status could be compromised.

It's important to remember that in 1962, the Guild, which had been founded by the same women who had made corsages to sell at Strawbery Banke's first fund-raiser, was only three years old. But in that time, it had already been remarkably successful in raising funds that eventually helped pay for the full restoration of the first two houses at Strawbery Banke—a total cost of over $200,000. It was an organization made up of individuals—mostly women—who believed deeply in the Strawbery Banke cause and who viewed support from the institution as acceptance and approval of the work they were doing. The board's decision came as a shock. Many Guild members viewed it as a rejection.

Astonishingly, though, the Guild's commitment to the cause never wavered. In spite of—and perhaps because of—the perceived slight from the Strawbery Banke board, the Guild struck out on its own. On October 1, 1963, the group incorporated separately as The Guild of Strawbery Banke, Inc., with the continued purpose of raising funds for the organization. Between 1963 and 1971, the Guild grew to become a fund-raising powerhouse, with extensive experience in staging successful events and managing large sums of money. It became a membership organization and was considered by many in the seacoast region to be a prestigious group to serve as a volunteer. When the Guild took over the Dunaway General Store in 1971, it knew just what to do and wasted no time in ensuring the venture would be a success.

A decade later, in the early 1980s, records show that Strawbery Banke had become dependent on the average $25,000 the Guild turned over to it every year, the bulk of which came from the Dunaway Store. It was an item in the budget, and if the Guild came up a few dollars short, the Strawbery Banke board was quick to ask why. That surely didn't help the relationship, but the Guild was in its heyday then. It had gone from five members in 1959 to over one thousand in 1980, and was enjoying immense success running needlework and gourmet cooking classes, as well as three successful shops.

Still, there was growing resentment among some Guild members that Strawbery Banke wasn't fully appreciating its efforts. Outside of the transfer of funds by the Guild and a perfunctory thank-you once a year from the board, there isn't much evidence of a cordial relationship between the two organizations in the 1970s or 1980s. At one point, Strawbery Banke even called the Guild "elitist." The Guild appeared to respond with hurt feelings and a cold shoulder. One former member I spoke to, who had been active in all three stores, remembers asking Guild leadership why it didn't bury the hatchet and move on. The idea, she says, was treated with derision. She was told in no uncertain terms that it was not under consideration—nor would it ever be. She never mentioned it again.

Barbara Widen is a former Dunaway Store manager and Guild member who began working in the store when it opened in 1967 and still works there today. She says she never understood why Strawbery Banke felt the group was elitist. "I never felt it. I have only fond memories of my time as a Guild member," she says. "But the Guild was doing things to raise funds that weren't usually done at that time, like sponsoring classes and running stores. They'd fill the Connie Bean Center in Portsmouth whenever they held a needlework workshop because they were able to attract nationally known experts to come here and speak. They were the first ones, at least in this area, to be doing these really great things, and I think the board just didn't understand it."

"Our stores had a wonderful reputation and a wonderful following," Barbara continues. "I still get customers at Dunaway who are looking for the needlepoint kits we used to sell. But in the 1980s, more and more organizations started doing the types of things we were doing and there was more competition. Also, many of our members lived outside the city and weren't traveling in as frequently as they once did. Our attendance numbers at events started to slip."

The stores still did well through the 1980s, but in 1990, Guild leadership, in typical businesslike style, decided it was time to call it a day and turn over all assets to Strawbery Banke. On December 31 of that year, the Guild of Strawbery Banke, Inc., ceased to exist. Over a period of thirty years, it had contributed more than $600,000 (well over $1 million in today's dollars) to Strawbery Banke's restoration work.

Of all the Guild's activities, only the Dunaway General Store has survived. Strawbery Banke has officially renamed it The Strawbery Banke Museum Shop, but has changed nothing else. I asked Barbara Widen why she has continued to work here every week for thirty-five years. "I've always loved it," she says. "Of course the look of the store has changed over the years, but not the atmosphere. Right now it looks again like it did twenty years ago, like it should look—like an old-fashioned general store. We haven't really planned it that way. Somehow the building seems to have taken over and become itself again."

Standing in front of Dunaway Store on a raw November morning, John Schnitzler, Strawbery Banke's restoration carpenter, is pointing at the roof of the store and shaking his head. "The roofline in this building is very funky. It's not historic in shape and there used to be a board running down the wall on the left side that tied with the roof. In 1990, we re-sided the building and took it out," John says, walking up to the side of the building. "Back then they were caught up in the colonial revivalist thing, and let's just say creativity flowed."

John came to Strawbery Banke in the early 1970s and got hooked on the ongoing maintenance of old buildings that now keeps him and a small crew of tradesmen busy year-round. He speaks with obvious authority about the houses at Strawbery Banke, because, in one way or another, he's worked on them all. He says he's mastered the job by learning how to read the buildings. "A lot of the work is piecing the building back together," he tells me. "You have to look at the chronology of the building through layers of paint or wallpaper. Multiple nail holes will tell you something probably has been moved and you have to figure out which holes are the originals. Paint shadows will tell you the same. This is when something has been moved and there are 'shadows' of the old paint left behind."

"It's difficult to put things back when they've been changed over the years," John goes on. "Old houses often have odd-sized lumber, so you can't go out to Home Depot and buy replacements. Just acquiring lumber is difficult. The labor it takes to put something back is time-consuming. There's more handwork on older houses than new ones. Today it's so easy. You buy something and plug it into a hole and you're done. A lot of carpenters today haven't hung doors."

John says the building will tell you its history, but you have to be willing to look for it by uncovering—literally—what's been done before, and in what order, before you can begin to restore the house to its original condition. That could require everything from taking down walls to replacing staircases. The work he's done on the store over the years, however, has been far less elaborate than anything he's done on the other houses. When you get down to it, Dunaway is just an old barn dressed up like a store. And like any old barn, maintenance is minimal. Inside, the timbers need periodic cleaning and painting. Outside, the building's siding is worked on once in a while, and the trim and porch get an occasional coat of paint.

John and I enter the store through its rough, unpainted door. Standing before the fireplace, he points to the wooden walls and beams overhead that give the building an authentically rustic atmosphere. "We don't know exactly how old the barn was when it was taken down," he says. "Timbers never tell their age, but you can look for clues. In earlier days, timbers were wider." He runs his hand along the broad timbers that make up the walls of the store. They're about twelve inches wide, washed lightly in cream-colored paint. "If there's one thing this building stands for, it's an example of early preservationist thinking. Today we wouldn't do this. We would've kept the house that was originally here, which would probably be about 150 years old now."

That's almost certainly true, but in order to have turned the original building into a store, which is what records show Captain Johnson was thinking, Strawbery Banke would have had to gut it, virtually obliterating most of the benefits of preserving it. At the time, it seemed easier—and less expensive—to build a new structure on the original foundation and to try to tie it in with the overall mission of the institution.

Today, the Dunaway Store may be the only nonoriginal building at Strawbery Banke, but at the very least, it likely has timbers of a similar age to other buildings in the compound. Over the years, it hasn't demanded a lot of the institution whose name it bears, but has certainly contributed much to Strawbery Banke's restoration. And at least as far as its structural materials go, it appears the Dunaway Store has never been an impostor.

# 8

## New England Marionette Opera

---

### "The Puppets Seemed to Have Minds of Their Own"

*F*or a small state, I'm always surprised at how long it can take to get from one side of New Hampshire to the other. After a two-hour drive, I know I'm in the right place by the legislative license plates on the dark car pulling out of the unpaved driveway ahead of me. Behind the wheel is a pretty blond woman wearing shocking pink lipstick. "Park wherever you'd like," she calls cheerily, waving me in.

When I ring the doorbell, state representative Ted Leach is there in an instant. He is a tall man, over six feet, with slightly hunched shoulders and graying hair that covers the tops of his ears and sweeps across his forehead. He's dressed comfortably in what is probably a favorite jeans shirt and khakis. I could style my hair in the shine off his penny loafers. His manner is gracious. His voice has a southern twang to it.

Several weeks earlier I had discovered Ted's web site, which briefly tells the story of the New England Marionette Opera (NEMO). The site is striking. It opens with a photograph of a *Madame Butterfly* marionette that sits against a black background and features other photos of the theater and its puppeteers. But what got me was the pop-up box that appeared over the first page. It said, "On January 1, 1999, at 12:22 P.M., a fire totally destroyed the New England Marionette Opera. . . ." This was hard to believe. I found ticket information, directions, even a complete schedule on the web site. But a second glance revealed it was from 1998.

Ted founded the theater in 1991, running it out of the Peterborough Baptist Church until New Year's Day 1999, when a fire raged through the building, destroying everything inside it. There were no human injuries, but the theater lost all but three of its cast of over two hundred handmade marionettes. Ted continues to run the web site as a kind of cyber memorial—to them, as well as to the theater itself—and still receives e-mail from people all over the country inviting the New England Marionette Opera to visit their town. "Oh well . . . ," he always says. Today, at his home in Hancock, he would tell me the entire story.

We ascend a narrow staircase into a room with long windows. As we settle into the plush floral furniture, the grandfather clock in the corner gongs ten times. Straight ahead on top of the television, among a collection of family photographs, I notice a framed picture of a geisha. She is wearing a white silk kimono and full geisha makeup. Upon closer inspection, I see it's the same *Madame Butterfly* marionette as on Ted's web site. Nothing in the photo is scaled, so she appears life-size, her features human. Ted picks up the photo and gazes at her like she's an old flame. In a way she is.

In 1973, Ted Leach was returning home from a business trip to Moscow when a flight delay stranded him in Salzburg, Austria. With time on his hands he decided to attend a performance of *The Magic Flute* by the world-famous Salzburg Marionette Theatre, the only one of its kind dedicated solely to opera. "It completely caught me off guard," he says. "What intrigued me the most was how quickly the audience bought into the performance emotionally."

Ted was so taken by the performance that all the way home he mapped out how he would build such a theater himself, but it would be almost twenty years before he would complete those plans. In the meantime, he soon left his job as a communications executive at an energy company in Tulsa, Oklahoma, to pursue another dream—owning a small country newspaper in New England. He bought the *Monadnock Ledger* in 1979 and ran it out of the 1843 Peterborough Baptist Church, which he also bought, until 1986, when he sold the *Ledger* to the *Concord Monitor.* He held on to the building, though, located on the corner of Main and Depot Streets in downtown Peterborough, and established the New England Marionette Opera there late in 1991.

"I made over four hundred calls over a six-month period that year to find out how to set it up," Ted recalls. "I guess this was my market research. My knowledge about marionettes went from zero to just about everything I needed to know. No one really encouraged me, because they had no frame of reference for what I wanted to do. A marionette opera had never existed in the United States before. I think many didn't understand the scale of my project. Those who did thought it would never make it. Some suggested that I start small and grow into this 'wild' idea."

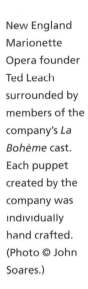

New England Marionette Opera founder Ted Leach surrounded by members of the company's *La Bohème* cast. Each puppet created by the company was individually hand crafted. (Photo © John Soares.)

I do not have the impression that Ted was particularly discouraged by this advice. He's an optimist by nature, and when he cares about something, he cares deeply and devotes himself to it. He tries to do everything right the first time, but recognizes he is only as good as the people around him. Those who know him well say he is a private man—intense, creative, demanding, visionary. They say he can beat a dead horse to drive home a point, but that you always know where he stands. (Former employees say they'd work for him again in a heartbeat.) Instead of discouraging him, I believe the negative feedback only strengthened his resolve.

At this point, Ted was ready to move ahead but was aware that he knew very little about the physical mechanics of making a marionette or building a theater. So in mid-1991 he contacted the University of Connecticut, which runs the only postgraduate puppetry program in the United States, and asked if there might be a student skilled enough to work as his artistic director. Ted figures it was fate that he was referred to the talented perfectionist Roger Dupen, who happened to have two loves: opera and marionettes. At their initial meeting, Ted says he hired Roger on the spot and immediately commissioned him with building a scale model of a marionette theater. Soon afterward, the two became completely engrossed in transforming the

Peterborough Baptist Church into the New England Marionette Opera, taking painstaking care to preserve as much of the historical ambience of the structure as possible.

One of the interesting things about building a marionette theater is the attention that must be paid to the dimensions of it so that the puppets on-stage appear life-size during performances. "One day I was sitting back looking at the stage, but it wasn't right and I didn't know why," Ted says. "So I removed a paint can that was sitting just off to the side. After that, the stage looked perfect again, and I realized the can had thrown off the entire scale of the stage because it had given me a known point of reference. When the lights go down, the perception has to be that the theater and marionettes are life-size. I can't emphasize enough how important scale is to a marionette theater."

The stage ended up being twelve feet deep and twenty-four feet wide including the side wings. It even featured an orchestra pit where a maestro puppet in a black tuxedo could "conduct." In photographs taken from the back of the theater, the stage, which is framed by a thick red velvet curtain, does indeed appear to be life-size. To create the illusion, Ted and Roger raised the original single-level floor so that each seat row was slightly higher than the one in front of it. Former audience members who had also visited the Salzburg Marionette Theatre said that NEMO's stage was better because you could see the stage clearly from anywhere. Basically, there were no bad seats in the house.

Ted's plan was to open the theater in May of 1992, but he knew he couldn't do that unless he found at least eight puppeteers who could become good enough to perform a full-scale opera within four months. So he ran an advertisement in a local newspaper in early January inviting anyone with an interest in marionette theater to attend an informational meeting. About twenty people showed up. "By the time of the meeting, the main part of the building was gutted, there were only a few clip-on lights, and there was no heat," Ted recalls. "We were looking for people to help us make marionettes, seamstresses, potential puppeteers, office people, whatever. Some knew each other, many did not. In that first meeting we picked up four people who were with us until the end."

A few weeks later, Ted and Roger held auditions. They knew they wouldn't find many people with professional puppetry experience, but they were willing to train. "We were looking for a sense of music, theater, desire, and dedication," Ted says. "I know we presented it as a very exciting venture, and several jumped on board. Our intuition was exceptionally good.

By getting people with no previous marionette manipulation experience, we could bring them up in our mold, so to speak."

As the stage construction and rehearsals progressed, Ted and Roger began crafting the marionettes that would serve as the company's stars. The puppets they created weighed between two and three pounds each and were between eighteen and twenty-four inches tall. Like all marionettes, each had four main parts—the control, the head, the body, and the costume. The heads were fashioned separately by various local sculptors, which was the most time-consuming aspect of the process, taking four days to complete. Ted says the sculptors never used the same face twice. Often the puppets resembled opera stars, including a considerably trimmer Luciano Pavarotti and a young Maria Callas with wistful eyes and jet black hair.

After the head was completed, Roger jointed the body using fifteen separate parts that moved as human joints would—with the exception of the head, which could swivel all the way around. For example, knees and elbows couldn't bend backward, and torsos only flexed forward. The reason was simple. Since a marionette's mouth cannot move, it must be able to express emotion through subtleties in movement—a kind of marionette body language. And it can do this only if its movements precisely mimic those of the human being it portrays.

Several NEMO staff members sewed the marionettes' costumes—with one exception. The *Madame Butterfly* costumes were created by the accomplished Japanese kimono artisan Masako Hayashi, who had created the same costumes for the New York City Opera's production of *Madame Butterfly* (she was living in the Peterborough area at the time). "She said she liked working with us better because a yard of fabric goes so much farther," Ted laughs. "In a marionette theater, there are no costume changes, because the strings go right through the costume. When a new costume is required, a new marionette comes out that looks exactly as the other one, only dressed in different clothing. We needed four marionettes to play the part of *Madame Butterfly*."

All marionettes have fourteen to twenty-four strings, each of which is eleven feet in length. Using them to manipulate a marionette looks much easier than it actually is, requiring impressive dexterity in the puppeteer. For example, there are six strings just for controlling the marionette's hands. The marionettes created by NEMO all had black strings because they didn't reflect light and became almost invisible in the theater's low stage lighting. The strings were attached to a wooden control in the shape of a T that fit in the puppeteer's hand and allowed control of the legs, while two subcontrols, one on each side of the T, manipulated the arms and hands. The company used an average of ten marionettes for each production and, over the course of its seven-year run, created a total of 212, including animals as well as humans. All were handcrafted individually on site. At the end, each was valued at between $750 and $1,500.

On May 15, 1992, the New England Marionette Opera staged its first production. Only twenty hours before, 135 red, crushed velvet chairs with teakwood arms had been delivered to the theater and quickly installed for the opening performance of Giacomo Puccini's *La Bohème*. (Ted says he hadn't planned to complete the house portion of the theater until the following year, but he was offered the $475 chairs for only $75 each.) It had taken six months of intensive labor to build the stage, create the marionettes, train and rehearse the puppeteers, plan the lighting and sound effects, and set up the administrative and financial operations of the theater.

With its infrastructure in place, Ted and Roger could begin to build the company's repertoire. Generally, they chose the most popular and well-known operas to produce, using a style that Ted calls "UFO"—user-friendly opera. He and Roger would listen to dozens of recordings before coming across one suitable for NEMO to use. The problem was that many operas are recorded live and include the sound of the audience clapping. Other recordings are simply too old to produce the right sound quality. Still others leave out whole sections of the music. When they finally found a clean recording of an entire opera, Ted negotiated the royalties to use it in his productions. Over the run of the theater, its repertoire grew to include *Carmen, The Barber of Seville, Tosca, Amahl and the Night Visitors, Madame Butterfly, La Bohème, The Magic Flute, Porgy and Bess,* and *Macbeth.*

Ted's biggest coup was obtaining permission to perform *Porgy and Bess* from the ultraprotective trustees of George Gershwin's estate. But before the performance could be permanently added to the theater's repertoire, it had to be viewed and approved by the trustees themselves. In addition, the estate wanted a fifty-performance contract, stipulating that all performances would have to be performed within one year. For a large theater company with a wide repertoire, this would not have been a problem. But for a small company like NEMO, fifty came close to the total number of performances it presented in an entire year.

Ted was so certain the trustees would be thrilled with the performance, however, that he invested the $86,000 in marionettes and costumes needed to make the *Porgy and Bess* production a reality. Finally, after months of preparation, the company staged the opera and the trustees arrived, including Gershwin's daughter. Ted says they were dazzled. In fact, they loved it so much that they wanted to include it in a documentary being filmed at that time about Gershwin's music. Unfortunately it was too late for that, but Ted won on another front. The trustees were willing to let NEMO stage the fifty performances over several years. *Porgy and Bess* was immediately added to the company's repertoire.

It's understandable why the trustees were so impressed. Before staging any opera, the company researched it meticulously and created a stage set that matched as closely as possible the original setting intended for it. This is important, Ted says, because many full-scale operas today don't do this. Instead, they modernize to fit the script. "There is a lot of 'experimenting' going on in the art world today," he says. "Self-made, supercreative directors take old operas and think they are improving them by putting them in new, and sometimes bizarre, settings. The 'nuevo theatergoers' then file in and cluck their approval. No one would dare suggest that the thing is stupid. Roger and I decided to stick with the way the opera was intended to be presented. Of course we had to take some liberties because we couldn't walk a marionette through a doorway, for example, or hand one a glass of wine."

Performances were kept to no more than two and a quarter hours in length, Ted says, because it's difficult for people to watch marionettes for long periods without straining their eyes. This meant cutting operas from an average length of three hours without sacrificing the quality of the production. "In opera, there's a lot of musical 'Hamburger Helper,' things you really don't need," Ted explains. "But you have to consider where the music begins and ends. You can't cut things off in the middle. Shortening can actually help a lot of operas. I had some audience members tell me we took the bad stuff out and kept the good stuff in."

When the music and sets were worked out, Ted experimented with the lighting to create the right effect for the production. "A big part of the opera is the lighting. It's absolutely key in a marionette theater," Ted says. "I knew what kinds of effects I was after, so I taught myself how to do them. I wanted the faces to come in and out of the shadows. If you don't do this and give full lighting, people will notice that the mouth isn't moving. You can also use lighting to distract from entrances and exits or add depth to the stage. But you have to be careful because in a marionette theater puppet strings break if they hit a hot light."

During performances, Ted worked from a state-of-the-art, computerized control booth (which he taught himself to operate) in the balcony, where he could see everything that was going on in the house as well as onstage. From there, he had complete control over all house and stage lighting, house temperature functions, sound systems, and the projection of translations, or "trans-titles," as Ted called them, in an area above the stage. "After I introduced the performance, I would disappear through the stage door, run down the steps leading from backstage through the lobby, out of the building, up the front steps of the building, and up the steps to the balcony," Ted recalls. "I'd have to excuse myself as I crawled over the balcony audience, who had been forewarned that I would be coming, and dash into the booth to take over the sound, lights, and trans-titles. At that point, Roger, who had been manning the controls, would leave the booth and go back to the lobby and supervise the preparation for intermission, as well as the phone and latecomers. I did the lighting for every production except one, *Madame Butterfly*, when I was performing on the bridge with a marionette."

Former audience members say they recall a suspension of disbelief that happened very quickly after performances started. "You entered right into the spirit of it without ever realizing you were doing so—you just completely forgot that these were marionettes," says Penny Warfield, who attended every production NEMO ever staged. "The orchestra pit was to die for. It had tiny Coke cans and Dunkin' Donut cups inside it—everything to perfect scale. Ted would come out and introduce each performance. He always wanted to know where people came from. Then the lights would go down and the conductor would appear. It was the incidental things that really counted a lot. The scenery transformed everything into something else. The lighting changed imperceptibly and altered the mood. Everything onstage was alive. And think about it. These puppets always had to look like they were singing. The subtlety of movement was extraordinary."

When most people see a marionette performance for the first time, they think it's all about the mechanical skill of working the marionette. That's a key element, but it's secondary. The best puppeteers know a lot about acting and have some type of theater experience. Some have studied mime. All, however, understand human movement. "Early on, all puppeteers attempt to get the marionette to do something that it simply cannot do. It's a gravity game, as well as a very loose-jointed operation," Ted explains. "Soon they learn that even though they can 'think' what they want their marionette to do, it simply isn't possible. The mechanical skills can be taught, but bringing the marionette to life cannot."

Although NEMO eventually developed a core group of what Ted calls "world-class puppeteers," the company held auditions for every production. What he and Roger primarily looked for was growth in the puppeteers as artists. For example, "teaching" a marionette to walk across the stage is probably the most crucial skill a puppeteer can master. It takes hours of practice to keep the puppet level with the floor, not sagging or floating above it. Over time, some puppeteers became better at handling male marionettes, which is particularly difficult because there are no skirts to hide the legs. After auditions, Roger assigned the roles, and while there were sometimes surprises about who got what, no one ever dropped out once rehearsals started.

Rehearsing was done in stages. First, Roger gave each puppeteer two copies of the script—the original (usually in Italian) and another in English. Then the group watched videos of the opera to take in the music and flow, and to study how human actors handled the roles. If the puppeteers didn't understand every minute of the opera, they wouldn't be able to match the movements of their marionette to the pace of the music.

In the six weeks that followed, the group rehearsed the roles onstage as though they were the marionettes themselves, developing each character, memorizing each bar of music, and determining how the marionettes would work together onstage. This was *before* they ever picked up their marionette. "The most important thing was the human reaction of the puppeteer," Ted says. "We would go through different parts of the opera during rehearsals and ask each other, 'How would you feel if this happened to you?' If the puppeteer cupped his hands over his head and said he'd feel terrible, that's the gesture he would use with his marionette. The movement had to be precise and refined, not exaggerated or overdone in any way. It had to be genuine."

By the end of the six weeks, the puppeteers began to transfer their character development to their marionette. "It's hard to explain how this happened; it was almost mystical," recalls Alana Korda, who attended that first orientation meeting in 1992 and worked with the theater during its entire run. "You just had to try to find something in your own experience to match the emotion. Getting used to the slight time delay for any movement to travel down the strings was difficult initially, but became second nature after a while."

In the ensuing month or so, the group worked as an ensemble, operating seven feet above the stage floor on two twenty-four-foot performing bridges that supported the eight to ten cast members. At this point, practicing pass-offs was key. These happen when a marionette must make its way to the other side of the stage but, to get there, must be passed from one puppeteer to another so that it appears the marionette is walking seamlessly. In any marionette opera production there are hundreds of pass-offs. In *Madame Butterfly*, for example, there were approximately 288 during each performance.

"We had one bridge, like a catwalk, in the front and one bridge in the back with the actual performing area in between the two bridges. There was about a two-and-a-half-foot-wide stretch between the bridges. You got so used to this space that you didn't think about it anymore," says Alana. "The puppets had to move from front to back, back to front, or past each other across the stage . . . it was an equally amazing performance on the bridge, more like a ballet. Some puppeteers didn't move their bodies much when manipulating and others were all over the place. It was tight quarters and you had to be aware of everyone around you, especially in crowd scenes."

In any creative organization there can be a natural self-protectiveness among its members simply because what is being brought to life comes from the heart and soul of the creators. It was no different within NEMO, although Ted says he had no tolerance for attitudes that rose above the group. "We had no room for defensiveness," he says. "We had a policy that if everyone felt a puppeteer should change something, that person would have to change it. We didn't want to hear excuses. There was no time for that."

Ted videotaped rehearsals, which proved effective because puppeteers could easily see what they needed to fix. "When I was in *Madame Butterfly*, I thought I was really good. But the first time I saw a videotape of the production it was a real eye-opener," Ted chuckles. "I was terrible. So I spent a lot of time alone at the theater with my own music learning how to do different things with the marionettes. That way, when I asked someone to try something different, they couldn't tell me it couldn't be done. It could because I'd just spent the weekend learning it."

Company members say the group was like an extended family, complete with spats, temper tantrums, and personality conflicts. Tensions rose typically around competition for roles, perceived favoritism, diva-ism, and differing styles of rehearsing and performing. The relationship between Ted and Roger was especially interesting because they appeared to be opposites—Ted being practical and businesslike, and Roger, by all accounts, tending toward the stereotypical *artiste*. "Both of Roger's parents were from the UK so he had a British accent," Ted says. "He was tall and thin as a rail; very intelligent—and he knew it. He didn't have a good grasp on handling people and could be a procrastinator. But he had creative genes flowing out of every pore in his body. This was vital to an operation such as ours. There was no 'book' on how to do a marionette opera, because we were the first in the U.S., so we were a constant work in progress. . . . I am convinced that there was only one person in this country who could have worked with me to develop a marionette opera and I found that person in Roger."

Alana agrees with Ted's description of Roger's character. "Roger had problems delegating. Someone would paint scenery and he would redo it. He was a perfectionist, but he mellowed over time as he came to trust us more. We knew there would be a tirade during various points in rehearsals, and we got used to it," she says. "One Friday night, the veteran puppeteers knew that Roger was going to yell at us whether we needed it or not. It was the opening of *Tosca* and he had just finished giving us notes. It was my birthday and the stage manager came up the stairs with a lit birthday cake for me behind Roger. Just then Roger launched into his tirade. So the stage manager stood there with the birthday cake candles melting as Roger, who was unaware of the stage manager with the cake behind him, went on and on. Finally Ted said, 'Let's go eat cake.' Now, it's a funny story. At the time, it made me wonder why I was investing so much of my time in the theater."

"Both Ted and Roger are strong-minded people, so of course there were clashes," she continues. "It was kind of like a marriage. They each had great respect for each other and they complemented each other well. Roger left six months or so after the fire. He comes back once in a while with little notice, breezes back into our lives, and breezes back out again. He now lives in Brazil and is not involved in theater, to anyone's knowledge."

By performance time, the group always pulled together. "Our call was for a half hour before curtain," Alana remembers. "This was the same time as when the house opened. We all did various stretching exercises to prepare our bodies, unbagged all our puppets, checked the strings for possible breaks. Some puppeteers practiced pieces with music before the audience arrived. For instance, when I was one of the dancers in *Amahl and the Night Visitors,* we always did the dance once before each performance, because it always went smoother in the performance when we did. Working with the marionettes was very physically demanding. It was like you had a weight at the end of your arm that you had to keep steady all the time. Roles that required the marionettes to stand around a lot were much harder and physically demanding than moving roles. Also, it was very warm on the bridges."

"There was always a great expectation before a performance," she goes on. "Nervous tension was prevalent in the early performances of the run, but by the end of it we could be downright silly and almost lackadaisical before the curtain went up, and then—bingo—we were focused. I only remember two times when a puppet dropped onto the stage area. When I think about it, I'm surprised this didn't happen more often. We also had to be incredibly quiet or the audience would hear us. After the performance we were exhausted but giddy, especially if it was a good one or if something happened that we had to work around. The biggest problems were getting your puppet caught on something—a part of the set or another puppet. If this happened, we had to keep the puppet singing and keep the gestures human. If that didn't work, we'd find a good time to slide the puppet offstage, where the stage manager could untangle it. This happened less and less as time went on."

When Alana said she "was one of the dancers" in a production, this was not a slip of the tongue. Over time, she said, the puppeteers would develop a relationship with their marionette that transcended the physical boundaries of simply making the puppet move. She describes the puppet-puppeteer relationship this way: "You get to know the quirks of each puppet very well. Sometimes they seemed to have minds of their own. In our group, the range of relationships between puppet and puppeteer varied from person to person. Some thought of them as little people, while others saw the character as the key thing. Some got into the roles too much and would stay in them off the stage, but everyone had to do different things to do their best. I come from a logical vein. I was fond of my marionettes, some more than others. Some had mechanical quirks, or I didn't like the costume. But it wasn't as personal to me as it was to some of the others."

Throughout NEMO's run, most of its puppeteers worked full-time "day jobs" and attempted to maintain family and other relationships while participating in two-hour rehearsals most weeknights, May through December, and performing in two shows each weekend. Although the puppeteers were paid minimum wage for each rehearsal hour, and double that for each performance hour, the time commitment to NEMO was tremendous.

"After hating opera growing up, I now love it," Alana says. "It was a very interesting and unusual job. I do miss performing. I regret not using the marionette manipulation that I learned since the theater closed. Looking back, I don't miss the amount of time it took out of my life, though it seemed normal at the time."

Ted acknowledges the toll the time commitment took on his company. "They were hitting the wall. I couldn't demand more from them than what I was already doing," he says. "They were a world-class group of puppeteers. When they had their characters fully developed, you could see the person coming down the strings. Everyone was attached to their marionette but in different ways. Some fought them, others embraced them. But the ones who fought their puppets I think missed them the most when the puppets were gone."

Was the privately owned New England Marionette Opera a business or a company of artists? In fact, it was both, personified best by Ted himself. Ever the consummate businessman, Ted followed the tried-and-true adage that to make money you have to spend it. Initially investing close to $200,000 of his own funds to start NEMO, he plowed all profits back into it so that he could continually "make a better product." Keeping it going was expensive—each production cost between $50,000 and $100,000. "Everything had to be completely professional," Ted says. "We even paid our ushers because we didn't want any issues about people not showing up or doing a bad job."

Over the course of seven years, the company performed eighty to one hundred times each year in four different productions, most of which were geared to an adult audience. During that time, only Ted, Roger, and a box office manager were full-time employees. Tickets cost $22 in 1992 and $26 in NEMO's final year. From the start, a portion of proceeds from sales was donated to two environmental groups—the Harris Center for Conservation Education, located in the Peterborough area, and Defenders of Wildlife, known for its mission to restore the eastern timber wolf population in the Adirondack Mountains.

In 1996, the company finally showed a profit and was financially healthy enough to take its productions on the road. Within two years, NEMO had performed at the International Festival of the Arts in Hamilton, Bermuda, the Nantucket Mozart Festival, Opera Omaha, the Cape Cod Opera, and the Nantucket Musical Arts Society. "We traveled with a twenty-four-foot long van. Inside were the two bridges, all lights, sound, marionettes, sets, drapery, and computer systems necessary to run it all," Ted says. "Our longest and most important tour was to Boston in the summer of 1998. We were there for three weeks at the Emerson Majestic Theatre and did *The Barber of Seville* and *Madame Butterfly*. Roger and I measured the entire theater four times and then scaled it down from 1,200 seats to 800 by pulling it all to the center. This was important to us because we wanted those sight lines to be good throughout the theater. We were building our audience at that time. We wanted the production to be successful."

And by all accounts it was. Ted and his puppeteers had charmed the sometimes stuffy critics of Boston's art world into raving about how lifelike the marionettes seemed. Many performances sold out. After six years of building, the New England Marionette Opera had finally made it. The Emerson Majestic was so pleased by audience response that it offered NEMO residency to begin the following year. Ted promptly accepted. The offer changed everything. The plan now was to move the company to Boston and use Peterborough as its summer home, like a kind of Tanglewood. There would be two casts—one in Boston and one in New Hampshire—and the company would spend twenty weeks each year traveling. Interestingly, Ted had always viewed Boston as his Great White Way, his ultimate yardstick for success, and had even written the city into his business plan with a time frame for getting there. By the time the residency offer came along, he was only thirty days behind his initial projected schedule.

To fulfill NEMO's ambitious plans, Ted recognized that it was time to take the company to the next level. He set up a nonprofit corporation to enable NEMO to seek grants and solicit tax-deductible donations, and established a six-member advisory board. Then he started negotiating performance contracts with theaters all over the country, including the Kennedy Center in Washington, D.C.

David Sobe, a Peterborough businessman who served on NEMO's board as its treasurer, remembers this period as a heady time for the company. "I know it would have been an inspiration to other companies if it had lived," he says. "I am sure it would have been an enormous success. The interesting thing was that people who love opera didn't see this theater as a substitute for the real thing. It wasn't second best in any way. It was a legitimate art form that stood on its own. I personally had never been interested in opera, but I was curious, so I went to a production and the quality immediately impressed me—the sound, lighting, attention to detail. After the first ten minutes, you were mesmerized—it was real life."

On January 2, 1999, the *Manchester Union Leader* ran a story on its front page reporting that a "Peterborough landmark and marionette theater" had been almost completely destroyed by fire the day before. "Long after dark, firefighters were still struggling to put the flames out," the article read. "With winds howling, and frigid air made more bitter by the thousands of gallons of water sprayed onto the large downtown building . . . firefighters from at least eight area towns tried to bring the fire under control. . . . some of the water used to douse the fire had turned to ice and clung to the sides of the building, turning the brick and wood into a kind of macabre-looking ice sculpture as the day wore on."

"I had no idea how much I was in love with the building—I'd gone there for twenty years," Ted recalls. On the day of the fire, he had arrived at the building in the morning, planning to reinstall the theater's computer system that he'd taken home to work on. When he got inside, he noticed the thermostat read fifty degrees. Usually, he didn't turn the heat on when he was in the building alone, preferring instead to keep his coat on and save the fuel. But on this day it felt especially chilly, and he flipped on the furnace before heading to the control booth in the balcony. A short time afterward he says he smelled smoke. He was wearing earphones at the time, so he didn't hear the smoke detectors screeching throughout the building. He ignored the smell and turned his attention back to his equipment. A few minutes later he smelled smoke again. Whirling himself around to face the stage, he found the entire theater full of smoke. He ripped off his earphones and could hear the smoke detectors. He has no idea when they first went off. Here is Ted's recollection of what happened next:

"I knew I had to make a fast decision. I could go out the front door, which was warped and sometimes wouldn't open properly in winter, or I could make my way to a fireproofed back stairwell, which would mean getting out of the balcony and crossing the floor through the smoke. I decided to go out to the stairwell, but then I had to decide whether to try and find the fire and put it out or go across the street to the convenience store for help. I decided to try to find the fire. In the kitchen I could see flames coming from the basement. The fire looked twenty feet wide and seemed like it was centered around a furnace. I thought one of the three furnaces was on fire.

"I couldn't see anything, because the smoke was so thick, so I backed out across a hallway and groped for the door. On the way, I picked up anything I could see. I had a sewing machine and a trash can that I'd put three puppets into to protect them. At this point, my lungs were saying the air is gone in here and you can't take in any more smoke. I knew I had to hold my breath until I could get outside. When I finally found the door, I pushed on it and was propelled out the door and onto my back in the parking lot. The fire chief said later that the force of the blaze probably expelled me from the building. The convenience store owner across the street told me I yelled, 'Call 911! I'm on fire!' I then went back to the building because I knew the sewing machine and trash can were right by the door. Someone tried to stop me. They thought I was going to go back inside. But once I got these things, I just collapsed into a snowbank and watched the building burn. It seemed like forever before the fire trucks arrived."

As the fire burned, Ted tried to comfort staff members who had begun to gather. "During that time, I relived all the years I had spent in that building," Ted says. "Every time a window blew out or something else exploded, it would spark some kind of memory." Friends say they were worried Ted would become hypothermic in the extreme cold. They tried to get him to eat candy bars to keep up his energy, but he was inconsolable. By 7:00 P.M. that evening, the building was devastated, a frozen mass of ice-covered brick. Inside, there was nothing left.

"I left at about 8:00 P.M. and went home for a drink. I couldn't even drink it," Ted remembers. "My wife tried to get me to eat some food. I just sort of sat there and stared at the wall. I know I was frozen solid and I spent three or four hours thawing out. About 11:00 P.M. the fire chief called and asked if I could come back. I did, and he explained what they were going to do through the night. I then stopped by the firehouse to thank the group there. I went back to the theater at 6:00 A.M. the following morning and set up my portable office in my car directly across the street from the theater. This was a heavy grieving moment, but I didn't have time to dwell on it. There were so many issues to be dealt with in closing things down. This was my base for the next seven days. I knew that we were into some big-time decision making and I was trying to equip myself for that as best as I could. I also had lots of theater people who needed reassurance, and I wanted to be there for them. I didn't know if we were going to try to restart the theater or not."

The day after the fire, the fire chief said there didn't seem to be anything wrong with the furnaces. Ted went down into the basement with him, and they examined the collapsed beams and wires with a flashlight. It appeared that a spark had gotten onto a beam and smoldered. When the furnace turned on, it brought oxygen in and the fire quickly ignited, although the beam may have been smoldering twelve to fourteen hours prior to the outset of the fire. A waitress reported smelling smoke the night before when she got off her shift around 11:00 P.M., but Ted isn't sure about this. "How come I didn't smell it when I entered the building the next day?" he asks.

A few days later he called a structural engineer from Boston and asked him to assess the damage. The repair bill was estimated at between $500,000 and $750,000. The building would have to be reconstructed, brick by brick.

. . .

Everyone associated with the theater was in shock. Thankfully no one was injured, but to Ted and his puppeteers, there had been 209 casualties. The marionettes, the life of the theater's stage, were gone. Only three—the ones Ted carried out in the trash can—had been saved.

On the weekend after the fire, Ted organized a kind of funeral for his theater and marionettes, inviting about twenty people. The temperature hovered around zero as the wind whipped through the blown-out windows of the ruined church. Ted directed his guests to safe spots within the ruins and asked them not to move. The center of the building had been roped off by the fire chief because the floor was covered with a foot of ice and was ready to collapse into the basement. Ted ran two hundred feet of electrical cord through the ruins, and as he read the name of each marionette, he played segments of the opera each had been a part of. Many guests wept openly. Outside, folks strolled by, curious. Some peered inside. After an hour, the memorial was over.

"Ten months later I made the decision not to restart the theater," Ted says. "The passion just wasn't there—we had the money, but not the energy." To rebuild the theater to its former glory, including the stage, bridges, equipment, and cast of marionettes, would have cost $3.2 million. Ted eventually sold the empty shell of the building to a nonprofit historical organization in Peterborough, but he still retains the New England Marionette Opera name. When I ask him if he will ever use it again, he answers flatly, "It's a closed chapter."

Later, I spoke to Alana about the fire and how it has been, coping with the theater's loss. "In the years since the fire, the hardest thing for me to hear—and I hear it often whenever I tell people I was part of the New England Marionette Opera—is, 'I'm so sorry I never got to see a performance,'" she told me. "I just want to say, Why didn't you? But I don't. I say, 'Yes, it is too bad.' After all, we all have them, those things that we mean to do someday."

## 9

# New Hampshire Daughters of the American Revolution

## "It Took a Lot of Card Parties to Pay for That Restoration"

*A*cross the wide boulevard that is the upper end of Elm Street in Manchester, I can see a trail of ladies causing a bit of a commotion at the front entrance of the General John Stark House. When I join them a moment later, a young-looking woman in her fifties wearing a paisley-print dress holds the heavy white door open for us. "You really should be entering through the side door," she teases us good-naturedly, as dry November leaves blow into the small entryway. "That's why we did all that work to the side of the house."

The woman is Diana Duckoff, regent of the Daughters of the American Revolution Molly Stark Chapter. Today she's presiding over the annual Good Citizenship Awards at the chapter's monthly meeting, which just happens to be on Veterans Day this year. She's too busy with the teenage award recipients to show me around, so she steers me toward the kitchen. Right now, that's where the action is.

The first thing most people notice about this room is the enormous open hearth that dominates it. Across from the hearth, under a framed antique American flag with thirteen stars, a square table covered in white linen is set out with bone china teacups and saucers—all different—that sit behind a neat row of silver spoons. On either side of the table, two women sit pouring—one tea, the other coffee—from sterling silver pots. A group of ladies stand nearby, chatting and sipping, occasionally eyeing the plate of Halloween-motif minicupcakes.

The scene reminds me of something out of an early Katharine Hepburn movie. In the 1990s, it might have seemed quaint, but now it's strangely comforting in its unabashed celebration of old-fashioned rituals. I ask one of the ladies if the chapter always brings out the china and silver at its monthly meetings. Why yes, she answers, as though it were the most ordinary thing in the world. And why shouldn't it be? The chapter started the practice back in the 1940s when the DAR raised money—a lot of it—by hosting formal "Silver Teas." Members enjoyed them so much that setting out the china and sterling have become a kind of tradition in the Molly Stark Chapter.

In the low-ceilinged meeting room, a few dozen women, many with stylishly cut winter-white hair, are delicately balancing teacups on their laps. The rectangular room is about forty feet long, richly paneled in caramel-stained pine, with an elegant grand piano standing at one end. Above it is a portrait of an older John Stark engulfed in a spectacular gilded frame. Hand tucked inside his coat, he peers out with the bemused expression of someone who isn't sure what the fuss is all about.

Diana calls the meeting to order and asks everyone to rise and face the flag standing next to the piano. We recite the Pledge of Allegiance and, afterward, the American Creed. I'm poised to sit down, but a spirited rendition of the national anthem follows (all of which the DAR has *always* done, Diana emphasized to me later). When the business meeting starts, several committee chairs are still out in the kitchen making tea sandwiches, but it doesn't matter. Everyone already knows what's going on. First there are the usual messages on internal issues from DAR national headquarters. Then Diana reads through a list of chapter announcements: a seamstress has volunteered to help them with period costumes in January; thanks to those who organized a Veterans Day parade the day before; sign-up sheets for the Christmas luncheon are in the hallway.

Then one of the ladies stands up to share an e-mail she received recently about flag courtesy. When she gets to the part about the meaning of each crease in a folded flag, a voice pipes up from the front row. "Where did you get that?" a lady in a blue jacket asks, irritated. Diana steps in. The e-mail wasn't meant to be taken as fact, she explains patiently. It was just something interesting.

Moving on, Diana reads off the impressive achievements of the five girls nominated by their high schools for a DAR Good Citizenship Award and hands each a certificate. They'll now compete on the state level and maybe win some scholarship money. Finally, in the last agenda item for the day, a local music teacher with an historical bent presents a talk on the mid-1800s Manchester Cornet Band, confidently stating the band had eighteen members. Actually, a lady in an aisle seat points out, there were twenty-one.

Clearly, this isn't the place to get your facts wrong.

. . .

A few months later on a chilly Sunday afternoon in winter, Diana and I are poring over the chapter's many scrapbooks in the basement library of the Stark House. All of the scrapbooks are numbered, with some dating back to the early 1900s. Midway through the afternoon, the phone rings. "No, I'm sorry, Molly Stark isn't here," Diana says into the phone. "She died in 1814." After a moment, she puts down the phone and returns to her work. Feeling my eyes upon her, she looks up. "Oh, that was Sears," she says.

What's interesting about the scrapbooks is that they include everything from newspaper clippings and photographs to official documents and correspondence. Using these bits and pieces, I'm tracing the history of the Stark House and how it eventually ended up on the National Register of Historic Places. In a nutshell, Archibald Stark built a small red house in 1736 out of tall-tree lumber taken from his eight-hundred-acre farm that is now part of the heart of Manchester. The family's home in Londonderry had just burned to the ground, and with eight children, including a newborn, it's likely the family was in a hurry to move into the new house and resume its daily routine.

Archibald's fourth child, John, was eight years old at the time, but he lived in the house for a quarter of a century until he left to fight in the French and Indian Wars around 1754. When he was thirty-two, he returned to it with his young wife Molly to care for his aging mother after his father died. Molly bore two of her eleven children here before the couple built a mansion a half mile away and moved there with John's mother a few years later.

The original house, built by Archibald Stark, which at that time was located on the banks of the Merrimack River near Amoskeag Falls, remained in the Stark family until 1821. Fourteen years later, it was sold to the Amoskeag Manufacturing Company. Over the next hundred years, the company rented it to tenants off and on but did little else to maintain it, so that by 1937 the house was in deplorable condition. It was around that time that the company heard about the Molly Stark Chapter's search for a permanent meeting place (the group had been getting together in members' homes for years). Aware of the historical significance of the house, and no doubt eager to avoid a public relations fiasco about its condition, Amoskeag Manufacturing deeded it to the chapter later that year and was done with it.

On the outside, this was a gallant thing to do. After all, the John Stark House was the oldest building in Manchester and essential, as a landmark, to the city's history. But in reality, although the ladies of the DAR were thrilled to have the house, it took close to sixty years and several major restorations to transform it to the near-original condition it is in today. The first restoration took place immediately, during the winter of 1937–38. It included removing whitewash from the walls to expose the original paneling, restoring the original pinewood floors, opening the bricked-up fireplaces, installing a modern kitchen, installing steam heat, and wiring the house for electricity. Any one of these projects would have been extensive, but the chapter also extended the ell, the rectangular room on the right side of the house once used as a shed and chicken coop, to provide space for a meeting room.

Later in the winter I spoke with Dot Wageman, who has chaired the chapter's House Committee for over twenty years. Dot lives only a half mile from the Stark House and regularly supervises routine maintenance of it. I asked Dot what she knew about the 1938 restoration, and she told me she had heard that cleaning up after those chickens had been nothing but a big mess. She also knew of a controversy about whether or not to stencil the walls. "Good Lord, it almost split the chapter in half," she told me. "There were those who said no way should there be stenciling on these walls. Others said it was historically accurate. They even solicited the opinion of a local historian, who said stenciling could have been on these walls." In the end, the prostenciling advocates won. "Some ladies are just very set in their ways," she said, sighing.

The women initially paid for the restoration through a reserve fund that quickly ran out as expenses crept into the tens of thousands of dollars. A high-interest bank loan paid the remaining bills. "It took a lot of card parties and rummage sales to pay for that restoration," Dot said. "That was a lot of money to raise back then. When I think of it I wonder, How did they ever do it?"

The second restoration was carried out in 1968. It was every bit as extensive as the first, with the added complexity of piecing the house back together after its relocation from a lot at the corner of Canal and Salmon Streets. The move came about when the state of New Hampshire decided to build a new Amoskeag Bridge partially on the plot of land, which was close to the east end of the aging bridge, that the Stark House had been sitting on for over two hundred years.

When the state notified the Molly Stark Chapter about the quandary in late 1966, it agreed to reimburse the organization for house relocation costs and another plot of land in exchange for the Stark House land on the river.

Diana Duckoff, DAR Molly Stark Chapter Regent, and the 1875 portrait of General John Stark that once hung in the Manchester mayor's office. It now hangs on the chapter's meeting room wall at the General John Stark House on Elm Street in Manchester, New Hampshire.

The caveat was that the house would have to be moved by June 1, only six months later. Without missing a beat, the chapter quickly polled its membership for relocation suggestions and found that the favored site was the northeast corner of Stark Park. But the ladies soon ran into trouble. Then–Manchester mayor Roland Vallee argued that placing the house in a city park would require the City Parks and Playgrounds Department to maintain it. Polite but firmly worded letters were exchanged until, on June 6, 1967, the mayor invited the chapter's six-member Stark House Restoration Committee to his office for a meeting. The goal was to resolve the impasse, but in the end, the mayor's will won out.

"From then on we tried to find a place for the house, but no one wanted us, poor orphan," House Restoration Committee chairwoman Marjorie Plaisted wrote in a later report. Fortunately for the chapter, the bridge plans were running a year behind schedule, but that still left less than twelve months to find a new site. Finally, Mr. Ezechiel Straw of the Brookside

Church on Elm Street approached the organization with an eleventh-hour solution: the church had a roomy east-facing lot on the corner of Waldo and Elm that might be ideal. It was in a quiet residential neighborhood with ample parking and public transport nearby, and perhaps best of all, the plot would have been part of Archibald Stark's original eight-hundred-acre farm. It didn't take long for the Molly Stark Chapter and the state, which paid for the lot, to negotiate the deal.

By this time, the organization had recognized that moving the house presented an unusual opportunity. Minor work had been done to it since 1938, but the time was right for a complete update. Over several months, the chapter's House Restoration Committee developed a plan that involved creating a granite foundation, renovating the kitchen, installing a new furnace, updating the wiring and plumbing, laying a brick sidewalk, building a cement ramp on the side of the house, and repairing windows, doors, walls, and ceilings. Nothing would be left untouched—the restoration would affect every aspect of every room in the house. First, though, was putting the house back together.

On October 17, 1968, the Dana Wood Company of Auburn, under state supervision, moved the rectangular ell of the house to 2000 Elm Street in less than three hours. A few days later, the main section followed. Before any further work could take place, however, the house's huge chimney and three fireplaces had to be fit to the new foundation. Over the ensuing year, the chapter spent $65,000 (about $335,000 in today's dollars) to complete the restoration, which demanded full-time supervision. "I never thought this was going to require me to get involved so deeply, taking so much time and energy, telephone calls, working with movers, architects, carpenters, engineers, plumbers, electricians, masons, the contractor, and the water department," wrote Mrs. Plaisted in her final report in 1969. "I have learned enough to start my own business." Indeed, she was reportedly at the house every day for well over a year, directing the entire restoration.

When the house finally opened on October 5, 1969, in celebration of the Molly Stark Chapter's Seventy-Fifth Diamond Jubilee, it made a big splash locally. Many community groups had volunteered time and expertise to the project, which had helped create a sense of public ownership, at least in terms of the house's heritage. The New Hampshire Department of Highways erected a platform in front of the house for the well-attended 2:00 P.M. ceremony, during which city, state, and DAR officials gave speech after speech. A year later, the house won a national award from the Federal Highway Administration as an "Outstanding Example of Preservation of an Historic Site." Both the New Hampshire Department of Public Works and the Molly Stark Chapter were honored for moving the house "out of the path of an urban renewal program."

But the story doesn't end here. In 1971, the chapter appealed to the state for assistance in listing the property on the prestigious National Register of Historic Places, the nation's official inventory of nationally significant historic resources. The following year, an historian from the National Park Service, which administers the program, inspected the property to validate that it had been restored to its original condition. After spending a long day with former House Restoration Committee members, the historian was satisfied and duly nominated the Stark House in late 1972 for inclusion in the National Register.

Several months passed with no word about the designation. When a chapter member inquired about the status, she consistently was told that the situation didn't look promising. But then quite unexpectedly, in June 1973, the chapter received a letter from the National Park Service. The nomination had finally been approved. Without further ado, the General John Stark House was promptly recorded as a museum and meeting place in the National Register of Historic Places on June 29, 1973, the same date as the Wentworth House in Portsmouth and the Weare House in Hampton Falls. Today, there are approximately 650 New Hampshire properties included in the Register's 75,000 listings.

The restoration of the John Stark House is typical of the type of work the New Hampshire Daughters of the American Revolution has done since its inception over a hundred years ago. In fact, all the DAR women I spoke to, while generous with their time, were a little surprised by my interest. After all, restoring historical buildings, placing monuments at significant sites, and otherwise promoting patriotism is what the DAR has always done. What's the big deal?

The National Society of the DAR was founded as a nonpolitical organization on October 11, 1890, and grew so quickly that it was incorporated by an act of Congress only a few years later. Open to any woman over the age of eighteen who can prove direct lineage to a man or woman who aided the cause of American independence, it has admitted close to a million members since 1890 and now occupies an entire block of buildings in Washington, D.C. Under its Act of Incorporation, it is required to report annually to Congress, and does so by delivering nonpolitical opinions that represent the views of its current 200,000 members on a wide variety of national issues.

New Hampshire was the ninth state to establish a DAR organization (members easily remember this because New Hampshire was also the ninth state to ratify the Constitution). When the first chapter was called to order in October 1892 in the living room of a prominent Manchester member, deciding on a name for the chapter was at the top of the agenda. Elizabeth Stark, one of the chapter founders, suggested the spirited wife of one her ancestors, John Stark. The group liked this idea, but it threw everyone into a temporary tizzy. John Stark had given his wife so many nicknames, including Madam, Debbie, and Betsey, that they didn't know which one to choose (her given name was Elizabeth). Finally they settled on Molly, as she was most often called, and the Molly Stark Chapter was in business.

Today the New Hampshire DAR organization has close to one thousand members spread over twenty chapters from Nashua to the North Country. Although it is relatively small, its chapters have made impressive contributions to preserving New Hampshire's historic buildings, including the 1736 John Stark House by the Molly Stark Chapter in Manchester; a 1770 schoolhouse by the Else Cilley Chapter in Nottingham; the 1834 George W. Pinkerton House by the Molly Reid Chapter in Derry; and an 1835 "Little Red School House" by the Reprisal Chapter in Newport.

Every state DAR organization elects a regent, who acts as president for a three-year term and, as part of her administration, chooses a project that all chapters contribute to throughout her term. In New Hampshire, some projects have been highly visible, like the restoration of Fort William and Mary in New Castle. Others have been less so—but equally as important— such as microfilming historic state documents so that anyone can view them. New Hampshire's current state regent, Maryann Wentworth, has developed an ambitious plan that's involving the direct participation of every DAR chapter in the state. Maryann wants the chapters to validate the historic markers in their geographical area, and add or replace them as needed. Then she wants the DAR to publish a modest reference guide listing every commemorative monument, marker, and plaque erected by the DAR in New Hampshire. No such resource currently exists.

To do that, DAR state historian Sylvia Getchell has asked each chapter historian to "wander around their area" to search out the markers, judge whether they need repairs, and supply her with a description of the historical significance of each. Sylvia is then validating the data and compiling it into a master list. "There are different types of markers," she told me. "There are big ones made of bronze or stone, for example, and others less

The General John Stark House lies buried in late winter snow, Elm Street, Manchester, New Hampshire.

permanent, like signs or markers at grave sites, that mark heroes and hero-ines of various wars. It's an unending chore to keep markers where they should be." It's also expensive. Fund-raising for the project is being carried out by all New Hampshire DAR chapters and likely will continue through the decade.

One of the charming things about the DAR is its unapologetic affection for military-style pageantry, which the entire organization particularly en-joys at its annual conventions. The national convention, called the Conti-nental Congress, is attended by four thousand members who, I'm told, often wear white gloves and appear awestruck during opening ceremonies. First there is a procession of all national officers, accompanied by pages car-rying the flags of each state and country where there are DAR chapters (fifty-four in all). Then, as the president general enters, a massive flag sud-denly unfurls from the ceiling while patriotic music stirs the crowd into an inspired swell of tears. (This is easy to relate to. I always get teary-eyed when I hear the national anthem.)

It should come as no surprise, then, that the DAR's elaborate hierarchical structure is not only evocative of the military—it is based on one principle alone: service. By default, service to the DAR means service to the nation. The two are interchangeable. To support the hierarchy, there are committees for everything. On the national level, thirty-eight committees cover everything from adult literacy to celebrating national commemorative events. When you add a chairman for each, plus a governing body comprised of twelve executive officers, twenty-one vice presidents general, and fifty-four state regents, you have well over one hundred women who serve the DAR on the national level.

The state DAR organizations mimic this structure, which can become a bit top-heavy in a small state like New Hampshire. At least 10 percent of the New Hampshire DAR membership is involved in some type of committee work, including national, regional, state, and special committees, with many members serving on several levels simultaneously. In the chapters, you see the same kind of dedication. For example, in the Molly Stark Chapter, which has 102 members (more or less—mortality is an issue in most chapters), there are nineteen active committees, all of which file reports that trickle upward, eventually landing on the desks of administrators at DAR headquarters in Washington, D.C.

Still, Diana Duckoff, a relatively new member with only ten years under her belt, would like to see a greater commitment from her membership so that everyone is pitching in to improve the chapter. But it can be difficult, she said, for newer members to fit into an organization where some members have been active for thirty or forty years. That's not good for any DAR chapter, because if members feel unwelcome, they won't attend meetings, or—worse—get involved in committee work.

Fitting in became an issue in the Molly Stark Chapter a few years ago when a new member from another state suggested creating name tags. Before then, this hadn't been necessary, simply because everyone had known each other for years. The request started a dialogue about how to make new members feel welcome, and now, on every second Monday of each month, Diana's vice regent stands at the side door of the Stark House where she can greet everyone as they enter. She can also subtly direct them to pick up their name tag, which is pinned on a cloth-covered bulletin board near the door.

One day I asked Diana if she would connect me with an active member who could give me better insight into who, actually, becomes a DAR member. She told me about Gail Forand, who also happened to be a John Stark descendant. I remembered Gail from the chapter meeting I had attended because, from across the room, she had resembled a four-star general gracefully pouring coffee from the silver service. She had been wearing a wide blue-and-white sashlike ribbon across one side of her chest that was completely covered with what appeared to be a plethora of medals.

Gail has been a DAR member since 1982 and is the official keeper of her family history. Sitting on the living room sofa in her Raymond home, she leafs through a gigantic black binder that traces her lineage back nine generations to John Stark. I tell her I've read some of his military correspondence in Tuck Library and that, contrary to the flowery writing of the letters he received, his were almost always one page and polite, but never effusively so. When I tell her my impression of John Stark is that he was frugal with words and emotions, generous with family and friends, but never anybody's fool, she readily agrees. "He was a real farm boy," she says. "He kept his communication short and sweet. He cared more about New Hampshire and the people here than pleasing the powers that be. He was a hero early in life, but he wasn't a political man. First and foremost, he was a frontiersman."

As we sift through Gail's lineage, my curiosity finally gets to me. Tell me about the medals, I blurt out. "You mean the pins?" Gail chides. "I'll go get them." When she returns, she lays down a piece of fabric that upon closer look is actually three sky blue ribbons sewn together with two white ribbons in between. The sash is about eight inches long and five inches wide, and it displays three long vertical rows of pins—about thirty in all. "You can tell what rank people are in the organization by the ribbon they wear," she says, and goes on to explain the complex system: thick blue, thin white; thick white, thin blue; and so on. At the end of it, my head is spinning.

In the DAR, there appear to be two camps: those who collect the pins and wear them proudly, and those who wonder if it's, perhaps, a little silly. Judging from reported mob scenes at convention jewelry counters, most members appear to fall squarely in the former category. There are many types of DAR pins, but, interestingly, not everyone in the organization is permitted to buy any type they wish. For example, an ancestor pin can be bought only by women from that family. Merit pins distinguish those who have served in office or on special committees. Then there are state, chapter, club, and honorary service pins worn only by participants in those groups. Commemorative pins, often used as fund-raisers to remember an aspect of American history, and campaign pins, displayed as a show of support during a president general's term in office (but *never* worn on the sash), however, are generally available to any DAR member. Members order pins through the national organization, which has a system for checking eligibility.

Gail's pins run the gamut, showing her service to the DAR across a wide range of offices that include a two-term stint as chapter regent and chairman of various state and regional veterans committees. (Her father is a World War II veteran, and Gail spends a good deal of her time volunteering through the DAR at veterans hospitals. For example, she and committee members have made and distributed hundreds of afghans to veterans hospitals.) Some members do scoff at the pin collecting, Gail acknowledges, but it gives those who wear them visible evidence of their service and dedication. "It makes you feel like you've done something," she tells me. "The pins are like a reward. The more you have, the more involved you obviously are."

Prices for pins vary. Pulling out a recent catalog, Gail points to a simple gold commemorative pin that retails for $335, or, "if you want to show off," for $2,200 bejeweled. But members can also buy used pins through the DAR at half the original price, which normally come from the estates of deceased members. This recycling system exists because the DAR requests that families return pins to the organization so that they don't fall into the wrong hands—or onto the wrong sash. In the Internet age, however, this is a problem. Pins are showing up in on-line auctions and going to the highest bidder. To counter this, Gail tells me, the DAR has formed a special national committee for the sole purpose of buying back pins.

I'm curious about the pin committee, so a few days after I meet with Gail, I call DAR headquarters to find out more about it. "Sometimes families don't always understand what the pins are or how the deceased got them," public relations director April Watkins explains, "so sometimes they put them up for sale in on-line auctions." To counter this, a five-member committee hunts the pins down and buys them back if they are priced reasonably enough. "Before the committee was set up, many members were buying the pins back with their own money and turning them over to the DAR," April says. "Now the committee corresponds with thousands of members who help them monitor these auctions for the pins. There's no way the committee could do this work without that kind of help."

Before I hang up, I ask April about another recently formed national committee called Women's Issues. My question is whether it's, perhaps, twenty years late. "This is probably true," she concedes. "But it was created because we started to hear that younger members wanted committees appropriate to them and their needs, such as how to be a mom and a volunteer, good nutrition for the family, breast cancer awareness, things that deal with women's lives." The DAR has been focused outwardly with its emphasis on service for so many years that, before now, she says, it hasn't looked inward at the issues its own members have been facing.

As we talk, I get the sense that these are more than organizational issues to April, and as much as she tries to hide it, it finally comes out. April is the daughter of the newly elected president general of the national DAR. She tells me her mother is an accountant and businesswoman who raised four children while working full-time and represents a different kind of leader in the organization—a generally younger member who is trying to open up the DAR and make it more "user-friendly," as April calls it.

One of the first things her mother's administration did was to eliminate the somewhat outdated social custom of referring to members by their husband's full name, as in "Mrs. John Stark." Not surprising, this has ruffled feathers among older members who see the custom as a sign of respect. "We expected those objections," April says. "We tell members: you are a member based on you and your own lineage, not your husband's. I think it's a generational issue."

Generational issues are common in many DAR chapters these days. Members are realizing that if the organization is going to endure, it must revitalize with younger members and try new ways of doing things—such as offering evening meetings to members who work during the day (many chapters still hold their monthly meeting on weekday afternoons). The old way may be the best way, many members are saying, but perhaps there is a need for some flexibility in choosing the road ahead.

In New Hampshire, State Regent Maryann Wentworth compares her role to that of a CEO. "It's the same as being the head of a small company within a larger organization," she says. "I believe in giving people a job and letting them do it. I've been successful with that as the regent in my own chapter."

But what is the everyday value in this day and age of a large, highly structured organization whose ways and means are described by some as more than a little outdated? "To be proud of your heritage and become knowledgeable about our country. That's the value," Diana Duckoff believes. "Our nation wouldn't have evolved to the present without our ancestors who fought hard for what we have today. I don't want to glorify the past, but this organization goes back to our founding principles. It brings us back to the basics."

From the outside, the John Stark House is a modest two-story building painted barn red with white trim, surrounded by a white picket fence. Inside, it's a treasure trove of donated Stark family antiquities. On a winter evening, Diana Duckoff and I are rummaging through desk drawers, back closets, and cabinets so she can show me what's here.

Diana grew up in a Gilford house built by her ancestors during the Revolutionary War and has a keen appreciation for recording historical artifacts. If she could, she says, she would work in the Stark House full-time cataloging its entire contents and creating labels so that visitors could better understand what they were viewing. For right now, though, it's enough that the house is clean and orderly and in good repair.

Starting in the meeting room, I ask Diana about the imposing portrait of John Stark that hangs at the far end. It turns out that it was painted in 1875 by Ulysses D. Tenney for the City of Manchester Centennial Exhibition of 1876 and represents Stark at seventy years old (Tenney re-created a number of portraits of eighteenth-century New Hampshire heroes and public officials based on the original works). For years the painting hung in the Manchester mayor's office, but it eventually ended up in the basement of City Hall. Around 1935, a janitor found it and brought it to the attention of the mayor, who promptly sent the painting to the Currier Museum of Art to be restored. A few years later, the city donated it to the Molly Stark Chapter when the organization acquired the Stark House.

In the nearby "best parlor," as the front sitting room was called in Stark's day, wide boards embrace the fireplace. This is unusual, because the house was built at a time when King George required that all thick timber be shipped to England for use as ship masts. It appears Archibald Stark wasn't interested. Across from the hearth, a massive blue guest book dates from July 20, 1938—the day the house was acquired from the Amoskeag Manufacturing Company—to the present. It's a good six inches thick and three-quarters filled with the musings and thank-yous of visitors from all over the world.

Diana calls me over to a large, dark wood secretary. Rifling through a small drawer, she has found an envelope with the cryptic message, "Be sure to keep this safely. History of the Blue Punch Bowl enclosed." Unfortunately the letter inside doesn't explain who donated the bowl or when, but the story goes like this: The bowl was purportedly taken from a pub by an American soldier during the French and Indian Wars after he captured the French soldiers who had been drinking from it. When the American soldier returned home, he presented it to his eldest daughter with the instructions that the bowl must be passed down to oldest daughters. Now Diana and I are on a hunt to find the bowl. Opening a back closet, she calls out the items—plates, teacups, old lamps, an 1834 sampler—but no blue punch bowl. Instead, she finds what members think are John Stark's tiny, slightly bent wire-rimmed eyeglasses. "There are so many treasures like this that we need to keep," she says, peering deeper into the closet.

In the corner of the room, a handsome grandfather clock from the 1600s with three round brass balls on top strikes eight times. It's a hard, tinny sound culminating in a loud, off-key clang that quickly returns to a lazy ticktock. Diana tells me the clock was made in Kennebunk, Maine, and that a "Mr. McNally" comes here weekly to wind it. He's kept it in fine condition for years.

Before we climb the steep, narrow staircase to what was once a loft area, I ask Diana how difficult it is to keep the house in good condition. In the 1980s, she says, they had the floors fixed because the panels had spread and members were catching their heels between the boards. The house springs a leak in the bathroom now and again and, right now, the walls are starting to peel in some of the rooms. She expects the stenciling issue to rear its ugly head again, but she is adamant that the house belongs to all the members and decisions about its upkeep should not be dictated by the tastes of a few.

Upstairs, there are two bedrooms. On the double bed straight ahead in the master bedroom is a handmade coverlet from the now-defunct DAR Submit Wheatly Chapter of West Lebanon, who donated it to this chapter in the 1930s. It's embroidered with the members' names and many patriotic symbols and images including flags, the Boston Tea Party, Paul Revere, and eagles. In most houses, the coverlet would be viewed as old, but here it looks positively brand-new.

Getting down on the floor, we open a chest of drawers and start pulling things out. "Just having things in drawers doesn't do much for history," Diana says. "If you want to find out where something comes from here, you just have to start looking for answers." In the bottom drawer we find a brass plaque that doesn't ring a bell with her, a crushed straw hat, and at the very bottom, buried in plastic, a taffeta wedding gown. It appears to be a petite size four and has hundreds of tiny covered buttons down the front. Next to it Diana holds up a small blue jar. Clearly many things in the house are old, and others just look old.

Downstairs, we end up in the kitchen, or "family room" as it was called, where the Stark family spent most of its time. In those days, if you wanted to keep warm this was the place to be—when the kitchen fire was started in early autumn, it didn't go out again until late spring. Near the fireplace is a smokehouse, which resembles a narrow cave within the house, where the family hung meats to dry. Diana says it was only discovered when the house was moved and that it complicated things immensely. Being essentially a gaping hole in the center of the house, it made all the surrounding walls unstable. There is also a low, four-foot-deep "beehive" oven for making breads and cakes, which was considered fairly high-tech in the eighteenth century, as well as a gadget for making toast. All of the fireplace tools, as well as the rifle over the hearth, are original to the house.

I ask Diana about the hand-sewn flag with thirteen stars hanging on the kitchen wall. She tells me it was donated by one of John Stark's granddaughters and was supposedly carried in the Battle of Bennington, where Stark definitively distinguished himself as a leader and soldier. The fight inspired Stark years later to send this toast to a Battle of Bennington veterans reunion: "Live free or die; to die is not the greatest of evils."

## 10

## Canterbury Shaker Village

---

"The Duck Speaks for Itself"

*T*he first time I see executive chef Leo Cuthbertson, it's through the swinging kitchen door of the Creamery Restaurant at Canterbury Shaker Village. He's orchestrating the Friday night preparation of a late-autumn candlelight dinner and he's got approximately five minutes before he's due to appear before his diners, Johnny Carson–style, to give his nightly monologue.

Precisely at 7:00 P.M., Leo emerges wrapped in a clean white apron. Holding the one-page menu, he goes through the four entrée selections and describes in just enough detail the inspiration for each. For example, he's added a touch of maple syrup to the squash soup to get us "interested in the autumn season." The duck, he says, "speaks for itself. It's wild and gamy." The baked acorn squash? "We didn't mess with it. It's right out of the garden."

All entrées are accompanied by a plop of garlic mashed potatoes and a cluster of candy stripe beets. Seventy-five percent of the produce in the meal comes from Shaker Village's own organic gardens, Leo explains, and all the bread is made here, too. "Can we have dessert first?" asks a man, who says he was here Leo's first night on the job several years earlier. Leo laughs and says we're in for a surprise. "I did something different with the crème caramel. I was looking at it, thinking, This needs something else. So I put currants on it." Concluding, he asks us if we're ready to eat. It's as if he's about to throw the first pitch. To applause he exits left.

A few weeks later I found a 1914 photograph of the Dwelling House dining room at the village, where most of the Shakers ate, that looked re-markably familiar. It showed two long rows of six-person tables set simply with white plates, cups, and saucers. On the center of each table was a small glass vase of fresh flowers. Within reach of every place setting were a creamer and sugar bowl, salt and pepper shakers, and condiment rack. (Back then, the idea was that no one's meditation should be disturbed by a sudden, and intrusive "Please pass the ketchup.")

The squarish dining room of the Creamery Restaurant is roughly the same size and laid out in a similar fashion with long, family-style tables and straight-back chairs. Even the dinnerware is white. Everything you need is within arm's reach, including big jugs of cider and fruit juices. The ambience of both rooms is austere, but simplicity means neither cheerlessness nor paucity in the Shaker tradition. Save for today's chatter of guests and soft Shaker music playing in the background, one's dining experience in either room would be alike: plentiful meals made from food from the Shakers' own gardens enjoyed in a relaxed communal setting.

But there's a small controversy brewing around the village's extensive expansion plans that began when it opened its new Visitor Education Center in 2001. Besides building restorations, the expansion calls for the likely addition of a bed and breakfast and a 150-seat restaurant that will replace the 48-seat Creamery, which currently closes during the winter. The new restaurant will stay open all year for lunch and the village's trademark "candle-light dinner" service.

Detractors of the expansion say the village may be crossing a boundary between upholding Shaker traditions and grabbing at the lucrative New Hampshire tourism trade. Village administrators, however, say it is Shaker-inspired. Not only is it an opportunity to reinvigorate the property to its previous prosperity under Shaker stewardship, but the expansion should increase annual visits to the village to well beyond the present 65,000. The core of the debate, however, isn't as much about expansion as it is about what Canterbury Shaker Village has become: a living, growing museum, or a different kind of place that should be preserved precisely as it is now?

The village has been struggling with these issues for several decades, but it's only been since the board hired its second-ever, full-time director that the discussion has taken on new significance. Dr. Scott Swank spent fifteen years as an educator at the Winterthur Museum in Delaware, renowned nationally for its museum education programs, before moving to New Hampshire in April 1990 to take over the directorship of Canterbury Shaker Village. In that time, he has slowly molded the institution into one that is espousing preservation while continuing to evolve.

In the last decade, Dr. Swank has overseen the steady restoration of twenty-five original Shaker buildings, created a fund-raising mechanism for future restoration and development projects, and balanced the budget. (The village was $500,000 in debt with no endowment in 1991, partly due to the installation of a villagewide fire suppression system that had drained funds.) He also initiated putting the village's remaining 694 acres under permanent conservation easement, which staff felt was very much within the spirit of the Shaker community. The easement allows the village to re-build Shaker structures on the same locations, as long as the buildings are architecturally true to the originals. Inside the buildings, staff are permitted to do what they need to in order to serve a modern museum.

Before making the move to New Hampshire, Dr. Swank first turned down a job offer from the Smithsonian Institution. "When I first came here, I said, 'This is my kind of place,'" he tells me. "It was clear that this was going to be the end. There were only a few Shakers left in 1990. I knew they needed to make the transition from a living Shaker community to a museum. There was the beauty and integrity of the place, and the challenge of the restoration and transition to carry on the Shaker tradition with re-spect to their point of view and values but within the context of modern scholarship. There was nowhere to go but up from here. Professional friends wondered why I would take this on. But I knew if I succeeded it would be honoring the Shakers and capturing an important part of Ameri-can life for the nation, New England, and New Hampshire."

I ask Dr. Swank how he intends to expand Shaker Village and still main-tain the tranquillity of the place, but I can see my question is off the mark. Tranquillity isn't the issue. What the village is trying to do is preserve a way of life that—compared with the complicated society of today—appears nostalgically peaceful and concordant. Because of that, any type of change here gives the impression of upheaval. "The Shakers had no dogmatic view toward religion, which has made it easy for us as a museum," Dr. Swank ex-plains. "They were a progressive people, not frozen in time. We decided early on that we would not be like Sturbridge Village, for example, doing things in costume using Shaker methods. Instead, we decided to embrace Shaker philosophy and blend the historic with the modern. The Shakers have a strong history of experimentation, and their philosophy was ste-wardship of the land. That's what we are doing now."

I'm wondering, though, how a modish new restaurant fits with the Shakers' view of "the world," as they called outside society. Dr. Swank ex-plains the village is actually harming the creamery building, which was built in 1905 for producing butter and cheese, by using it for cooking because moisture has built up in it over the years. It's also smack in the middle of the village, forcing delivery trucks to enter the village through a dirt path-way originally constructed for use by humans and animals. "This wouldn't have happened when the Shakers lived here," he assures me. "The commercial aspects of the village were located along the road."

And that's precisely where the new restaurant also will be situated: on the west side of Shaker Road, on the foundation of the village's former blacksmith shop. Dr. Swank's office is cluttered with rolled-up blueprints, but he easily finds the one for the restaurant. It's a simple three-story structure that looks almost identical to any of the other buildings in the village today. The 7,400-square-foot building will feature two dining floors that will allow the village to offer more dining options to guests by accommodating, for example, larger groups as well as couples who might not want to sit elbow to elbow with strangers as they currently do now. "But we have to keep some aspects of the Shaker communal dining table," he says. "Maybe we'll have one communal table for those who want to meet new people. We're taking our time in making decisions."

The Creamery Restaurant has a history of hiring inexperienced young chefs and giving them the physical and creative space to make themselves stars. It hasn't been intentional. When the Creamery's first chef, Jeff Paige, prepared his inaugural meal here in the late 1980s, his main charge was to establish the restaurant as a quality establishment known for New England regional cooking. But he took the dictum to heart, being the last person trained in Shaker food traditions under the tutelage of the Canterbury sisters. A decade later he had made enough of a name for himself to launch his own successful restaurant in an old textile mill in Manchester.

Leo Cuthbertson's career, so far, is following a similar path. He didn't know when he started working for Jeff Paige in 1999 that within five months he'd be promoted to executive chef. For the then-twenty-five-year-old, that was heady stuff. But what his predecessor had ingrained in him in only a short time was that Shaker cooking had less to do with a set of recipes than with an attitude toward food and how it is treated. Several years later, Leo already has proved adept at translating those values into the preparation of fresh, wholesome meals for the real world of today's picky diners.

"Presentation wasn't in the Shaker mix," Leo tells me. "They weren't into impressing anyone. That was their food philosophy. It's where I have to restrain myself. I could give you the architecture of how a meal should look, but this restaurant became what it is by honoring Shaker food traditions. And I respect that."

Leo sports a neat goateelike beard and a single gold hoop earring. He says he started in the restaurant business when he was fifteen, washing dishes at a country club near his home in North Carolina. But the chef there took a personal interest in Leo's career and mentored him into the first-rate Culinary Institute of America. "He taught me I would only get out of it what I put into it," Leo says. After graduating, he worked for seven years in the five-star kitchens of Florida's resorts, before reversing the route of the snowbird and moving his family to Concord.

I try to ask Leo about his cooking standards, but today he's all worked up about the garden. He talks about vegetables as if he's talking about dessert. The heirloom tomatoes "taste like sugar cubes." Another type suggests "a hint of peach." Dave Bryant, the land manager who tends the village's extensive gardens, has just hammered out a plan that will keep Leo deep in organic greens throughout the summer, and Leo's ecstatic. So I ask him how he and Dave collaborate. "I work around him and what's being harvested," he replies. "He's doing such a service for me. I can say, 'I need 120 pounds of potatoes by tomorrow afternoon.' And here they are. This summer we'll be taking the greens out of the ground, washing them, and putting them on the plate. I can't wait. He'll also throw some herbs in there for me. It's such a novelty to have them—crisp, delicate, . . ." he trails off.

In any given year, Leo figures he serves about 18,000 people: 15,000 individual lunches and 72 candlelight dinners. In season he has twenty employees that include pastry chefs, kitchen attendants, wait staff, bakers, and dishwashers spread over the Creamery, the less formal summer kitchen, and bakery. While he accepts that his employees may use different methods in the kitchen, he says the results must be consistent. "I get very upset if someone throws a tomato or onion on the counter. Vegetables can bruise," Leo tells me. "When my staff are washing greens, I want them to get all the greens out of the water and not leave any behind. These were grown for us. We also use every piece of the meat. I have certain standards in my kitchen. There's always a way to improve what you are doing. I try to get my staff to see this as a positive thing."

The Creamery's kitchen schedule on a typical busy summer day is similar to that of any full-service lunch-and-dinner restaurant. Starting around 7:30 A.M. staff begin the prep work for the menu items that take the longest to complete, such as smoking ribs or baking beans. Midmorning, they move on to preparing for lunch. When lunch is over, work for the 7:00 P.M. candlelight dinner starts with preparation of sauces, desserts, and vegetables. Sometimes, though, lunch drags on to 4:00 P.M., causing a crimp in the rhythm of the day. "Lunch is supposed to stop at two o'clock, but I always honor the waiting line," Leo says. "I try not to turn anyone away." All the while, he is juggling phone calls from the summer kitchen, his bakery staff, and a reservationist scheduling groups. And somewhere in all this the Creamery is scrubbed thoroughly between each meal.

Besides making full use of the village's gardens and orchards—a rare luxury for any chef—Leo tries to buy as much food as possible from local sources. For example, all of his hams come from a smokehouse down the road, where he can work with the purveyor on the precise cut. It's a bit tricky, Leo says, because the Shakers used less desirable cuts of meat like shanks and shoulders. "That's why Shaker cooking often calls for braised dinners, although that's not necessarily what all of our clientele is looking for. Yes, people want the Shaker experience, but there's a line we have to cross. Our best-seller is veal osso buco, but we have to use modern methods to make the meat soft."

Compared to many chefs, Leo takes somewhat of a backward approach to menu planning. "The type of ingredients don't really matter," he tells me, matter-of-factly. "It's what you do with them. You have to make them work with each component on the plate." So instead of focusing on the meat, for example, he examines his garnishes and finds harmonious blendings that complement, but are able to stand on their own. "Like fried leeks. If you don't do them right, they're oily. I take the leeks and look at what kind of fish will go with them, not the other way around," Leo says. "With dinners, I like to keep everyone guessing. I want to make them wonder, How did he make that tomato taste like that? I like to marry one flavor with another . . . and then explain to everyone how to enjoy the meal best. That's the fun part."

I suggest that Leo is, perhaps, expecting a lot from his guests who, after all, just want to enjoy a good meal and a nice evening out. "If I'm not giving something to the customer that is true, I'm not doing what I should be doing," he responds. "People expect Shaker-style food, but I want to give them a special experience." He asks me what my experience was like in his dining room. I tell him that I thought I didn't like beets, but the candy stripe variety opened my eyes. I say it was like being in someone's living room, that it was cozy—perhaps because I didn't have much elbowroom. "That's what I'm trying to create," he says. "A homey experience for every guest."

So won't that be impossible in a larger restaurant? "No," Leo replies. "It's taken a long time to get to where we are now." In the Creamery, he explains, they are working in a building that was made into a restaurant. The new

Leo Cuthbertson, executive chef at the Creamery Restaurant, Canterbury Shaker Village, gathers fresh summertime produce from the village's organic gardens. (Courtesy of Canterbury Shaker Village.)

building will be constructed specifically to be a restaurant, which he thinks will afford a better experience for everyone—both guests and kitchen staff. "You're talking about constructing a building that portrays Shaker food traditions over centuries."

Leo says he has been very involved in the design of the new restaurant and is adamant about one thing: he doesn't want a lot of clutter in his workplace. "My thing is simplicity so that I can clean. If something isn't necessary in the kitchen, I don't need it," he says. "It has to be streamlined and easy to work in. There doesn't need to be any more confusion in the kitchen than there already is."

Dave Bryant's blue fleece jacket has fragments of brown leaves all over it. He's just come in from the orchard, where he and a crew of volunteers are getting the trees ready for the next growing season. Dave is a refugee from the high-tech world, where he once worked out of a cubicle the size of a small tractor. Now in his fourth growing season as Shaker Village's full-time land manager, he oversees 694 acres that include 500 acres of forestland, 80 acres of fields, organic vegetable and herb gardens, flower beds, five ponds, and an apple orchard. He has straight brown hair and the bright eyes of someone who spends most of his days outdoors. His wife Donna is a respected herbalist who teaches popular classes here in the summer and fall.

Dave is a doer kind of guy, and it takes some time to get him warmed up to talking about his work. He tells me his calendar looks something like this: In January he plans the gardens for the next season, buys seeds, researches Shaker methodology, and works on the village's organic certifications; February means prep work in the orchard and greenhouse; in April he and his three employees finish the garden cleanup and start digging perennials; in May and June they plant; July through September he relies on twenty volunteers to help with the constant weeding and harvesting; October through December they're cleaning and cutting back. In December they decorate the village with fresh swags and wreaths. Then the cycle starts all over again.

In highly productive gardens, like those at Shaker Village, timing is everything. All summer, Dave successions the planting so that something is always ready for harvesting. For example, he plants early-, mid-, and late-season potatoes, for a total of nine varieties, to ensure a steady supply. (Potatoes are, by far, the village's most popular crop, as they were when the Shakers lived here; the Creamery Restaurant will use more than one hundred pounds of them in one busy summer weekend.) Dave recounts how, in his first year, he overplanted with seven types of lettuce. "I didn't do that again," he laughs. Now he works with Leo on what he needs for the next growing season. "We experiment with new varieties to give people a chance to try things they wouldn't get to try elsewhere," he says.

All of the vegetable and herb gardens at Shaker Village are organic, which, on the simplest level, means synthetic fertilizers or pesticides aren't used. But most organic gardeners will tell you it's not merely about what you don't do. Organic gardening encompasses a way of thinking that involves the entire ecosystem of a garden—from the soil to the water supply to the insects and wildlife that surround it. Gardening organically requires working with nature to sustain the garden's delicate balance, which tips any time a foreign substance is introduced.

It begins with attention to the soil. Organic gardening calls for regular composting, which provides an ideal natural fertilizer for replenishing any resources the garden consumes. Another important element is choosing plants specifically suited to a particular site. Plants that are adapted to the climate and soil conditions are much more likely to thrive with relatively little attention than plants that need their natural defenses boosted to stay healthy and productive. (It's no different from a person who moves to Alaska with only a summer wardrobe.)

I ask Dave if he thinks the Canterbury Shakers would have been organic gardeners if the community were still active today. He says he has no doubt that they would have been, especially given that the Shakers had already eschewed some pesticides long before their use was outlawed. Personally, Dave is a strong advocate of organic gardening. "You're giving the plant what it needs to grow," he explains. "If you aren't gardening organically, you're leeching out the life in the soil, like the worms and microorganisms that thrive there. If you're killing bad insects, you're killing good insects, too. But with organic gardening, the soil is alive, which produces a healthier vegetable. All gardening was organic at one time."

The village is in the process of transposing its orchards to organic, a process that takes three years from when organic methods are first introduced. Dave is following a similar course for the village's forests through a sustainable forestry program called SmartWood, which leads to a "green" certification. But before the latter can happen, he will develop a fifteen-year land management plan that analyzes the ecosystem of the entire area, including water, trees, wildlife, endangered plants, and the archaeological value of the land. "When we're out here, we're always thinking, Would the Shakers do this?" Dave says about his plans. "The idea is to use as much of the property as possible—to get people back here after they've visited the buildings. We want to keep the place productive, but there's a lot of give-and-take."

Like the Shakers, Dave and his crew use the most modern equipment and methods. For example, they make their own compost from kitchen scraps, mulch, straw, and anything else that's "not too weedy, stocky, or thick." Dave says he wants to churn out compost as quickly as possible so he can add it to every bed when it's needed most. At the height of pest season, though, the crew uses an effective, if decidedly low-tech solution. "Sometimes we just get out there and pick the bugs off by hand. I call them bug patrols," he says. They also use lightweight row covers that let plants develop pest-free, as well as organic sprays—but only as a last resort. "In general, I can live with mild pest problems."

The water supply for the beds draws on one of the village's five mill-ponds through a line that also allows Dave and his crew to use a drip tape system, as well as to water each bed individually. Interestingly, the ponds were created by the Shakers in the 1800s, because, at that time, there were no naturally occurring streams on the village's original three thousand acres. The Shakers created nine ponds in all, between five and thirty acres in size, each of which rose above and flowed into the next. They also dug a two-mile canal, dubbed the "long ditch," which fed the ponds through water reserves located north of the village. The ditch flowed north to south and became a steady, year-round source of water for the eighteen mills the Shakers had built on the ponds. Archaeologists still consider the system bold and farsighted for its day.

On another agricultural front, the Shakers were among the first to package and sell seeds. It turned out to be a lucrative endeavor for them, although the actual work behind it was extremely labor-intensive. First they pulled the seeds; then they washed, dried, sorted, and packaged them, and then marketed them through catalogs. The village no longer packages seeds, but Dave says he tries to use as many Shaker plant varieties in his gardens as possible, including many older ones that have been all but forgotten. "The Shakers experimented a lot with plants," Dave says. "If a new variety came out, they would try it." Last year the village tested two hundred varieties of herbs and over one hundred different vegetables in its four-acre production garden, which has been feeding the kitchen from the same location since 1795.

Several times during our talk, Dave has alluded to the village's one-quarter-acre flower beds, but I get the feeling he doesn't want to appear frilly by spending too much time on the subject. With a little prodding, though, he tells me he loves sunflowers. So much so that he plants twelve varieties. "I had to cut back a few years ago," he says, chuckling. "I got a little crazy." He says he tries to plant low-maintenance flower varieties that also happen to look good. Visitors enjoy them, and growing them lets Dave's crew deliver fresh bouquets to all the buildings in the village a few times a week. "But the fun part about maintaining all the gardens," Dave tells me, "is watching people take pictures. One year we grew oats, and people were out there in the middle of them taking pictures."

Perhaps the biggest news concerning the gardens at Shaker Village is the re-creation of the 1816 botanical garden that grew only herbs. The garden spawned a highly profitable herb business for the Canterbury Shakers that included scented waters, medicinal applications, and, most sought-after of all, the Shakers' own sarsaparilla syrup, a one-bottle-heals-all digestive made from a dozen types of herbs and roots. To re-create the garden, Dave and his crew have cleaned up three of the original hillside terraces. Now they're working from a hand-drawn plan of it—the only existing map—to figure out what went where. To select plants, they're using the 1854 Shaker seed catalog, which listed over 150 medicinal herbs. Another small section of the garden will be devoted to "modern" herbs Dave believes the Shakers would have grown, such as echinacea.

"My first priority, though, is Leo—to get produce to the restaurant," Dave says. "The vegetables can't be fresher. It's a positive thing for visitors. They're eating fresh, organic produce that just came out of the garden. The gardens are a large part of the visitor experience here."

Canterbury Shaker Village was first called to order in February 1792, when a local farmer invited a few believers to share his hundred-acre farm as a communal living place. Only fifty years later, the community had grown to three hundred believers who eventually constructed over one hundred buildings on three thousand bountiful acres that supported everything from holsteins to extensive orchards.

Stewardship of the land was a basic tenet of the Shakers. They followed a few guiding principles that are as effective today as they were when the Shakers farmed this land: aim for perfection, work faithfully, don't rush, nurture the soil, use the most efficient tools, take care of your tools, and grow useful plants. Their ideal garden was well ordered and high yielding. To support this, they didn't hesitate to try new farming practices and were always improving labor-saving devices. During the peak of the Shaker movement in the mid-1800s, they were often at the forefront of many leading technologies of their day.

But the businesses the Shakers especially excelled in were those tied to the soil. The Canterbury Shakers planted apple, pear, peach, plum, and cherry trees that, over time, became vital to their economy. They experimented with maple trees, ultimately producing thousands of pounds annually of maple sugar products. They began selling medicinal herbs here in 1824 and garden seeds in 1829. It's not by coincidence that Shaker businesses were so successful. They were run by smart people who understood efficiency and weren't afraid to take calculated risks. And in a time of few standards, the Shakers built a strong reputation for fair-minded business dealings and high-quality products that the public came to trust.

In Shaker communities, both genders were considered equal, but everyone was expected to pull their weight. Men worked the heavy machinery, while many women were employed in what the Shakers called "household industries." This included harvesting the production gardens and orchards, canning and storing the yield for the winter, and all food preparation. In the Dwelling House, where the Shakers ate their meals, the female kitchen team rotated every month or so. It was led by a head cook who planned the menus and cooked the meats, followed by a second cook who washed and cooked the vegetables, and a third cook who prepared special dishes for the community's elderly and sick.

In typical Shaker fashion, mealtimes revolved around work. Most accounts show that they rose between 4:30 and 5:30 A.M., depending upon the time of year (earlier in summer, later in winter), giving them a half hour to wash up and tidy their rooms before breakfast. They ate in several shifts to accommodate all members of the community. After breakfast the community went directly to work. At 11:30 A.M. a bell would toll, giving everyone a half hour to put aside their tools and ready themselves for dinner, the main meal of the day. Consisting of meat, potatoes, and two vegetables, it was served promptly at noon for a half hour and fortified the community until everyone finished work at 5:30 P.M. They then returned to the Dwelling House at 6:00 P.M. for supper, the final meal of the day.

If you peruse any Shaker authored cookbook, you are immediately convinced that the Shakers loved a hearty meal and valued good cooks. They saw the preparation of meals, as they saw all service to others, as a form of prayer offered lovingly to God and fellow believers by hand and heart. The Canterbury sisters used an informal apprentice system to teach young women how to cook. From a young age, girls assumed simple cooking duties and were rewarded with more challenging tasks as they matured. Girls also were expected to observe and imitate the older sisters so that by the time the girls were old enough to bake pies and cakes, they needed little supervision.

Typical of the way the Shakers approached any job, they quickly adopted new kitchen technologies that saved time and labor. In the late 1800s, the Canterbury Shakers already were using a revolving bake oven, patented by a Shaker, that could hold sixty pies. In 1909 they remodeled the Dwelling House kitchen and equipped it with two new ranges and a broiler. Fifteen years later, they bought a used, oversize KitchenAid electric mixer that they sometimes used to make ice cream. The following year they bought a meat slicer and installed a refrigerator. Photos from this period show the sisters in their simple dresses, aprons, and bonnets grinning happily in their fully equipped kitchen that resembled any you might find in a small restaurant today.

Darryl Thompson remembers the Dwelling House kitchen well, having eaten many meals in its dining room as a youngster in the early 1960s (at that time there were only eleven sisters left in the community). He says everyone—hired help and sisters alike—would first gather in a parlor before filing from the oldest to the youngest into the dining room separated by gender. "This was the custom," Darryl explains. "We would first go over to the parlor and then go to the dining room in a procession. It was connected to nineteenth-century practices." Each person sat at a designated table and seat. When it was time to leave, everyone did so together, this time led by the youngest. Shaker dining style was "four square," which meant that four people shared the same pitcher and condiments, precisely as it's done in the Creamery Restaurant today.

Darryl is the son of Charles "Bud" Thompson, the man who guided the sisters in preserving the village and whose collection of Shaker artifacts established its museum. When I first contacted Darryl, he didn't understand why I wanted to talk to him instead of his father. After all, it's certainly safe to say that without Bud Thompson, Canterbury Shaker Village would not have survived as the important historic and cultural landmark that it is today. But I was interested in Darryl because he is the only person alive who absorbed this place as a child when the sisters still breathed life into it. His first memories are here. His recollections are unique because, when he lived here, he knew of no other home.

Darryl is a round man with large hands and soft brown eyes. He is well spoken and reflective. In 1959, he came to live here with his parents when he was only a year old. His father, who had been a folksinger in search of undiscovered music, had worked for the sisters over the two previous summers in exchange for their teaching him Shaker lore and music. After two years, the sisters asked him to work for them permanently. He agreed, moved his wife and young son from Roslindale, Massachusetts, and stayed for thirty years. Eventually Darryl's parents divorced, and he moved from Shaker Village with his mother and younger brother to Gilmanton. From the time he was eight, Darryl then spent most weekends and every summer here. He's been a tour guide ever since he was thirteen.

There had not been any children at Canterbury Shaker Village in many years, so it was quite unusual for the sisters to have Darryl and his brother around. Darryl says they looked after him and his brother as if they were the sisters' own. As a result, he became close to them, especially Eldress Bertha Lindsay, the last senior member of the community, who died in 1990."Next to my parents, the sisters were the most powerful influences in my life," Darryl tells me.

I ask him how the experience of growing up here has affected him in his adult life. "It's my intellectual center point," he answers. "It unifies every branch of knowledge in my mind. Anything I study enriches my knowledge of the Shakers. But it goes beyond that. My choice of career as an historian, my friendships have come out of here, my religious life. I'm a perfectionist in my work. I hope it's affected the way I treat people. Scholars have written a lot about the Shakers, but much of that is peripheral. What's often been overlooked was their kindness."

Darryl continues to be involved in the village researching, training, and helping to develop new programs. He's a welcome sight to village tour guides, because his presence adds an authenticity that historic buildings alone can't create. I ask him how it has been over the years watching the village transition from home to museum. "People come up to me all the time and say, 'It must be so difficult to witness all these changes!'" he responds. "But it has not been hard for me . . . the most difficult thing has been the loss of my Shaker grandmothers. I lost them one by one and I miss them greatly. But my memories of them are so happy and I am so grateful for the opportunity to have had them in my life that I dwell in the mansion of gladness, not in the habitation of loss."

"It is a very odd experience to see an article of clothing worn by a person to whom you were very close, or an object possessed by them, staring out at you from behind a glass museum case," Darryl continues. "Despite the fact that I'm constantly around such objects in cases, I never quite get used to it. Nevertheless, I'm absolutely delighted that at least these items have been preserved. But, with the exception of these . . . things, the transition has been a highly positive experience for me. To understand my attitude, one needs to understand the outlook of the Canterbury Shakers. The sisters were not people who sat around waiting for the hearse. They were vibrant, forward-looking, and highly positive individuals. Yes, they had feelings of nostalgia and all the other various emotions experienced by any older person who has outlived most of his or her contemporaries. But they also kept up with current events, planned for the future, maintained their daily routines and rituals, cultivated a variety of interests, engaged in projects, maintained wide-ranging friendships that included some friends of much younger ages, enjoyed life, and always, always continued to learn."

Recently, Darryl completed a master's degree in history from the University of New Hampshire, where, not surprising, he specialized in Shaker studies. For his thesis, he drew from the research of many Shaker scholars around the country to identify twenty-four plant varieties developed by the Shakers, only a handful of which had been previously discovered by other historians. "Some of these plants had wonderful qualities, but as horticulture became more commercialized, they weren't productive enough for wide-scale production," Darryl says. The upshot was that at the end of the day, the Shakers simply selected the hardiest plants with the best commercial prospects.

"Gardening was something the whole community could do together," he continues. "To some, it was something pure. The idea of stewardship and protecting God's gifts was strong. You can see the same drive for improvement in Shaker gardening as you do in Shaker inventions. . . . Their knowledge of plants and herbs was incredible. They were amongst the greatest horticulturists in this country in the nineteenth century."

# 11

## New Hampshire Historical Society Tuck Library

### "The Story Was Hidden Here All Along"

*I*'m sitting in the back of the reading room at the New Hampshire Historical Society's Tuck Library in Concord on a cold, blustery day in December. It's a pleasant place right out of the early twentieth century, with rows of tables each bedecked with tall Windsor-style chairs. Across from me is head librarian Bill Copeley, who has worked in this room every day since 1973. Considering that history was his least favorite subject in school, he seems somewhat surprised about the outcome of his career. "It's accidental that I'm here," he tells me. "I've always liked books, but I was motivated more by the reality of earning a living. Now I can't imagine doing anything else."

Behind thick, rimless glasses, Bill's eyes occasionally dart around the room, surveying the landscape for patrons or volunteers who need help. He reminds me of a college professor in his green wide-wale corduroys and slightly scuffed wing-tip shoes, but, in fact, Bill started out studying chemistry. After a few years as an MIT undergrad, he decided "the world had enough chemists" and ended up as an American Studies graduate student at the University of Wyoming. When he applied for a job with historical societies all over the country, the New Hampshire Historical Society snapped him up. Since then, he's spent the better part of thirty years working with the vast resources of this respected research and genealogical library.

From the outside, Tuck Library is an imposing granite block that anyone might be dissuaded from entering just by contemplating its sheer weight. But once you get through the door, it's surprising what is here. Since 1823, when the New Hampshire Historical Society was founded, the library has been collecting a wide variety of New Hampshire–related materials, including genealogies of New England families, histories, vital records, church records, maps, manuscripts, business records, photographs, and newspapers. After so many years, it now contains the most extensive collections of historical records in the state.

On any given day, Bill and two other librarians might hear from patrons writing town histories, researching the history of their home, investigating ownership of a particular building, or, most often, tracing their family history. "Often someone calls and if they can make that one link, they can go back five more generations," Bill says. "Genealogy is like an addiction. Once you get into it, it hooks you. I started asking questions about my own family and I found a lineage that dates back to the 1600s. I tell people to start when they're young because family members aren't around forever. I started in the late 1970s and I'm still working on my family's history. It's helped me a lot with my job."

Every year Bill teaches a one-day genealogy class at the library (at the start of this year's class, he went through the entire list of twenty participants and quickly identified which were New Hampshire surnames and which were not). He says genealogy has grown in popularity so much that it's now the second most popular hobby in the United States (next to gardening), with over half of all Americans pursuing it on some level. New England genealogists are particularly blessed, however, because the best and most plentiful historical records in the country are located here. The farther west you go, Bill says, the harder it can get to find links.

Most library patrons don't think much about how a library's resources are cultivated, expecting only to find what they are seeking on the shelves. But part of a head librarian's job is building the institution's collections. Every year Bill supervises the addition to Tuck Library of about three hundred items that staff find through major genealogy publishers, out-of-print book dealers, and the Historical Society's own bookstore. Sometimes the library receives gifts, which are as likely to be a single box of books as an entire collection of family papers spanning several centuries. An Historical Society staff acquisitions committee meets frequently to consider all purchases and donations, analyzing the items' relevance and relation to New Hampshire, overall condition, and whether the society already has similar items in the collection. It also considers practical issues like storage and space limitations. Ultimately, the defining question is—What does this item tell us about New Hampshire history?

I ask Bill what is different today about the type of items the library collects from what was collected, say, a hundred years ago. He tells me the thinking about what to collect hasn't changed a lot, although the library is actively collecting more business records and annual reports now than at any time in its history. The difference has more to do with the methods used to preserve collections. Quality of paper is the issue. Before the Civil War, most people used rag paper, made literally from rags chopped into fibers. If you look at documents from those times, the paper is thicker and sturdier than what we use today.

By 1870, the industrial revolution was in full swing and cheaper, mass-produced wood pulp paper had taken over for daily use. What people didn't realize, though, was that this paper had a higher acidity level and, because of that, it aged faster. "There was a great resurgence of interest in history at the turn of the twentieth century, and that's when people began to understand that the type of paper they use makes a difference in its preservation," Bill says. "I'm much less concerned about documents from the 1700s, because the quality of paper from then was very high. It comes down to the scientific aspects of what the paper is."

Because so much of the library's more recent collections—meaning anything from the twentieth century—are on wood pulp paper, the Historical Society installed an expensive climate control system in the building in 1997. Before this, Bill says, he noticed that many old documents were wearing out faster than they should due to uneven and too-high levels of heat and humidity throughout the building. Now library staff can focus their preservation efforts on repairing material in the collections, some of which is done in-house by the library's two volunteer "book doctors," who commonly repair broken bindings and covers. When fragile pages are torn or bindings fall apart, Bill sends the books out to professional conservators, who have the tools and experience to handle delicate repairs.

To understand where Tuck Library's collections fit in with other New Hampshire–related document collections in the state, you have to know something about what is kept where. The New Hampshire State Library, a state agency partly set up for use by state legislators and employees as well as county and municipal governments, is larger than Tuck. It contains many government-related publications and mostly nonhistorical materials about New Hampshire. The State Archives, on the other hand, stores several million public records created by New Hampshire's two hundred state agencies.

Tuck Library once collected many public records, but stopped doing so when the State Archives was established in 1963. I ask Bill how much overlap there is among the State Library, the State Archives, and Tuck's collections. "There is probably some overlap," he says, "but here the focus is history and genealogy. Our strength is that we have a lot of privately produced, nongovernmental records, many of which are handwritten or typed."

But for any collecting institution, it's not good enough only to collect. The point is to make the institution's resources available to the public, wherever they might live. In that respect, technology has made a tremendous impact over the last ten to fifteen years by making it possible for libraries and museums to put their entire collections on-line. Tuck Library placed its 50,000-item catalog on-line through the Historical Society's web site in 1996, a project that took ten years to complete. In 2001, the library wrapped up a twelve-year project that put 800,000 pages of New Hampshire newspapers from 1756 to 1900 on microfilm. Before that, access was limited mainly because many of the newspapers were too fragile to handle.

"We're in a transition in the library world between everything being in the card catalog and everything being on-line," Bill says. But the point, he says, is to make the library—overall—more user-friendly. "People tend to think that everything is on-line and of course it's not. Two-thirds of our patrons are researching family history. Most of them are beginners and are learning how to discriminate between reliable and unreliable sources. They don't always realize that they need to come to libraries like this because many records can't be found on the Internet, so they're getting only part of the story. Many things here are one-of-a-kind sources."

Architectural historians call Tuck Library one of the finest examples of classical design and granite construction in the United States. It's a symmetrical building reminiscent of its slightly older and grander cousin, Boston's Museum of Fine Arts, crafted by the same architect, Guy Lowell. When you enter the library's cool, airy rotunda, you can't help but notice the dark gray veins that twist through the marble walls. Straight ahead, perched on the staircase landing, is a gigantic gold eagle from 1818 that once roosted on the State House cupola. Over the rotunda, a dome rises forty-five feet above both floors, filtering a soft natural light that reflects off the marble below.

Before the New Hampshire Historical Society moved to this building in 1911, it had occupied the former home of the Merrimack County Bank on North Main Street in Concord since the 1840s. But by 1900 the three-story brick structure had become so crowded and unsafe that Benjamin Ames Kimball, a former Historical Society president, decided to approach the international philanthropist Edward Tuck about funding a new building.

The interesting thing is that Kimball had never met Tuck, but he knew that several years earlier Tuck, who was a native of Exeter, New Hampshire, had donated a large sum of money to establish the Amos Tuck School of Administration and Finance at his alma mater, Dartmouth College (he had named the school after his father, who was also an alumnus). Kimball was so sure the Historical Society project was right for Tuck that when he approached Tuck by letter, he spelled out the requirements: the society wished to move to a permanent home created only for them, preferably constructed in the Greek style of architecture.

At that time, Tuck had retired to a chateau outside of Paris with his wife Julia, having made a fortune in the gold and silver markets. He appreciated Kimball's forthrightness, being of similar temperament, and was immediately intrigued by the opportunity. Eventually he became so inspired by Kimball's as well as others' passionate pleas that he agreed to become the sole donor to the Historical Society's building fund. His only caveat was that he would not permit financial involvement from others except in purchasing the land. By 1906, he had corresponded with Kimball enough to feel comfortable appointing the seventy-three-year-old former railroad executive as the society's building committee chairman.

Kimball gladly accepted the challenge and quickly went to work, quietly buying several lots he had already identified on the corner of Park and North State Streets. Kimball had played a significant role in placing the State Library and federal building close to the State House, and he likewise felt that the Historical Society building belonged among what he saw as the great institutions and buildings of New Hampshire.

The choice of an architect was equally uncomplicated. Guy Lowell, who was just completing a contract with the Museum of Fine Arts, had fulfilled many important commissions for such institutions as Harvard and Brown Universities and was very much in demand. But the Historical Society contract was something of a dream job for Lowell. Tuck wanted him to utilize only the best materials and the most advanced technologies of the day to erect the classically styled structure.

The exterior was constructed of local granite quarried from Rattlesnake Hill in Concord—the same source of granite used to build the Library of Congress in Washington, D.C. On Tuck Library's interior, the rotunda walls and ceiling came from marble quarried by monks in Siena, Italy, the only known source of this particular type of stone. To embellish the building with sculptural effects, Lowell hired sculptor and New Hampshire native Daniel Chester French, best known for his seated Abraham Lincoln sculpture in Washington, D.C.'s Lincoln Memorial. There is no doubt that

Librarians *(left to right)* Bill Copeley and Philip Abbott confer over a genealogical query in Tuck Library's late-nineteenth-century first-floor reading room.

Lowell and Kimball did, indeed, employ the best craftsmen, materials, and designs to build Tuck Library.

As in most large projects, there were problems from the start, but finally, after three and a half years, the building was dedicated on November 23, 1911. It had cost well over the original estimates, but Edward and Julia Tuck were thrilled with the results. At the dedication, Tuck called his involvement in the project "perhaps the happiest inspiration of my life . . . of which we and our successors will never cease to be proud."

If you follow the staircase at the back of the rotunda down a flight, you'll come to a dark oval table in the center of the special collections reading room. Before visiting here, I didn't understand how different this part of the library is from what is in the book stacks upstairs. Special collections librarian David Smolen set the record straight. "It's a library's special collections that distinguish it from other libraries," he tells me. "The books upstairs can overlap with other libraries, but it's a library's special collections that make it stand out." Special collections are, in effect, just that.

David, who is in his late twenties, is the first full-time special collections librarian at Tuck. He calls himself an archivist, which is different from a librarian who primarily handles printed materials such as books. As an archivist in this library, David works with everything from the extensive map collection to the unpublished records of often-prominent New Hampshire individuals, families, businesses, and organizations. For example, if you wanted to view the papers of John Stark, Daniel Webster, Mary Baker Eddy, or the Abbot-Downing Company, makers of the Concord Coach, David is the person you would see.

Most items in Tuck's special collections can be categorized as primary sources, which in an historical society library are often the unpublished bits and pieces of past lives. A few years ago, David organized a workshop for sixty high school seniors to prepare them for the Advanced Placement Exam in American history, where he covered, among other things, how primary sources are the living stories behind every event in history. As an illustration, he showed them an 1852 letter written by the famous writer and poet Walt Whitman, addressed to John Parker Hale. Hale, a former senator and representative from Dover, was the first U.S. senator to speak out against slavery and had just been nominated for president of the Unites States by the newly founded, antislavery Free Soil Party.

As Hale hesitated, Whitman urged him to accept the nomination, saying that his party, as well as the nation, needed him. Hale eventually did accept, but lost the election with only 150,000 votes to another New Hampshire native—Franklin Pierce. "The letter from Walt Whitman was already a 'wow' to these students," David says. "But the story it told was equally impressive." In fact, the workshop was so successful that the library plans to take it directly to high schools around the state in the future.

All collections, some of which contain thousands of items, must be processed and preserved so that anyone who needs them can easily find what they are looking for. Processing is no small task and can take months, or years, depending on the amount of material. Sometimes family papers are donated to Tuck in unordered boxes, with no hint about what's inside. Staff and specially trained volunteers must then sift through the papers and organize them into a collection.

One of those volunteers is Lea Stark, who at this moment is quietly sorting papers at a small table across the room. Lea has filled many volunteer roles with the New Hampshire Historical Society over the last forty years and was one of two volunteers who spent five years processing the Kimball-Jenkins papers, the library's largest collection of family documents.

Acquired in 1984, it contains twenty thousand items that span almost two centuries—from 1753 to 1930. Even though her work on the project ended a decade ago, she still talks with enthusiasm about it.

While David answers a patron's questions, I ask Lea how she started, considering the voluminous size of the collection. The first thing the volunteers did, she tells me, was to separate all items into two categories: personal and business. When that was finished, they started the arduous task of figuring out who in the family was whom. Lea says it was especially difficult to decipher handwriting, but she couldn't let that slow her down. All twenty thousand items had to be read and logged. "You'd open a letter and a piece of hair in a ribbon would fall out," she says, laughing. "This family saved everything. We opened and flattened every document, and then organized letters, financial papers, invitations, note cards, playbills, personal IOUs, small slips of paper, checkbooks. Everything."

It was time consuming and required much patience, but Lea says reading through the correspondences put her in direct contact with how people were thinking about important events, as well as the values people espoused, over a span of 177 years. "There were several hundred letters just from the Civil War era," she recalls. "One of the most striking things about them was that they hardly ever mentioned the war. Most were from women, and the things they talked about were deaths of family and friends, illnesses, and education. Other interesting letters came from a lawyer in the family in the 1700s. Judging from the number of lawsuits, I could see we were a litigious society even then." Lea says that sometimes she felt a bit like a voyeur. "But in boxes, the material is useless. Only after it's been opened and organized can anyone make any sense of it. And that's when the stories start coming out."

One of the more interesting, if obscure, areas of special collections is the ephemera collected over the last hundred years. These are the everyday items like train tickets, brochures, advertisements, and postcards that capture the essence of the times. I'm curious about the types of ephemera the library is collecting that will one day give patrons a glimpse of daily life from today. Walking over to a series of folders, David shows me a program from a special service held at St. Paul's Church in Concord dated September 14, 2001. "A hundred years from now, I'm sure someone will ask for material related to September eleventh," he says.

Taking out a bright yellow brochure printed by a group of local businesses, David says he likes it because it has a complete list of businesses inside, as well as a map. Another pamphlet is from the Concord bus system. This is important because it can be analyzed to reveal all kinds of insight into daily life—traffic patterns and rush hours, ticket prices, and where the largest pockets of Concord's population live today.

I ask David if he would have collected different items a hundred years ago than what librarians before him collected. "No," he replies. "When I look through these collections, I feel a real connection to librarians before me. There's a continuity in why they collected what they did. This doesn't change. We still know what is important, no matter the type of document. The problem today, though, is that there is so much material to choose from. We really have to be selective about what we collect." He says he often has to restrain himself "because you can't collect it all."

The New Hampshire Historical Society has a reputation for being a forward-thinking, innovative, technologically savvy institution. This in itself isn't particularly surprising unless you consider the fact that New Hampshire's Historical Society—unlike those in most other states—receives no state funding, instead operating as a member supported, private nonprofit organization. Even with limited funds, the Historical Society manages to maintain extensive, high-quality collections through Tuck Library and the Museum of New Hampshire History that are widely considered to be in the same league as those of its well-funded peers.

As recently as twenty years ago, however, the New Hampshire Historical Society was a different place. A decidedly aristocratic society from its founding, the organization had an elitist image that persisted well into the 1980s. But all that changed in 1987, when the society's board hired a dynamic new director named John Frisbee, who had history and museum management degrees and two decades with the National Trust for Historic Preservation under his belt. Outside of New Hampshire, he was a big name, but inside the state, he differed from his predecessors in one fundamental way: he wanted to fling open the doors of the institution and welcome everyone in. "For 175 years we had done well in collecting information, but not necessarily in communicating it and disseminating it," John told me a few months before he passed away in 2002 (he directed the Historical Society for fifteen years). "I'm not just talking about facts and data, but why this institution is important and how it enriches our lives."

Not surprising, the institution started to grow, and by the early 1990s it had once again outgrown its headquarters. At that time, it was operating its evolving museum, library, and operations from the Tuck building. But space was limited, and staff were concerned the society wasn't offering exhibits and programs on the scale that it should have been. In 1994, the institution bought an old stone warehouse off Eagle Square in Concord, moved its collections there, and one year later opened the Museum of New Hampshire History. At the same time, the Park Street building, which had served as the society's headquarters for eighty-four years, was restored to its original purpose and became Tuck Library.

All of these changes have had positive repercussions not only for the society's members and visitors but also for the staff, who say the museum could not exist without the library. When I asked John Frisbee how important Tuck Library is to the overall institution he answered, "The library is central to everything we do. The museum gets most of the press, but if someone said you have to stop everything you're doing except for one thing, I'd say keep the library. I don't see how we could do research on New Hampshire without using our library."

Donna-Belle Garvin, the society's research director, agrees with that assessment. One of her major tasks over the last twenty-five years has been cataloging, which has meant spending long hours in Tuck Library researching and validating the origins and history of many objects in the society's collections. But objects come from people, and in order to establish a connection between items and owners, Donna-Belle has also had to delve heavily into genealogy. Without the validated connection that traces the life of an object, its historical context and value aren't as great.

On the day we meet, Donna-Belle is wearing a stylish nut brown dress that meets her ankles. Her silver hair, parted in the middle, is swept softly off her face. She is earnest in disposition and has a formidable reputation for scholarship. Besides being the editor of *Historical New Hampshire,* the society's academically oriented journal, she is also one half of this state's Power Couple of History. She is married to New Hampshire State Architectural Historian James L. Garvin.

Donna-Belle has prepared for our talk by setting out three neat stacks of books and journals on her desk, but it's a bulging white binder on the far corner that gets my attention. Bookmarks are protruding from it like tiny yellow flags. Inside, the pages are covered from every angle with handwritten notes. Donna-Belle tells me the binder contains four hundred pages of transcribed diaries of an eighteenth-century Stratham, New Hampshire, farmer that were recently published by University Press of New England as a book, *The Years of the Life of Samuel Lane, 1718–1806.* Working over a period of three years with a University of New Hampshire history student, who transcribed the diaries as his Ph.D. dissertation, Donna-Belle edited the manuscript down to a more manageable two hundred pages for publication.

The book is only one of several Donna-Belle has worked on for the society over the years, but she tells me this one was particularly interesting. In 1984 the Lane family donated the dairies to the society hoping that one day they would be published. The diaries are extraordinary, she says, because they span sixty years and are one of only a handful of similar collections in the state that give such a complete view of daily life in New Hampshire from that time.

As we talk, I can see Donna-Belle's work has become somewhat addictive over the years, and she looks at me quizzically when I ask her what has kept her here so long. "I like rediscovering obscure or less well known people in history because I often find surprising connections as I research," she tells me. "These people may have been forgotten, but I don't see them as lost forever; it's just that their tracks are a little harder to trace than more prominent people."

Sometimes she'll come across something in her work that hooks her curiosity so much that she'll pursue it on her own time to solve the puzzle. That's what happened with the story of Hannah Wilson, an early-nineteenth-century weaver from Farmington, New Hampshire, whose exceptional blue-and-white hand-woven coverlets have turned up in important museums all over the country, including the Smithsonian Institution. A former employee of the Smithsonian donated one of Wilson's 1842 coverlets to the Historical Society, prompting Donna-Belle to begin researching its history of ownership. Within a short time, however, she ran into roadblocks.

No one knew the name of the weaver. Unlike other coverlets from the time that were commonly marked with the maker's name, these were carefully inscribed with the owner's name, a number denoting a series, and the date of manufacture. As Donna-Belle researched, she found more coverlets from this weaver, all of which had lost their histories.

Finally, after a few years, she came across a coverlet in the Wadsworth Atheneum in Hartford, Connecticut, that was numbered 177, appeared to be dated 1839, and included the initials "HW aged 72." Donna-Belle knew this was the only coverlet bearing the weaver's initials, which suggested that the weaver knew it to be her last. "But it was only after some unproductive searching in the census for an 'HW' who was seventy-two in 1839, and only after learning from the Wadsworth Atheneum that their files actually list the date of the coverlet as 1859, that we began to get anywhere with solving this puzzle," Donna-Belle recalls. "A little bit of the thread on the '5' had worn, which made the date look like 1839."

From here, it took some genealogical detective work in Tuck Library for her to unearth the rest of the story. She found that Hannah Wilson had lived in the Farmington-Tuftonboro area for most of her life and had never married. In 1829, she changed her name from "Hannah Leathers" to Hannah Wilson, which explains why Donna-Belle had difficulty finding birth records for the family. (It was common at that time for people with the Leathers surname to legally change it. Historians say the name was associated with poverty and carried a stigma that those bearing the name often wished to escape.) Hannah Wilson also bore an illegitimate son, earned enough money from her weaving business to buy her own home, and produced 177 coverlets, only 18 of which have been identified to date. Most are now in museums.

"It was bothering me," says Donna-Belle, who pursued the mystery for six years. "I wanted to find the whole story and bring life to this object, the coverlet. I wanted to bring it back from obscurity, and it turns out the story was hidden here in our library all along."

Over several weeks of visiting Tuck staff, I've heard a lot about the library's stacks and vault, but now my curiosity has gotten the better of me. I ask head librarian Bill Copeley to show me some of the library's treasures himself.

Once again, we are sitting in the reading room. "I'm constantly shifting things around," Bill says. "Librarians are always doing that. I try to keep the genealogy-oriented materials in the reading room because that's what most of our patrons come here to see." He points out family and town histories before heading up a back staircase that feels a lot like a secret passageway. When we reach the top, we're in a large square room overflowing with long rows of bookcases—at least eight aisles. It smells faintly musty, but it's comfortably cool at sixty-seven degrees. The lighting is dim. It's completely quiet.

I ask Bill to show me what he finds interesting up here. Pausing only for a moment, he turns and walks quickly down an aisle, stopping in front of a pile of thin boxes. Reaching for one, he opens it to reveal yellowing leaves of happy-looking sheet music. It's from the 1840s, and the cover sheet says "Songs and Glees of the Baker Family." The mid-1800s sound a lot like the 1960s when Bill explains that some families took their message of social reform to the stage, performing at concerts with an abolitionist bent. "But the Hutchinson family was more famous than the Bakers," Bill says. "They were social reformers from Milford who traveled around the country, singing after speeches by people like Frederick Douglass. I think they were a little too broad-minded for New Hampshire at that time."

We're slowly perusing the next aisle over when Bill pulls down a brown leather volume with gold lettering from 1746. Bracing the book's spine on his forearm, he opens it carefully. The pages are tanned with age, but you can clearly read through each handwritten list of baptisms and marriages. From a genealogical standpoint, Bill says church records like these are an excellent way to trace family members. Most church records from the 1700s are Congregational, the most established church in New England until the early 1800s, and the Congregationalists were very good at keeping track of their members.

Next to the church records are published sermons covering most of the 1800s. "Pastors liked to publish sermons if they thought they were doing something particularly good," Bill says. "Sermons were extremely popular reading and right up there in the top ten of reading-list material for everyone. The interesting thing about reading them today, though, is that you can trace broad trends in American religious practices through them."

I'm wondering if the society ever deaccessions material because there is simply too much of it. Bill tells me it does. Last year he weeded out eight hundred biographies, including four shelves on George Washington and even more on Abraham Lincoln. The need for space is always pressing, he says, but deaccessioning isn't a casual thing. Three levels—a staff committee, a board committee, and finally the director—analyze what stays and what goes, according to the amount of material that's already been collected. When deaccessions are approved, the material is often sent to other libraries in the state.

In the school records section, Bill brings up an interesting issue. For many years, New Hampshire was a national leader on the private school front, and the Historical Society collected records from these schools as a genealogy tool. But today's schools, Bill says, are more concerned than ever about privacy. "It's important for us to collect these types of records because no other organization does that. But right now, no existing schools are giving us records. It makes me wonder what we'll end up with from this era in a hundred years."

But wouldn't privacy also be an issue for families who donate entire collections of personal documents? Surprisingly, Bill says, it's less of an issue. In earlier decades, people often concealed records of illegitimate births or unmarried partners living together, but not so today, although families sometimes do place restrictions on donated materials. Recently a prominent family gave Tuck Library a collection of papers and requested restricted access of the documents for the next fifty years. "There's a family secret in there somewhere," Bill chuckles. "But we try to discourage restrictions because the material in the library should be for use by all patrons. Occasionally there is a good reason, but not often."

From the stacks, we descend to another floor that houses the library's vault. It looks like a bank vault like those you might see in the movies, only this one is painted a rosy gray, which Bill finds awful. He twists the combination lock several times, turns the metal wheel, and then tugs heavily on the door, coaxing it to open. Inside, the room is small, like a closet. It smells strongly of old leather and paper, but, like the book stacks upstairs, the room is cool.

Bill says he doesn't come in here often, so he's typed himself a memo and taped it on the wall opposite the door to remind him what's here. It says:

> Books to be kept in vault:
> 1. NH imprints, 1801 or earlier
> 2. American imprints, 1750 or earlier
> 3. European imprints, 1701 or earlier

He climbs up the small ladder that rests against rough wood shelves built into the wall and hands me a few volumes. As he does this, I notice that he is handling these books the way veterinarians often handle animals—carefully, but with the confident hands of someone who knows he will not hurt the spines. From the ladder, he hands down Franklin Pierce's personal copy of the *History of the American Tribes of the United States,* dated 1857. It's a large book, about eighteen inches tall and four inches thick, heavily bound in textured black leather with the owner's name and the imprint of an eagle—both in gold—on the front. Rich purple velvet lines the inside of both covers.

Picking up a previous discussion about preserving old books, Bill shows me a copy of *The History of New England* from 1720, which has a completely new brown leather binding. The original pages rest snugly inside the new spine. Some conservators don't like to change the bindings, he tells me. Instead, they rely on a dressing made with lanolin oil to treat and recondition the leather. He says this is controversial, though, because if the dressing isn't applied properly, it can leak onto the pages and ruin the book. Even the best conservators have problems with this.

In a corner I notice a rather chunky looking book sitting on a small shelf. Bill says it's the Philbrick family Bible loaned to the library in 1930. Dated 1583, it's the oldest item in Tuck Library's collections and easily weighs ten pounds. Bill thinks its coarse binding was made from the thick, rough leather once used to make belts. He thoughtfully checks the Bible over and points out the places where tiny nails have been hammered into the top and back to hold it together. In another place, it appears that the binding was hand sewn. Obviously well used, the Bible's metal clasps on the front and back suggest to Bill that a strap was once attached to keep the book closed.

Before placing the Bible back, Bill opens the front cover and finds a sheet typed on an old typewriter that recounts the family's connection to the Bible. He reads and smiles. "I don't know about that," he says, shaking his head slightly. After all these years, he can quickly decipher historical fact from fiction. "You have to be somewhat skeptical about family histories because legends sometimes are presented as facts. But any information about a book is important. It's all part of the book's life."

## 12

## Lake Umbagog National Wildlife Refuge

---

### "For Many, Umbagog Was the Last Stand"

*I*t was in mid-December that I first asked Lake Umbagog National Wildlife Refuge staff biologist Jennifer Tietjen to drive me around the refuge and tell me about it from a biologist's point of view. "You really should come back in the summer," she advised. "You can only access most areas on the lake by boat." I would do that, but I first wanted to see its geography in winter, without foliage, to get a sense of what this place is about.

On a clear afternoon we set out in a rugged four-wheel-drive vehicle that would haul us up icy roads to an overlook in Upton, Maine. While the lake straddles both states, with most of it in New Hampshire, one of the best views of it is from this spot. Facing due north, we could see its entire length—long, slim, dragon-shaped. Petite Mount Dustan, the highest point on the lake at 2,845 feet, rose like a goose bump to the west. Umbagog (pronounced Um-BAY-gog) is an Abenaki word that means "clear water," and on this day there was no question why. The sky was pale blue, but the water was the color of sapphires.

Looking at the shoreline, you would never guess that 120 years ago, the 7,850-acre, ten-mile-long lake was much smaller, at only 1,000 acres. But as the westernmost lake in the six-lake Rangeley chain, Umbagog eventually swelled to its present size when five dams were built on the interconnected water system in the middle to late 1880s. (One dam, the Errol Dam, built in 1852 and 1888, is in New Hampshire; the rest are in Maine.) The dams helped maintain high year-round water flows while minimizing flooding, so that the growing logging industry could float logs more evenly throughout the year, not only when natural water levels were high. Much of the water in the Rangeley chain ultimately flows into shallow Umbagog Lake through several sources, and then funnels into—

and becomes the headwaters of—the Androscoggin River. (While the refuge is called "Lake Umbagog," topographical maps refer to this body of water as Umbagog Lake.)

Today Umbagog Lake, located thirty miles south of Canada, is widely regarded as New Hampshire's most pristine water body and wetland ecosystem, containing some of the richest and most productive wildlife habitat in the Northeast. For example, Umbagog is home to eagles, ospreys, peregrine falcons, northern harriers, great blue herons, merlins, Canada geese, and a wide range of waterfowl. When the loon population was nearly depleted in New Hampshire, it held on here. Umbagog is now the most productive breeding territory for loons in the state. Moose, bear, deer, bobcat, pine marten, and other wildlife roam the area. According to the Northern Forest Alliance, an organization working to protect the 26-million-acre Northern Forest (the largest remaining contiguous forest in the East), there are twenty-nine species of rare plants that thrive at Umbagog Lake.

Much of the land around the lake is now protected within the boundaries of the Lake Umbagog National Wildlife Refuge, which includes an unusual blend of state and federally owned land as well as conservation easements. The lake's significance, however, already was recognized in the late 1800s, when the conservation movement was in its infancy in this country and ornithologists started flocking here to gather wildlife data. In fact, Umbagog Lake is one of the few places in the country where it is possible to trace wildlife trends over decades. This is thanks primarily to William Brewster, the most prominent New England ornithologist of this period, who made annual, month-long trips to the area for years. While visiting Umbagog he recorded his observations, eventually amassing six hundred pages of documentation (published posthumously by Harvard University in 1924). Brewster died in 1909, but others picked up where he left off, and records of one type or another exist for Umbagog for most of the years since.

Soon after touring Umbagog Lake with Jennifer, I read an article in the New Hampshire Aubudon Society's newsletter about bald eagles in this state, which are on the federal list of threatened species, but listed as endangered in New Hampshire. According to Audubon, Umbagog is the state's longest continuously occupied eagle territory, but there were no successful eagles' nests here in the thirty-nine years prior to the discovery of a nest in 1988. At that time, a pair had built a two-by-four-foot nest in a white pine that was only six feet away, in the same tree, from where another pair was spotted nesting in 1949. In the decade that followed, during which time

Umbagog boasted the only eagles' nest in the state, the territory produced sixteen young eagles.

To find out more about the eagles' return to Umbagog, I talk with Audubon senior biologist Chris Martin to ask him what this says about the area. "When you see an extremely rare species that declined over the years, then disappeared, then begins to establish itself again, it tells me as a biologist that it's the optimal habitat this species could have. That it has all the features they need to thrive there," Chris tells me. "Eagles consider fifty to one hundred square miles as their territory. That spot in the pine allows them a 360-degree view where they can observe their habitat." He points out that there are now two nesting eagle pairs on the lake—one in the north and one in the south. The southerly pair surprised naturalists because it had been thought that development on that section of the lake would keep eagles away.

Chris heads the Friends of Umbagog, an advocacy group started by Audubon in 1997. Every year the group helps organize the small but event-packed Umbagog Wildlife Festival in early August, which offers guided canoe tours and bird walks, freshwater fishing instruction, and an enjoyable loon-calling contest—all for the cause of raising awareness about the wildlife that live here. He's been involved with protecting Umbagog in one way or another for over a decade and is the keeper of the voluminous unofficial files that document the events that led to the establishment of the Lake Umbagog National Wildlife Refuge. Before poring over them, I ask Chris to tell me a bit more about the area's biology. What is it exactly that distinguishes it from other wildlife habitats in the state?

"It's the mixture of habitats, the wide variety of wildlife that thrive on different types of systems," he says. "It's not an area of uniform species." Many species come together here simply because the land is so varied with forests, a bog complex that comprises the most extensive freshwater wetlands in New Hampshire, and a major river flowing through. But as the ecosystems in the region have changed, due mainly to the damming of the Androscoggin, so have some of the species that thrive here. "Animals and plants adapt or disappear depending on the conditions of the ecosystem around them," Chris explains. "For example, the palm warbler breeds in this bog, but they wouldn't if it weren't a wetland. Likewise, there were probably some upland creatures that lived here two hundred years ago that no longer do because the area is now a wetland . . . the thing to remember is that it's all habitat. If the water is lower, it's not good for some animals. If it's higher, it's not good for others."

I'm wondering then how the habitats of endangered species are managed when the face of the land can change, becoming dryer or wetter over time. "The question is what do you do if there's an endangered species on preserved land—do you preserve the species or the ecosystem?" Chris says. I'm surprised to hear that it's sometimes decided case by case after biologists and other specialists study the local causes of why a species is threatened. This is because, despite new approaches to wildlife management that protect entire ecosystems, there is still pressure to manage habitats for specific species, especially charismatic ones like the eagle. "The point is to keep the right habitat balance before things become endangered so that these decisions don't have to be made," Chris says. After that point, biologists must study what the ideal habitat for the species is and then decide where it makes the most sense, realistically, to support it. "It's not always a biological decision," he tells me. "Sometimes it's political."

The land around Umbagog Lake has a long history of ownership by timber and paper companies. Logging continues in the area, and in the winter, you can see the patterns created by culling. It's been a struggle here, as it's been in other parts of the state, to equalize human and wildlife use of the land. No matter how well intentioned, one or the other must give. I ask Chris about the timber companies and the land they managed. Does he feel they were good stewards? "No question is a yes-or-no answer, but in the case of Umbagog, the stewardship was generally good," he says. "There was a succession of companies and harvesting was done on an appropriate scale with environmental concerns in mind for over a hundred years."

"In terms of sustainability for the future," he continues, "good stewardship may be one of the reasons Umbagog has been so rich in wildlife. The land hasn't been greatly altered over the years. If you took a map of this state and pointed to different parts of it, you'd see that there are many places where wildlife is not sustainable. There might be ten-year-old saplings on it, but you would say, 'It would take a long time before this land could be made into a habitat for wildlife.' That's not the case at Umbagog. If we protect the whole range of species in an area, we are creating a balance. But it takes a lot of work to maintain the balance."

Driving into the unpaved parking lot of the Society for the Protection of New Hampshire Forests is like entering a nature reserve. Indeed the society owns one hundred acres here with hiking trails open to the public. Inside its rustic, solar-powered Concord headquarters located on a bluff overlooking the Merrimack River, the building looks like a large sauna with

A bald eagle nest with two nestlings, Lake Umbagog National Wildlife Refuge, Errol, New Hampshire. (Photo by Michael Amaral, U.S. Fish and Wildlife Service.)

windows—all wood and light. From its deck in winter, you can see the State House dome gleaming in the distance.

I'm here to talk with Forest Society senior director of research Sarah Thorne, who was part of the original task force that helped make the Lake Umbagog National Wildlife Refuge a reality. Sarah has been with the Forest Society since 1983, and Umbagog was one of her first projects. In a small conference room, she's laid out maps, geological surveys, and wildlife reports that confirm my hunch: unraveling the refuge's story isn't going to be simple.

"Umbagog is considered a semiwild lake," she tells me, by way of introduction. "Maine has many such lakes, but in New Hampshire we have only this one. The impetus for creating the refuge always came from New Hampshire. For many in the conservation community here, Umbagog was the last stand."

In the three decades prior to the refuge's creation, Umbagog underwent a long succession of threats that, looking back, make one wonder what people were thinking. First there were two proposals in the 1960s and 1970s to mine the bottom of the lake for diatomaceous earth, which is the fossilized remains of organisms that's used, among other things, to control pests in a wide variety of products. Opposition to the plans registered strongly enough, however, for the state to reject the proposals. More recently in the mid-1980s the Swift River/Hafslund Company, an energy development business based in Portland, Maine, proposed building a hydroelectric plant nearby that would require digging a four-mile-long tunnel under the lake. Fortunately, that, too, was rejected.

By this time, though, another, more insidious threat was looming. Ownership of the timberlands around the lake was becoming unstable as large tracts were being sold to the highest bidders. Sarah says the rush to buy lakefront property was especially strong, as were bids for some of the islands. In 1983, the Forest Society purchased 156-acre Big Island, the largest island on the lake, but Sarah says it was only a matter of time before the entire shorefront would have gone the way of many New Hampshire lakes. "It may not have developed to the palatial extent of Lake Winnipesaukee, but we would have lost habitats of the wildlife around Umbagog," she says. "By the mid-1980s it had become clear that we needed to do something more to save this lake."

Prior to her present job, Sarah was land acquisitions director of the Trust for New Hampshire Lands, an organization set up by the Forest Society and its partners in 1986 essentially to inventory the best of remaining undeveloped lands in the state and to address conserving them. One of the Trust's tasks was to educate the state legislature, as well as the public, about the New Hampshire Land Conservation Investment Program (LCIP), which, if passed by the legislature, would give the state funds to purchase lands with conservation value to protect them from development. One of the interesting things about the LCIP was its concept. Prior to this, there had been no specific state-sponsored program to acquire conservation-related land. But because there was no history, legislators were wary. They liked the idea of the program, but they didn't want to pay for its administration.

The Trust's founders were aware of the legislature's reservations. To counter them, the organization agreed to help implement the legislation by paying the salary of an LCIP administrator and a team of land acquisition specialists. All the legislature had to do was appropriate the funds to buy the land. By the time the legislation was drafted and filed in 1987, there was such broad support for it that it was assigned the prestigious Senate Bill 1. The bill passed overwhelmingly with an initial appropriation of $20 million, allocated from a budget surplus. (Appropriations in succeeding years brought the grand total for LCIP funds to $48.5 million, all of which went directly to protecting New Hampshire lands.)

With state funds now available, the Trust could spend the bulk of its time meeting with landowners, responding to inquiries, and expediting the application process for LCIP funds. Not surprising, competition for the money was intense, but there was only enough to protect approximately one-third of the priority acreage identified. Near the top of the list was Umbagog Lake. During the Trust's earlier lobbying activities, it had fashioned Umbagog into a symbol of state identity that typified the type of land that could be saved through the LCIP. The threat to Umbagog was so obvious that it drew an emotional response across much of the state. Once the LCIP funds were in place, the drive to save Umbagog intensified.

In 1988, the Trust and its partners pulled together the Lake Umbagog Study Team comprised of such organizations as the Forest Society, New Hampshire Audubon Society, Loon Preservation Committee, the Nature Conservancy, New Hampshire Fish and Game Department, U.S. Fish and Wildlife Service, Land for Maine's Future, and landowner representatives to conduct a thorough analysis of the region. Their task was twofold: to identify which lands around Umbagog were most important to protect and to determine how best to conserve them. From the outset, the shoreline and hillsides with views of the lake, as well as the wetlands, were most obviously threatened. But funding acquisitions in the area was an issue. The LCIP would cover only part of the lands the study team identified.

After months of analyzing options, the group proposed a rather inventive two-pronged funding strategy that had never been tried before and would eventually protect about 16,000 acres around Umbagog. First, it recommended that the state focus LCIP funds on purchasing conservation easements on the lake's shoreline and hillsides. (When landowners sell the development rights to their land, but retain ownership and use of the land, the legal transaction is called a conservation easement. On land under easement, development is forbidden, but nondevelopment uses, such as logging and farming, may be permitted by the landowner.) The Trust/ LCIP agreed and quietly began negotiating with the largest landowners around Umbagog, which at that time were the James River Corporation and Boise Cascade (both paper companies), about putting their land under easement. But the Trust quickly found that while the owners were willing to give up development rights on their lands, they were not willing to give up timber rights. Other issues surfaced. Traditional land use at Umbagog had included not only logging but hunting, fishing, and camping. Many local people equated conservation with losing access to land that, in many families, had been enjoyed by three generations. Clearly, it would take compromises from all parties to reach an agreement on how best to use the land in the future.

Finally, the LCIP and James River agreed to a plan that proposed the state purchase a five-hundred-foot buffer along the western shoreline to protect the lake's water quality, forested habitat, and natural beauty. Conservation easements would protect an additional 2,258 acres behind the shorefront buffer to prevent development, but still allow owners to continue harvesting trees. It took a few years of negotiations, but in 1992 four landowners agreed to accept about $3 million in total from the LCIP for the shoreline buffer and easements covering 3,348 acres. Interestingly, the LCIP was criticized for allowing the landowners to continue to manage their timber. Even now, Sarah wonders why. "We weren't talking about virgin forest here," she says. "This forest had been heavily managed for years."

The second part of the study team's plan called for the U.S. Fish and Wildlife Service to purchase approximately 7,500 acres of wetlands that would form the core of a national wildlife refuge. This wasn't the first time the federal government had taken an interest in Umbagog. In 1972 the U.S. Interior Department designated the area as part of the Floating Bog National Natural Landmark, an honor that recognized Umbagog Lake's significance to the nation's natural history. A few years later, in 1979, the Wildlife Service published a wildlife management plan for New Hampshire that again identified the region as an important natural area threatened by development.

After more analysis, the Wildlife Service announced during the summer of 1990 its intention to establish a national refuge at Umbagog. The *Manchester Union Leader,* which had been covering the study team and its activities for several years, ran a front-page article on August 2, 1990, that reported the Wildlife Service would release an environmental assessment—a detailed wildlife management plan—for the area in mid-September. The article also stated there would be at least three public information hearings held throughout New Hampshire, with at least two in the North Country,

The pristine waters and shoreline of Umbagog Lake, Errol, New Hampshire.
(Courtesy of Lake Umbagog National Wildlife Refuge.)

and that a thirty-day comment period would follow. The Wildlife Service would then release a final proposal for the refuge based on the feedback it had received. All of these procedures were, and still are, standard for establishing national wildlife refuges.

But when the Wildlife Service released its initial plan, it was met with immediate and strong local opposition. Residents of the towns near Umbagog said there hadn't been enough local involvement in drafting the original proposal and accused the Wildlife Service of being less than up front about its intentions. At an initial hearing in Berlin, many stood up to state for the record that they did not want to be told how the land around Umbagog would be used, preferring, instead, to decide for themselves. Finally a young biologist in the crowd reminded everyone that they didn't own the land, that a paper company did, and that they could be sure of one thing—the landowner wasn't going to ask for their input. It seemed to strike a responsive chord. The meeting ended on a more positive note, with townspeople asking the federal project manager for the refuge, Dick Dyer, to solicit more feedback from local people before developing the final refuge proposal.

By all accounts, that is what he did. Over the next six months, Mr. Dyer met with small groups wherever they would have him—living rooms, clubs, town halls. By the time the final refuge proposal was rolled out in the autumn of 1991 there was still tension, but it wasn't nearly as fierce as it had been a year earlier. In fact, many local residents had changed their minds and could see that if the region was developed, it would no longer be a desirable place to live. The following year, the Lake Umbagog National Wildlife Refuge was established with a $5 million appropriation through the 1992 Interior Department Appropriations Bill, which allowed the refuge to purchase its first land parcel. (At about the same time, the LCIP legislation expired, and the Trust for New Hampshire Public Lands disbanded.)

Since 1992 the refuge has grown to encompass 16,300 acres, but initial anxiety about establishing it has been replaced in some circles by anxiety about its expansion. "Anytime you talk about a federal presence in this state, you have to do so with great care," says Charlie Niebling, senior director of policy and land management at the Forest Society. "You have to consider a number of things. What is the tax impact? How do communities view their own growth? What is the long-term impact of a refuge on economic development in the area? What implications will federal ownership have on recreational uses of land? Land coming out of commercial timber production is a big concern to people up there. When the federal government has come in, local people have traditionally lost control. Growth of the refuge is an issue, and it should be."

Ironically, Charlie points out, the more people who visit a refuge, the more likely the area around it will become built up. "You put a national wildlife refuge on a map and it automatically becomes a destination," he continues. "We've spent millions to preserve this pristine environment, but I think there has to be a certain ethic followed that's different from, say, Winnipesaukee."

So far, the truce between the refuge and local towns has held fast. But I'm wondering how Errol, which has a population of only three hundred, feels now—more than a decade after the refuge was established. "Problems are far fewer than expected," Errol selectman Fran Coffin tells me. "The refuge staff have gone out of their way to be involved in the town. That helps us all build up a good relationship . . . it's a cooperative effort now. We're a gateway community for the refuge."

Fran has lived in Errol for close to twenty-five years and runs a local oil and gasoline business. He says that at first he had reservations about the refuge. "The whole thing was cloaked in secrecy. The initial announcement was the first thing locals heard about it. It was a done deal, and that raised the hair on our necks. It's like any kind of change. Not involving the local people wasn't the way to plan it and establish it." Now, however, Fran says the community has rallied around the refuge because of its potential benefits.

Indeed, last year 35,000 people visited Umbagog—10,000 more than the previous year—and signs show those numbers will continue to increase. The inflow of visitors has changed the face of many businesses in the area. For example, when Fran started his company in 1986, 70 percent of his business came from forest-related vehicles and equipment and 30 percent from recreational visitors. Now those numbers have reversed. Fran says high visitor numbers have also led to at least twenty business start-ups in the region, many of which are recreation-oriented.

To address the commercial growth, local leaders established the Umbagog Chamber of Commerce, which didn't exist before the refuge arrived. In addition, a number of local groups, including the refuge, have come together to form the Upper Androscoggin Advisory Committee, a local task force working to develop a vision for the region that considers both conservation and economic development issues. "Since the advent of the refuge, we've seen a tremendous influx of people into the area," Fran tells me. "Everything that's going on is fantastic, but we also want to protect ourselves from overdevelopment. We're already starting to see lights in the rearview mirror. But we don't need other groups dictating to us: 'This is how it will be.' People draw lines around you that you have no control over. We want to be able to control our destiny. To channel growth where it's suitable."

"We need an economic engine, and it's obvious that it's tourism and recreation," he continues. "It's a double-edged sword, though. We need to use the land, but we also need to protect it. It's hard to stand so close to the problem and plan for twenty years from now."

Unless you live within thirty miles of Errol, you have to *want* to reach Umbagog Lake. The area isn't remote in that craggy Alaskan Big Nature way, but to those of us who live in this state's small southern towns it surely feels Out There. You first notice it halfway between Berlin and Errol, when your attention starts to drift away from the road toward the wide, black Androscoggin River. Closer to Errol, the scenery transcends from merely lovely to astonishing. It may not be virgin territory, but it appears as people say—pristine.

The refuge headquarters is a few miles up Route 16, housed in a small building on the Magalloway River, one of the waterways that flows into Umbagog Lake. On this day I'm meeting with refuge manager Paul Casey, who has worked at the refuge for about half of its history. He is wearing the brown uniform of all U.S. Fish and Wildlife Service employees and has the ruddy complexion of an outdoorsman. He's a New Englander—it's impossible to miss his Massachusetts accent. When he's not out on the refuge, he works from a sunny office with a view of the river from all windows.

We talk a bit about the refuge's past, and trust, and why those two things have sometimes been at odds. "The public had apprehensions that we would come in, put up signs, and keep them out," he says. "We've had over a decade of living up to our agreements. We've probably facilitated more use of the land and have proactively helped to put Errol on the map. Trust has come with doing what we said we would do. If we hadn't, the trust would never have been built. We've put a face on the refuge. All of us live in the community here and that has helped because people know us. Distrust hasn't completely disappeared, but I would say the majority of folks up here recognize the refuge."

The refuge is part of the Wildlife Service's Northeast Region, which covers thirteen states from Maine to Virginia and seventy refuges, four of which are in New Hampshire. Compared to more established refuges with larger territories, the one at Umbagog is relatively small. It's also relatively new. The National Wildlife Refuge System has been around since 1903, when local conservationists in Florida hatched a plan to protect the last breeding area of brown pelicans along Florida's east coast. The idea was so popular that it prompted President Theodore Roosevelt to establish the first refuge on three-acre Pelican Island. By the time he left office in 1909, he had established fifty-five more. Since then, the system has grown to encompass 94 million acres—all of which was acquired from willing sellers—on close to six hundred refuges located throughout all fifty states and U.S. territories. Ninety-eight percent of refuge land is open to the public.

As a refuge manager, Paul sets the direction for the refuge through an expanding staff that includes a deputy manager and two biologists. Outreach is a big part of the job. System rules require the refuge to report to the public on the condition of various species on the refuge, and that, in turn, requires building partnerships with organizations such as conservation groups. The point is to combine resources. "We're all working in the same field, we're all generally short-staffed, and we all want to make the best use of time spent in the field," Paul says. "We recognize that we can't do everything. The goal, though, is to make and follow through on priorities."

The top priority for all national refuges is protecting wildlife. Second is facilitating the six federally stipulated priority public uses: hunting, fishing, wildlife and nature photography, environmental education, wildlife observation, and environmental interpretation. Paul says these activities were set apart from other potential uses because they foster appreciation and understanding of wildlife and the outdoors. "We'll facilitate these uses, but everything else is secondary, like waterskiing, boating, or jogging trails," he explains. Not all refuges permit every public use, mainly because habitats are different from state to state. For example, a refuge without a body of water on it obviously wouldn't be a place to go fishing. The Umbagog refuge currently facilitates all public uses except fishing, which Paul says will be opening up within the next few years. In the meantime, it provides fishing access points and hosts an annual "Let's Go Fishing" day that offers participants instruction and free one-day fishing licenses.

Studying a map of the Umbagog refuge is like studying a weather map—it changes frequently, and sometimes the outcome is confusing. Even the boundaries aren't as they appear. All refuges actually have two: a legally designated acquisition boundary that encompasses the land the refuge seeks to protect within publicly approved limits, and an actual boundary that surrounds the land currently owned by the refuge. Most perplexing is that the acquisition boundary can include land that is protected and managed by organizations other than the refuge. For example, a quick inventory of the Umbagog refuge's acquisition boundary includes easements held by the state of Maine and the New England Forestry Foundation, and land owned by the Forest Society and the state of New Hampshire, including a ten-acre state park. With the exception of a tiny five-acre easement, all of the land held by the refuge itself has been purchased outright.

What's important is that refuges seek to acquire land within their acquisition boundary only when it is put up for sale. This means that all land already protected by other organizations within refuge boundaries is managed cooperatively with the refuge, with the overall goal of conserving it. Twenty years ago, this kind of arrangement was almost unheard-of. Refuges normally owned all the rights to the land within their boundaries and gradually expanded as land came up for sale. But in the last decade more and more refuges have begun to resemble the one at Umbagog, which has served as a model for what is now the way the Wildlife Service does business.

"It's much more difficult to manage this type of refuge," Paul tells me. "It's like any private business that has to relate to everything around it. We have to do that, too, while getting the best out of it. That's our mission. The days of only worrying about water levels are gone. The Refuge Improvement Act gave us our marching orders." Paul is referring to the Wildlife Improvement Act passed by Congress in 1997, which clearly states that at America's national refuges, wildlife and wildlife conservation come first. While this might sound like stating the obvious, it is the first national legislation of its kind to use phrases like "environmental health" and "conservation of ecosystems." Specifically, the act calls for the Wildlife Service to inventory and monitor federally threatened or endangered species, institute comprehensive conservation planning, and apply the latest scientific research to refuge management.

On a daily basis, these mandates have greatly changed the way national refuges are managed. Prior to the Endangered Species Act of 1973, most refuges focused on protecting waterfowl production and migration areas. After 1973, refuges shifted priorities toward protecting endangered species and their habitats. Now, however, refuges are taking a Big Picture approach and attempting to protect all species and habitats within their boundaries. To accomplish that, the Wildlife Service has encouraged refuges both to expand and to form cooperative arrangements, similar to those at Umbagog.

But the fact remains that no refuge can expand beyond the boundaries set forth in its conservation plan without a full public review and comment period. When I ask Paul about his strategy for Umbagog, he tells me, "We don't need the land today. We'll be here a long time. It took ten years for this refuge to acquire sixteen thousand acres. Whether we are able to expand will depend also on the willingness of sellers." And the willingness of the federal government. While every refuge in the system receives basic operating and capital project funds each year, not every refuge receives land acquisition funds. Which refuges receive them is a competitive—and political—process that's handled by the Wildlife Service's regional offices. The upshot is this: refuge land acquisitions tend to happen slowly.

Occasionally, though, a landowner is ready to sell when a refuge has no acquisition funds available. If that happens, the Trust for Public Land (TPL) sometimes steps in. As a large, national nonprofit organization, TPL works with organizations like refuges all over the country to protect tracts of land with conservable value. When a key piece of real estate comes up for sale, TPL may buy it and hold it until funds are available, thus ensuring the land is protected. In 2001, TPL helped the refuge at Umbagog acquire an additional 6,218 acres from the Hancock Timber Resource Group for $3.2 million, allowing the refuge to almost double its size to 16,300 acres.

Another important provision in the 1997 Wildlife Improvement Act was requiring all national refuges to develop a fifteen-year Comprehensive Conservation Plan (CCP). Paul spent most of 2002 doing just that, even handing over daily management of the refuge to his deputy, Laurie Wunder, so that he could concentrate on the plan. Similar to a corporate strategic plan, the CCP gives a long-range view of the desired future conditions of the refuge, specifying goals and objectives to guide management decisions in getting there. Paul says it covers the gamut of refuge operations—staffing and facility requirements, cooperative wildlife management, expansion opportunities, partnerships, water level management, hunting and fishing—even where future nature trails should go.

For input, he's worked closely with a planning team comprised of experts from New Hampshire Fish and Game, Maine Department of Inland Fisheries and Wildlife, the Wildlife Service's Northeast regional office, and other state and local groups. After it's drafted, the CCP will be accessible for comment through public meetings and other outlets. "We'll need to bring in public input to make decisions on where the refuge should be going in the future. Compatibility"—of refuge use that's in line with its mission—"is a huge issue," Paul says. "It's important to remember that we're public servants. This isn't my refuge. I'm managing the public trust. It's also not Errol's refuge. It's a national refuge. The public has spoken, and they want national refuges. It's my responsibility to fulfill that."

Later on I talked to Laurie Wunder, a zoologist by training and former educator, about the new direction of refuges and what kind of opportunities it has created for the refuge at Umbagog. "It really is about ecosystem management—not about always trying to increase the population of species," Laurie told me. "The point is to sustain balance throughout the entire ecosystem of the refuge. Sometimes that might mean reducing populations or removing foreign species that are upsetting the balance. But there is no wildlife without the health of the ecosystem around it."

Laurie said she feels fortunate to work for this refuge because it's new enough to allow staff to make an impact on its future. "Older refuges are pretty much set," she explained. "Here's it's still in the formative stage. Paul has a vision for the refuge that's maybe broader than other refuges. We're asking, 'How can we contribute to the Northern Forest ecosystem? How can we interact with other land managers to help on a larger scale?' Our refuge is small, but we can work with the White Mountain National Forest and other landowners to have a larger impact. Wildlife move on and off the refuge. To protect them, we have to work with other land managers. And that's different from the way many other refuges in the system are managed."

# 13

## Pats Peak

## "It's the Feeling of Winter in New Hampshire"

*F*inally there is snow. In a winter notable for its lack of precipitation, Pats Peak in Henniker is reporting conditions as "beautiful" as its parking lot fills on a weekday morning in late winter. Minivans and SUVs skid to a halt, skiers hop out, and everyone clambers up to Pats' big, brown, alpine-style lodge, as though the snow might melt before they're able to get to the top of the mountain. Everyone is smiling.

It's been twenty-five years since I last skied here as a teenager in the 1970s, and I'm amazed at how little it appears to have changed. The original stone hearth inside the lodge still burns bright. Sleds still decorate the walls of the aptly named Sled Pub. And in the cafeteria, thank goodness, a long row of Pats' famous six-inch M&M cookies sits waiting to be inhaled by hungry skiers.

But these are only first impressions. The reality is that, in these years, Pats has refused to go the way of most small family-run ski operations that opened in great numbers around New England in the 1960s but fizzled out by the 1980s. In fact, as the largest ski area left in New England still owned and operated by the same family, you could say Pats is the last one standing. Its secret? Pats decided early on that small is indeed beautiful, but that small doesn't have to mean dull. Over the years, it has followed a simple strategy of staying on top of ever changing ski industry technologies and delivering a consistent product.

In that, the company has been hugely successful. Pats operates one of the largest ski schools in New England, boasting over ten thousand students every year, a popular fifty-four-team racing program, and a ski club that has churned out several Olympic skiers (Pam Fletcher, who competed in the 1988 games, and Holly Flanders, who competed in 1980 and 1984, both are former members). But when you talk to Pats Peak staff, you quickly see that all of these progressions are merely an outgrowth of the company's core value: commonsense frugality. There is little mystery here. If the mountain isn't open for business, there is no business. Period.

When I first meet with Pats Peak mountain manager Walter Read, I tell him his title sounds exotic, but he clearly has no idea what I mean. Walter has worked in the ski industry for over twenty years and has come to specialize in lift maintenance. On this day, probably like most others, he is wearing a clean red sweatshirt that says "Pats Peak Operations—Walt" on the left side. In the winter, he has fifty guys working for him—everything from lift attendants and mechanics to snow groomers. With his direct gaze and a tendency toward straight talk, there is little question about who is in charge.

I ask Walt how the trails at Pats have changed over the past forty years. He reaches into a drawer for a map of the mountain and explains that by studying it you can more or less trace the history of modern skiing. "These are classic 1970s trails," he says, running a finger along the map's left side. The three trails he is pointing to are tight and winding, almost snakelike, each about seventy-five feet wide. "It used to snow back then, and groomers only had to pack it down with snowcats, which gave them a base of about two to three feet. But the necessity to make snow changed the way trails are made. Making snow on narrow trails is hard because the snow is made in piles that have to be smoothed out." Since the number of trails at any ski area is limited by the mountain's physical mass, most areas have simply widened their trails to accommodate new and better snowmaking and grooming technologies. At Pats, the map shows broader trails toward the center and right of the mountain.

But cutting a new trail or widening an older one is a tedious and time-consuming project that takes months to complete. For example, a few years ago, Pats finished widening its Twister trail, a favorite route down the mountain in the 1970s, that was barely being used by the 1990s because it was too narrow for snowmaking equipment. Walt's crew started the work in July and completed it just before Pats opened in December that year. "Work on a trail starts with a hike in the woods, when we mark off where the trail should go," he explains. Then they "drop the trees with chain saws and pick the rocks off the trail for days" before it's smooth enough to plant grass. "It's like building a golf course. It has to look like a fairway. That's what Twister looked like when we finished."

Once the land has been worked over, Walt's crew carves out a drainage system and hauls the four-hundred-to-five-hundred-foot snowmaking pipes straight up the mountain. These will carry the necessary air and water mix up the slope to strategically placed snowmaking guns. A third component is installing night lighting. "In the old days, guys would climb a tree, string up lights, and there you go—night skiing," Walt says. Nowadays standard utility poles are used, but placement is critical. Before positioning the poles, they first ski with a light meter to see where light falls naturally on the trail. This is to avoid creating dangerous light patterns that can actually smudge the boundaries of the trail at night.

My knees quit skiing years ago, but I remember attempting to navigate some of the more advanced trails at Pats, and I ask Walt how trail difficulty is determined. There are different types of technical rating systems, he says, but Pats uses a common international system of green circles for the easiest trails, blue squares for more difficult, a single black diamond for most difficult, and the double black diamond for experts only. Trails are rated according to the best conditions normally encountered on that trail during the ski season. "But the thing to remember is that you're using the system against your own trails," Walt points out. For example, a double diamond slope at a larger mountain with more varied terrain and steeper slopes would probably be more difficult than a similarly rated trail at Pats. That's not to say that Pats' seven double diamond trails are easy. Pats' ski patrol deals often enough with novice skiers who are attracted to expert trails because of the sheer danger of them.

For one of the smallest ski areas in the state, Pats' statistics are good. It has twenty-one trails on seventy-three skiable acres (the vertical drop is 710 feet, with a 1,400-foot summit elevation) and eight lifts. Trail difficulty is fairly evenly distributed among beginning, intermediate, and expert trails. But with 110,000 skier visits a year, it's not clear to me how Pats prevents bottlenecks and safely manages its traffic on the mountain. "We put 1,500 kids a night here through our ski school. No one has traffic like us," Walt says emphatically. "The way we've created our flow is to keep beginners away from the more advanced skiers and vice versa."

Walt is referring to the chairlift Pats installed several years ago after novices in the ski school and 200 to 300 adults in the racing program started plugging up the system every evening. There was only one chairlift to the top at that time, and everyone was competing to use it. "You know how racers are. They're always in a hurry," Walt says. "The wait at the chairlift was driving everyone crazy." So Pats bought a secondhand double chairlift from a company in Vermont, disassembled it, rebuilt it, installed it, and called it the Vortex. Now racers can bypass beginner trails and skiers altogether by going directly to the expert trails this chair services. (In the process, Pats saved $300,000 by doing the work itself.)

But a ski area can't buy a used chairlift from, say, 1970 and start transporting skiers on it. It must update the lift to meet today's standards in accordance with strict codes enforced by state inspectors, which involves upgrading the cables and towers as well as the chairs themselves. Then the lift must be spliced into the existing power system and tested thoroughly for safety. In fact, all of Pats' lifts are examined every autumn by state inspectors who visit the mountain for two full days. Part of the inspection is carried out in a cage that transports inspectors along the lift cables, allowing them to check each tower individually (the towers hold the cables above the ground). "The only way to get ready for it is to be working your butt off in maintenance all summer," Walt says, laughing. At the same time, an independent inspector examines the cable by taking measurements of its width and length. As cables get older, they stretch and become narrower. After about twenty years, they start to wear out and need to be replaced. "There are a lot of eyes on chairlifts," Walt assures me.

Thirty years ago, mechanical failures at New Hampshire's small ski areas were a fairly common occurrence, as were heavy snowfalls. Now, though, an area can have the best equipment money can buy, but if it can't make enough snow to open the mountain, there is no point in showing up for work. It is not possible to overemphasize the importance of snowmaking to modern ski areas. As recently as ten years ago, a dry winter like the one in 2002 would have meant financial disaster for many New Hampshire mountains. But with the help of rapidly evolving snowmaking technologies and a vigorous cold snap, a ski area can make enough snow to open the majority of its trails in only a couple of days.

Making snow requires only two elements: water and compressed air. Putting both together, the issue becomes how quickly a mountain can pump out snow, which is measured in gallons per minute per acre. For example, Pats, which was the first ski area in New Hampshire to make snow and claims to have one of the highest snowmaking ratios per acre in the state, is able to go from being 15 percent open (not much better than being closed) to being 60 percent open in only two days flat. It can cover 90 percent of its trails in five days.

To do that, Pats needs water—25 million gallons per year, to be exact. While that may sound like a lot, larger mountains in New Hampshire routinely use 250 to 350 million gallons for snowmaking in a typical ski season.

Water access is important to ski areas because the more they can use, the quicker they are able to make snow and open trails. In 1998, Pats hired an engineering firm to help it locate an additional 15 million gallons of water to supplement the 5 million gallons it was already storing on its own property. Using a state permit, Pats now draws water from a nearby pond, and has agreed to cease pumping when it has drawn the pond down three inches.

In any given year, it takes five hundred hours to keep Pats Peak in snow from early December through March. Using a mix of tower, fan, and ground guns, most of which remain in fixed locations, Pats' snowmakers move 2,500 gallons of water per minute through the system. In the 1960s and 1970s, snowmaking machines were designed to be backup or secondary systems to natural snow. Now, however, they've become the primary systems at most ski areas, including Pats Peak, which has added more than 150 tower guns over the years to its original arsenal of 15. Sixty to 70 of them run most nights in season, supplied by 350 hydrants that pump air and water through close to twenty miles of pipeline.

But the conditions have to be right for the snow to fall like soap flakes in piles along the trails. Low twenties and dry are good. Low thirties and humid are not. Conditions can vary dramatically at different locations on the mountain or even from one snow gun to the next. Much of the work of snowmaking is mental—figuring out where the best conditions on the mountain are, using them optimally, and making snow only when you know it's going to stick around. The physical part kicks in with the grooming, done with heavy machines to create what Walt calls "that classic corduroy pattern."

I tell Walt that grooming seems to be a matter of pushing snow around, and he agrees that this is often true—at least at the start of the season. "In December you're creating a road that's two to three feet thick because you want to open the mountain," he says. "Later in the season, it becomes like mowing your lawn. Every groomer develops their own technique. What they're doing is chewing up the trail, putting air back in the snow, packing it down, and smoothing it over. We call groomers snow farmers."

The connection between farming and snow grooming isn't strange, given that the first generation of groomers were little more than glorified tractors that dragged a large roller to flatten the snow. It wasn't until the 1980s that snow grooming came into its own through innovations that let operators handle a wider range of conditions on more varied terrain at higher speeds. Technology continued to improve, making machines more reliable—and comfortable—so that operators could stay out on the slopes longer. By 1990, snow grooming had hit its stride, evolving from a mainly background activity to a fundamental part of the product.

Altogether Pats owns five grooming machines, but bragging rights come with its recent purchase of a Piston "Park Bully," which some mountain managers are calling the Mercedes Benz of grooming machines. One of only five such machines in New England, Pats' Park Bully is part of the new wave of equipment designed specifically to handle the moonscape requirements of all-terrain snowboarding parks. Before making the purchase, Walt spent two years evaluating grooming equipment for the opening of Pats' freestyle Turbulence Park in 2001.

I must admit that all grooming machines look somewhat alike to me, so I ask Walt why there is so much hoopla about this one. "For terrain parks, you have to be able to create all the odd surfaces and then maintain them on a daily basis. This machine does that," he explains. Then he gestures as if he is doing the hula to illustrate the range of surfaces a Park Bully can actually create. He even sent three of his groomers to Mammoth Mountain, California, where there is snow year-round, to learn how to build hits, jumps, quarter-pipes, and other things I have never heard of. "It's an exotic machine," he concludes, offhandedly.

On March 17, 1963, the *New Hampshire Sunday News* ran a story about three brothers named Patenaude who were wrapping up their first season—successfully—as the owners and operators of Pats Peak in Henniker. It was only a year earlier that Merle, Jr., twenty-nine, David, twenty-seven, and Stuart, twenty-two, had thought it was a fine idea to buy a couple of hundred of acres around the 1,400-foot Craney Hill off Route 114 and establish "a real ski area," as they called it, that would attract families from all over southern New Hampshire. With an initial investment of $200,000, the only issue was that they were going to have to do the work themselves.

First, though, they broke the news of their bright idea to their father, Merle, Sr., who upon hearing it didn't seem terribly surprised. The family had a long history of entrepreneurship. Starting and running businesses was what they did. But that didn't mean Merle liked the concept. "I told them they were crazy," he quipped to the *Sunday News* reporter. Nevertheless, as the three boys worked outside at breakneck speed laying out trails, installing steel towers, and bulldozing the slopes, Merle, Sr., accepted one responsibility. He agreed to design and build a thirty-by-eighty-foot structure that would serve as the fledgling ski area's base building. By the time he

Mountain manager Walter Read with one of Pats' all-terrain Bombardier snow grooming machines. (Courtesy of Pats Peak.)

was done with it, the rustic wood frame structure, reminiscent of alpine lodges in Europe, had open beams, pine paneling, a cafeteria, and a stone hearth for roaring fires.

From its first season Pats Peak, which opened for business in January 1963 (the name comes from Patenaude—as in multiple), was fully operational with a double chairlift, a T-bar lift, a rope tow, a small ski school with certified instructors, and a good mix of novice, intermediate, and expert trails. It cost adults $2.50 to use the rope tow all day. A season ticket cost $65 for adults and $40 for children. Propitiously, the *Sunday News* predicted the ski area would become one of New Hampshire's most successful.

Eventually a fourth brother, Wayne, joined the company; he is now sole owner and still actively involved in the business. Wayne's niece, Amy Patenaude, was born the year before Pats Peak opened and remembers begging her parents to teach her to ski before she could barely walk. Out of all the Patenaude cousins, she figures she's probably the most avid skier, having done so on mountains all over the country. She still races at Pats every winter. "Pats has always had a real family feeling and it hasn't changed much over the years. Lots of people who learn to ski here later come back as coaches or instructors," she told me by phone. "I love the small mountains. You don't have to go to the big, fancy resorts for good skiing. Small mountains have something for everyone."

In the late 1990s, Amy helped draft legislation that made skiing New Hampshire's official state sport. She was serving as a state senator at the time and viewed the legislation as a way to boost the ski industry's economic engine. "We thought it should be the state sport, because, unofficially, it really already was," she told me. "I wanted to be involved because my family's skiing roots are so deep in New Hampshire." Amy still has a picture of herself when she was six years old standing in front of the fireplace in Pats' lodge holding a ski trophy. "Every winter I see that picture repeat itself in the same place with other six-year-olds," she said.

On another day over lunch in Pats' Sled Pub, I mention Amy's family memories to marketing director Doug Peel and ask him how they connect with Pats' "classic skiing" campaign. But as soon as I get the question out, I realize it is moot. We are surrounded by a veritable sled museum, walls decorated with antique sleds in all sizes and colors that were bought over the years by the Patenaude family. Frank Sinatra is singing "Mack the Knife" a little too loudly overhead. A wood-burning stove is stoked regularly by staff. Classic skiing is all of this, isn't it? Doug is devouring one of Pats' homemade sandwiches, but he nods his head and pauses for a moment searching for images. "It's the stone fireplace from the 1960s," he finally says. "It's coming inside for cocoa and cookies after a day of skiing. There's something special here. It's the feeling of winter in New Hampshire."

Doug skied these slopes in the 1970s as a teenager as I did, and we wager that our paths have most likely crossed before. After attending nearby New England College and working at Pats as a ski instructor, he basically never left. (He keeps his old Pats season passes—three decades worth—in his desk's top drawer.) Doug calls his decision to stay a "lifestyle choice," but he is not referring to nonstop skiing. Like the rest of Pats' twenty permanent employees, he routinely works eighty-hour weeks in season, grabbing the odd hour every so often to hit the slopes. "It's for love of the sport that we're here," says Doug, who is now teaching his own kids to ski. "Every time I pull into the parking lot and see the lifts going, I get excited. There's something about a ski area that brings people together. My fondest child-hood memories are of skiing as a family."

Later on I ask Doug if competing with the big mountains was ever part of the picture at Pats. "We can't compete with Killington in terrain," he tells me matter-of-factly. "So we want people to come to Pats and say, 'The bur-ger tasted better here, we were greeted by the lift attendants, the snow was great, and guess what else? We got a free bowl of popcorn in the pub.' You don't have to be a 'glitz and glamour' ski area for people to expect a lot. At the end of the day, the question is, Did you have a good time?"

And for most snow lovers, that is indeed correct. But many industry in-siders say skiing peaked in the 1980s and has become a bit passé to kids who are now primarily interested in snowboarding. I ask Pats' general manager, Kris Blomback, what he thinks. "Skiing is a mature business, but I'm not a doomsayer about the industry," he replies. "We're not only competing against other ski areas, but also hockey rinks, cruises, Chuck E. Cheese, even Disney. A lot of the time, skiing wins. I hate to bring it down to the al-mighty dollar, but that's often what it is. Skiing has sex appeal. It's still a happening industry."

Kris was only thirty when Wayne Patenaude promoted him to general manager in 1995. He is originally from Long Island, but worked in ski area operations in Vermont before coming to Pats in 1991. He is punctilious in the way engineers often are, and his managers praise him for his knowledge of snowmaking technologies. In a building next to the lodge, his office is tucked away behind the ski services desk, where he can hear everything that's going on without being in the middle of it. Most days he brings his aging golden retriever, Kasey, to work with him.

"There's an old saying in the ski industry: 'How do you make a small for-tune in this business? By spending a large one,'" Kris says, settling into his chair. "Over the last five years, Pats has invested $2.5 million in technology upgrades for lifts, machines, buildings, and equipment. We've had to invent ways to make money—we've had to ask ourselves, Are we a winter business, a ski business, a four-season business? We've got this huge facility that's sit-ting here unused for 250 days a year. We realized we should be using it." This train of thought led to installing air-conditioning in the lodge and suc-cessfully courting the wedding and event industries. In fact, Kris has be-come rather well known in the business as someone who understands the importance of diversifying his income stream. He's written articles about it, and managers of other ski areas have asked him for help in applying his ideas elsewhere.

I'm wondering, though, why so many ski areas closed in the 1980s. Was it truly the lack of diversification, or was it fewer skiers making more expensive demands on already cash-strapped mountains that are open for business only a hundred days a year? "I really feel that the shakeout in the industry with so many mom-and-pop ski areas closing was because these small areas couldn't modernize their facilities," Kris says. "There is tremendous pressure in this industry to do something new every year. The first question skiers ask every year is, 'What's new?' If that press release doesn't list at least six new things, they're not interested. You have to be creative. If you're not, you'll stagnate in this industry."

Pats' Turbulence Park is a perfect example of what Kris is talking about. In the late 1990s, Pats started planning a state-of-the-art terrain park for snowboarding, which its customer base was starting to clamor for. Although Pats already had a terrain park, it was small and on the mellow side. At that time the company had neither the high-tech groomers nor the expertise to take the park to the next level. Then Kris went to a ski industry conference out West, where he heard about a terrain park on a small mountain in California that sounded like the one he wanted to build at Pats. After the conference, he rented a car and drove out to see it, spending several days taking photos, measuring every inch of it, and talking to staff.

As soon as he got back to Pats, he showed the photos to his managers. "I told them, 'Guys, we're building this,'" he says, laughing. The next step was to approach owner Wayne Patenaude about buying a Piston Park Bully to build and maintain the park. Kris says Wayne didn't hesitate. "The park has been a big success," Kris says. "People go to bigger areas and tell us ours is as good as those." (The name for the park, by the way, was suggested by the eleven-year-old snowboarding son of Pats' accountant.)

Small family-owned companies can be difficult to work for, and I'm wondering what it's like being part of a business that still involves many Patenaude family members. (Every time I visited Pats, there were always nieces and nephews around.) Kris says he shares the family's Yankee convictions about growing slowly and keeping a sharp eye on the budget. "With a hundred-day season and big requirements for a lot of heavy equipment, those are good policies to follow," he says. "I talk to other managers who spend hours on conference calls talking to ownership, but I deal directly with Wayne. When he promoted me to general manager in

1995, he was like a nervous father that first year. But it's worked out well. He's frugal, and so am I."

On his days off out of season, Kris likes to hike local ski areas. In season, he's more of a snowboarder than a skier, and he's kidded about it by the die-hard skiers on his staff. "I'm not a person who feels passionately about a lot of things, but I've got a real passion for this industry," he tells me. "My ultimate fear is losing that passion. I think, What would I do next?"

Entering the ski patrol building, which is located to the rear of Pats' lodge, you can't miss the orange stretcher in the hallway. Just behind it is the sickroom with three full-size hospital beds and anatomy posters on the walls. Pats' seventy-member ski patrol operates from here, and this is where they bring injured skiers.

The urge to serve the ski patrol first hit director Bob Wright in 1981 when he and his daughter Jennifer witnessed an accident at Pats. He sent her to get the patrol while he stayed with the injured skier, and afterward he chatted with the patroller. The conversation stuck with him, and the next year he joined Pats' ski patrol. He's been patrolling ever since and took over as director in 1998. His daughter is now the assistant ski patrol director.

One of the most important things this duo does is teach and implement the highly regarded safety and emergency care programs of the National Ski Patrol (NSP), which counts 98 percent of all patrollers in the United States as members. Chartered by Congress in the 1940s, the NSP was set up as a training organization to build patroller skills and make mountains safer for all skiers. Now the NSP offers a wide range of courses to patrollers on many levels, covering such topics as avalanche awareness, mountain travel and rescue, patroller enrichment, mentoring, outdoor first care, and toboggan enhancement.

Most people think of ski patrollers as good skiers with first aid skills, but this only describes basic patrollers, all of whom have passed the NSP's foundation course called Outdoor Emergency Care. Bob teaches the eighty-hour class to new patrollers at Pats every year and requires those returning to take a yearly refresher. One step up are the senior patrollers, who have demonstrated they can ski on any mountain in their division and are able to organize emergency scenes. Fifteen of Pats' patrollers, including Bob, have reached this level. Certified patrollers—a rare breed that has passed a tough and lengthy examination—are advanced skiers able to manage disasters where there are casualties, such as avalanches. In addition, there are auxiliary members of the patrol who have medical skills but don't ski. (Many of Pats' patrollers are emergency medical technicians or other types of emergency workers, and all are certified in advanced CPR.)

During the week, Bob's twenty paid patrollers work the slopes, but on weekends he relies on fifty volunteers, who exchange hours for free lift tickets and passes. All patrollers at Pats spend long hours on the mountain. "You need a lot of certifications and training and you buy your own equipment," says Bob, who is also an unofficial safety adviser to the New Hampshire Safe Kids Campaign and safety adviser for the New Hampshire Region National Ski Patrol. "You don't make much money doing this. You really have to like it to be here."

The best kind of day for a patroller is a day without accidents, but a typical day goes more like this: Three patrollers and one first aid specialist open the mountain by 7:30 each morning by riding every lift to the top and checking it completely for safety. While they're on the lifts, they use the high vantage point to examine the trails for fallen tree limbs and other safety hazards. Then they ski or snowmobile down every trail to ensure it is safe to open. If any trail is unsafe, they'll either fix the problem or close the trail by pulling a rope across it. Finally, they post necessary warning signs, call in their lift reports, and describe conditions to Pats' main office.

"And then at some point the accidents start happening," Bob says, "You never know when that will be. It might be someone fell in the parking lot and cut their lip. Whatever happens, we have to be prepared for any accident." Throughout the day, more ski patrollers arrive so that by the time the afternoon school programs begin, there are at least six of them on the mountain. When there are no accidents, patrollers often practice training drills, such as toboggan runs and first aid for serious injuries, to keep the multitude of medical and equipment-related procedures they must remember fresh in their minds. On days after a snowfall, they often repair fences. (Pats' patrollers are easily identified by their red jackets with a large white cross on the back.)

A hot topic of discussion among ski patrollers in recent years has been how much caution to exercise when treating snow-sport emergencies. It's an issue because so many of these injuries are related to the head and spine and sometimes don't become apparent until hours or even days later. In most cases, if they're treated immediately, the damage is less, but many people refuse treatment by signing a form. I tell Bob I read a message in an on-line ski patroller forum from a father who complained that a patroller had used what he viewed as extreme caution when his daughter collided with another skier and reported feeling back pain. The parent said it ruined the day because his daughter "obviously wasn't seriously injured." What does he think of that?

Bob pauses for a moment. "If someone complains of pain in their neck or back, we have to assume there is an injury there," he says evenly. He tells me about a young man who came into the ski patrol building a few years ago with a slight bruise to his head after causing an accident. "He said he was fine, but he just didn't look right to me. A few minutes later he got sick, a definite sign of concussion." Bob called the rescue squad, and on the way to the hospital the boy went into convulsions and full respiratory arrest. If the boy's mother had taken him home, as she had wanted to do, Bob says he probably would have died. "That's the best example I know of in defense of using caution," he says. Case closed.

When I ask him about the type of equipment ski patrollers take with them on the slopes, he shows me a well-worn black fanny pack the size of a small watermelon. It's filled to overflowing with a whistle, notebook and pencil (ink freezes), dressings and Band-Aids, CPR equipment, a pipe cutter to cut ski poles, markers for the accident area, tweezers, a flashlight, latex gloves, and, of course, a Swiss army knife. And that's just the top section. All of his patrollers wear such a belt. Bob even keeps a list of suggested items to store in it. On the mountain, there are toboggans stashed in key places, each equipped with a back board, two blankets, and splints and cravats for setting broken limbs.

In a side room where the patrollers store their gear, we study the color-coded charts Bob has generated that break down this year's 650 accidents—a normal year—into an assortment of statistics. For example, 60 percent of injuries were sprains, strains, bruises, and abrasions; 30 percent were concussions and fractures; the rest were dislocations or frostbite. Sixty percent of the injured walked into first aid on their own. Sixty percent were snowboarders, who commonly injure their heads or wrists. Not surprising, most injuries took place between 2:00 and 4:00 p.m., peak time on the slopes.

I tell Bob I've come across quaint National Ski Patrol posters from the 1940s featuring vigorous young men rushing down a mountain, braving the elements, doing whatever it takes to reach that injured skier. Does this sense of mission still exist? "There is an esprit de corps," he answers. "To some patrollers it's a way of getting free skiing. But for others it's a way of using medical skills and helping out. I enjoy doing this. I like the idea of being able to help people."

. . .

A few days before the season ends, Pats Peak ski school director Bertie Holland is telling me how she got her start here. Twenty years ago she was taking lessons from Doug Peel, who watched her get better and better, and eventually convinced her to become an instructor in the same ski and snowboard school she now manages. Her two kids grew up here, she jokes. Last year her son ran Pats' racing program.

Bertie is a spirited person with short blondish hair that tumbles over her ear-warmer headband. She has a natural gung ho enthusiasm that sets the rhythm and pace of the entire 10,000-student ski school. Most years she supervises 300 full- and part-time instructors who, judging from the boisterous sounds outside her small office, are much like her. "Sixty percent of them return every year," she says. "We're sort of in a time warp here." Every weekday, her instructors work with 1,500 adult and child students—250 an hour—on everything from basic skiing skills to snowboarding to racing techniques. (To put these numbers into perspective, many large mountains have only fifty instructors and a few thousand students.)

Each year Bertie's job starts in mid-September, and for the next two months she spends most of her time visiting schools, talking with kids and teachers about Pats' ski and snowboard programs. Then she trains her new instructors, who are hired as much for their ski ability as their communication skills, in areas such as teaching styles, leadership, and risk management. "It's not just teaching students how to go left and right," she says. "We tell the kids how to dress in layers, make them wear eye protection and hats. We tell them about terrain and how conditions change through the day. We talk about fatigue and accidents."

And safety. Pats' ski school runs an aggressive helmet program that Bertie says has drastically reduced the number of injuries over the last few years. In addition, she works closely with Bob Wright, who provides her coordinators with safety information that is then passed along to students. He also gives her videos and other materials that she takes with her when she meets with schools and parents. "We feel that the better-educated students are, the safer the sport will be," she tells me.

Ski instruction has come a long way since the days of the "ski bum," who went from resort to resort year-round, teaching at each for a while before moving on. Most ski schools today hire only certified instructors and follow the national teaching standards and curriculums of the Professional Ski Instructor Association. Pats is no different. All of its instructors hold some level of certification that has involved testing them on skiing and teaching skills as well as technical knowledge of the sport. There is a weekly goal for each class, and instructors track students' progress on a report card.

Of course, teaching kids is different from teaching adults. "Adults are more technical. They want to know why the ski does what it does," Bertie says. "Kids don't understand this. So we'll tell them they have a peanut butter ski and a jelly ski so they learn when to move each one. We teach all of our skiers the skier responsibility code"—which stresses courtesy, safety, and control—"and how to use safety straps. We teach them to ski in control and to yield to others. Every class is different. You can't take things for granted in skiing. Conditions on the mountain can change quickly."

Some skiers jokingly remark that skiers who snowboard have switched to the "dark side" of winter sports, a quip that comes from the early days of snowboarding when there was, to put it mildly, some hostility between the two communities. (It's best summed up in a still-popular poster of a masked, twisting snowboarder in black with the caption: "Proudly annoying skiers since 1972.") I ask Bertie if this is still a problem today. She explains that when snowboarding became popular in the late 1980s, there was little, if any, etiquette in the sport. It created so many problems that, eventually, skiers and snowboarders didn't want to be on the same mountain.

That's changed now that snowboarding has hit the mainstream and evolved, since its official debut in the 1989 Olympics, into a sport with its own rules and teaching certifications. Bertie says Pats hired its first snowboarding instructor in 1989, who gave only a half dozen lessons that season. Now, snowboard instruction is 40 percent of the ski school's business. "Snowboarding has pulled in high school kids who otherwise might not have come here," she says brightly. "The terrain parks have brought back excitement to the sport."

## 14

## Mount Washington Hotel

### "Pride Is the Wave We're All Riding On"

**O**n a day between seasons the Mount Washington Hotel in Bretton Woods is at once commanding—castle white, flags flapping in a stiff breeze—and retiring, nestled dreamily into the base of its namesake. A sign posted at the start of the hotel's long drive says, "You are entering Bretton Woods, the Famous White Mountains Resort." If you had never been here before, you might think you were entering Shangri-La.

Inside, however, the ambience is unaffected. On this day, small bands of well-behaved children have completely taken over the cavernous main lobby, which extends to the right down a long avenue to an equally cavernous ballroom. On the left, past the reception, the hotel splits into a V, with one corridor leading to the main dining room. The other takes you past staff offices to a spacious corner suite occupied by the hotel's CEO and president Joel Bedor. It's a room without much of a view, which is a shame because the most distinctive thing about it is its large, wide windows. Meeting me at the door, Joel motions me to sit in the burnished wooden chair he received from the Littleton People's Bank, where he once served as a board member. Inscribed on its back under his name are the words, "For 21 Years of Service."

Joel is dressed in a classic navy blue suit, crisp white dress shirt fastened at the wrists with gold cuff links, and a tastefully patterned gold and blue tie. He has silvery white hair and carries himself with the imperturbability of a purveyor of fine goods, which, in a sense, he is, but with no hint of pretension. Several times in my visits to the hotel I have seen him in the hallways talking casually with guests and staff. He always appeared relaxed and he was always wearing a suit.

Growing up in Littleton, Joel says he never expected to be running a hotel. His first career was as a self-employed accountant, a business his wife Cathy assisted him with for years. (They are both University of New Hampshire graduates.) The couple's experience with historical restoration began in 1983, when they and another local family decided to purchase the Mount Washington Cog Railway. The partners appreciated its history and liked the idea of restoring the landmark, which was in terrible disrepair, back to its original condition. The project went so well that a few years later the families explored buying the Mount Washington Hotel. But they quickly found, Joel says, that it was "well beyond our means."

In June 1991, the families got a second chance. A year earlier, the hotel had been acquired by the Federal Deposit Insurance Corporation, which had pumped over $1 million into it before putting it up for auction. At that time, the Mount Washington Hotel was operable but in serious enough disrepair to make many in the area doubt whether it could ever be fully restored. Teaming up with three other New Hampshire families, the Bedors bid on the hotel. "The Mount Washington Hotel had many problems, the least of which was financial," Joel tells me, pausing to sip a caffeine-free Diet Coke. "We didn't think we had a prayer at the auction, but there were only a few serious bidders. In the end, we won." The hotel was theirs for $3.15 million, 50 percent of which was financed through the partners' own resources. (Considering that in 1902 it had cost $20 million in today's dollars to build the hotel, it's fair to say the price it fetched in 1991 was reasonable.)

Interestingly, none of the partners had an ounce of hotel experience. All became involved in the hotel in some way, but it was the Bedor family who handled much of the day-to-day financial and restoration management. Cathy Bedor put the hotel back on the map as marketing director through most of the 1990s, and Joel took over as CEO and president. On the couple's first day, Joel tells me, it was hard to know where to begin. Many of the rooms had orange shag carpeting. Rust had taken over the bathroom pipes, and the claws on the vintage bathtubs were raw and unpainted. At that time it was common for guests to return to the front desk several times before finding a suitable room.

"Our immediate plan was to stabilize the hotel. It had been losing $2 million a year for several years," Joel says. "We came in with not huge expectations, you could say. Our first few years we treaded water trying to maintain the staff and building." They also spent a lot of time and resources restoring the traditions of the dining room, which had been reduced by prior owners to little more than a very fancy roadside café.

Given all that, Joel says he was surprised by the loyalty of guests to the hotel. By 1994, the partners had built the business back up to a level where they could start planning realistically for their long-term goal—opening the hotel beyond summer for year-round service. But in order to sustain the business through the North Country winter, the partners realized they were going to have to buy the ski area, which they did in 1997. "The hotel feeds the ski area and the ski area feeds the hotel," Joel says. By owning it, along with the hotel, Cog Railway, and an additional two thousand development acres, the partners could now operate as one resort throughout the year and control the quality of each business.

The hotel completed a comprehensive $10 million winterizing project in the spring of 2001 that involved replacing 800 of the hotel's 1,200 windows with double-pane insulated glass, installing thermostats in its two hundred guest rooms, and upgrading its still-functioning original 1902 heating system. So far the gamble is paying off. "It was a risk. We had to ask, What would entice someone to come here in the winter?" Joel says. "We were convinced the same experience that draws people here in the summer would draw them here in the winter. There are a lot of people who want to ski, but don't want to drive to the mountain."

I ask Joel how he manages to run a luxury-class hotel in an historic building, where guests come to enjoy its character and grace, but are not necessarily looking for an authentic turn-of-the-last-century experience. Joel says that the hotel asks guests what they need, but that respect for the historic nature of the property comes first. "Some historic hotels have said they won't modernize the hotel in any way, like having TVs in the rooms. But it didn't take us long to figure out that many guests want a TV. We've been very aware of having all the modern conveniences." As testimony, he points out, the hotel recently installed high-speed Internet access in all rooms.

But the real difference, Joel says, is that he and his staff must be cognizant of tradition in a hotel like the Mount Washington. "Not all management principles used to run and manage a modern hotel can be applied here. We have to realize the needs of the staff and their importance to the longevity of this hotel. It's the local staff that gives this hotel its personality," he says. "Guests don't come here for the experience of a hotel built in the last few years. And our staff can give them that difference in experience. Extended families come here year after year. They feel safe here. It's like they left the world behind on the bridge after leaving Route 302. Everyone here makes the effort to meet guest expectations. We as owners look at it this way and we're fortunate that our staff does, too."

In a way, I suggest, the hotel is in the business of selling history—its own, as well as that of an entire era. "My guess is the hotel would not have survived if it hadn't been for its history," Joel agrees. "Had it not been for that, someone would have decided it was easier and more financially feasible to get rid of it. The location is prime, here in the mountains. The history of this place is paramount to its future success."

He doesn't say it directly, but I get the feeling that owning and operating this hotel may very well be Joel Bedor's greatest adventure. A few years ago, he stepped away to let others run the business, but after watching a series of general managers come and go, he's back holding the reins temporarily. "Let's just say we've recognized the importance of having an owner in the shop," he says, chuckling. "So I've regained the corner office for now."

I ask Joel what it's like to drive by this majestic place and know that you, in fact, own it. He pauses. "I have to step back because owning this hotel can be somewhat ordinary," he says, finally. "But that's not hard to do. This is an amazing place. Everyone who comes here is part of its history."

Room 13 in the Mount Washington Hotel's basement is the size of a walk-in closet. It was once Cathy Bedor's office, but it's now in the process of becoming the hotel's archives. I've been given access to the room for a morning, since staff aren't quite sure what's in here. Boxes are stacked on top of each other with notes that identify which cover which years. Most of the material relates to the present owners, but I've found a few gems in an overflowing black file cabinet. One is a newspaper article dated January 1, 1904, announcing the death of this hotel's builder: "Mr. Stickney's Fortune Left to His Wife—his bequests to others, although liberal, were relatively small." Another is a 1990s letter from a seventh-generation family member asking the hotel for assistance in organizing a Stickney family reunion.

Joseph Stickney was born in Concord, New Hampshire, sometime around 1820 (records vary on the precise date) and eventually ended up in New York, where he made a considerable fortune in coal mining and the Pennsylvania Railroad. His first venture in the hospitality industry was the Mount Pleasant Hotel, located across the street from where the Mount Washington Hotel stands today, which he bought in 1881. Old photos show that the Mount Pleasant, although smaller than the Mount Washington, boasted a similar palatial facade. (The Mount Pleasant was torn down in 1939 when its owner, a distant relative of Stickney, could no longer afford to keep it open.)

In addition to the Mount Pleasant, Stickney bought ten thousand acres of land with impressive views of the surrounding mountains—reportedly for one dollar per acre, a bargain even in those days. But Stickney was the kind of man who, when inspiration struck, didn't waste time dreaming. His idea was to build a kind of Super Hotel, similar in scope and entertainment value—comparable for its time to anything you might see in Las Vegas today. It should stand out, Stickney told friends, as simply the best, biggest, and most socially significant grand hotel in the region.

First, though, he trudged through sections of his newly bought acreage to find a location for the hotel, finally deciding on a tract that would make any structure built on it appear to be settling back into the base of Mount Washington. Next he promptly hired and transported a crew of 250 master craftsmen from Italy, who specialized in wood and stone construction and broke ground for the hotel in 1900. Stickney wanted the work done quickly, so he created a tent city on the boulder-strewn lot for the men. For the next two years, they labored year round to complete the project by July 1902. Similar to other industrialists who were building great structures during this era, Stickney spared no expense in the quality of materials he instructed his architects and contractors to use—from Tiffany stained windows to mahogany-paneled doors.

As the construction progressed, Stickney pondered a name for the hotel, eventually choosing the obvious. But an informal history of the hotel says that he later had second thoughts. Shortly before it opened, Stickney reportedly attended a local dinner party where a guest suggested calling the hotel "The Bretton Woods," after the original name of the area. It was too late at that point to change the name, but Stickney liked the idea so much that from the day it opened, the Mount Washington Hotel's location was always listed as Bretton Woods. (The town of Carroll was called Bretton Woods until 1832, when residents changed the name to honor Charles Carroll, one of the signers of the Declaration of Independence.)

Historians define a grand hotel from this era as one that could accommodate at least two hundred guests, had an architecturally lavish style, and offered an eclectic array of dining, recreational, and social opportunities. The Mount Washington Hotel certainly met those standards, although it opened just after the peak of the grand hotels, when two hundred of them peppered throughout the White Mountains region had welcomed an astonishing twenty thousand guests each summer. That was when the region had the highest concentration of grand hotels in the country and attracted many wealthy families who stayed for three and four months at a

The castle-like Mount Washington Hotel and Resort, Bretton Woods, New Hampshire, nestled into the base of its namesake. (Courtesy of the Mount Washington Hotel.)

time. By 1902, though, some of the smaller grand hotels had closed, leaving the new, stately Mount Washington in a category of its own.

The summer of 1902 was a disappointingly cool and rainy one in the North Country, prompting many regular guests to go elsewhere for their annual retreat. But when August arrived, hotel proprietors were caught off guard by the influx of visitors that flocked to the area at a time when the season was normally winding down. It would not be a stretch to guess that the onslaught was due to the July 28 opening of the Mount Washington Hotel. Interestingly, there is little evidence of hype around its debut, as you would see under similar circumstances today. Instead, historians say, word of mouth built the hotel's reputation—quickly at first and then slowly over time. "People were interested because this was the first hotel in the area built as an original to actually be a grand hotel," amateur historian and North Conway native Dick Hamilton told me. "Most of the other hotels had started out small and grew. The Mount Washington Hotel ended up being one of the last of the grand hotels, and it offered new amenities like private bathrooms and well-appointed rooms"—both of which were virtually unknown in other grand hotels at the time.

So when the fully booked, 235-room hotel finally opened, it was, indeed, the event of the year. At a total cost of about $1.5 million in 1902 dollars, it was so technologically advanced that it was completely self-contained, operating its own heating, plumbing, electrical, phone, laundry, and sewage treatment systems. It had fireproof lathing, inside and out, and steel supports in its wood frame that made the structure as resistant to fire as was possible for those days. All of these technological details were big draws in a time when steam heating was still unusual in public buildings and wooden structures often burned to the ground.

In addition, noted New Jersey architect Charles Alling Gifford had designed the Spanish Renaissance Revival–style building on the north/south axial line so that every room not only would have a view but also would be splashed in sunlight at some point during the day. Photos from this period show the hotel's windows bedecked with dark shutters, which to my eye gave it an almost Gothic heaviness. Shutterless today, it's easier to admire the hotel's beauty and graceful lines without the external clutter.

From the start, the Mount Washington Hotel was exclusive. With other hotels in the area charging five dollars a day, Stickney had a keen grasp on the wiles of the wealthy—being exceptionally so himself—and figured he could rent more rooms if he charged four times that (about the equivalent of what it costs to stay at the hotel today). He was correct, and the Mount Washington Hotel easily filled its rooms in its first few decades. "Who can resist the call of the mountains—the grandeur of giant peaks—the wonder of vistas into the very heart of nature's wilds!" declared an early brochure. But while it is true that the natural landscape was what drew most guests to the hotel, it was the social landscape that made them return year after year.

What guests especially liked about the Mount Washington Hotel was the unparalleled opportunities for "amusements," as leisure-time activities were called then. The hotel had its own forty-horse stable and employed a professional riding instructor. There was golf, hiking, tennis, and croquet. Guests could rent a rowboat on Lake Carolyn, a man-made pond in front of the hotel named after Stickney's wife. If you felt like taking a drive, you could hire a car with or without driver from the hotel's automobile livery and follow any one of "10 delightful tours" highlighted in a free auto map given out by the hotel. You could go on a rail excursion organized by the hotel or take in a baseball game at the hotel's diamond, where employees from competing hotels played each other twice a week.

On stormy days, you could play billiards, described in a brochure as "unusually attractive rooms, open for ladies as well as for men." Or you could bowl in either of the hotel's two state-of-the-art bowling alleys constructed with soundproof walls. But a favorite area of the hotel, rain or shine, was its indoor, basement-level, steam-heated pool—the only one of its kind in the country. It was busiest between 11:00 A.M. and 12:00 P.M. every day, when swimming instructors employed by the hotel gave lessons to children and adults. There were also frequent water polo matches, sometimes drawing as many as four hundred spectators.

I asked Dick Hamilton, who is also a serious collector of grand hotel memorabilia, what a typical day would have been like for one of the Mount Washington Hotel's six hundred guests. "Guests would eat, take a walk, change clothes, eat, take a walk, change clothes, take tea, walk or sit on the promenade, eat, dance, go to sleep. That was pretty much it," he laughed. "But out of all the activities available to guests at the Mount Washington Hotel, probably the most popular was the promenade."

Dick was referring to the guests' well-entrenched daily custom of walking along the hotel's nine-hundred-foot, one-sixth-mile veranda after taking afternoon tea. Guests would either sit in one of the white wicker chairs pushed back against the veranda wall or stroll along arm in arm, engrossed in conversation, pretending, of course, to be unaware of onlookers. "The veranda on the Mount Washington Hotel was the longest and widest of any of the grand hotels and it gave the hotel bragging rights," Dick said. "That's what you did. You wanted to see and be seen. It was part of the entertainment. You had to show off."

Inevitably, the day would end where it began—in the hotel's European-style, octagonal dining room, described by historians as without peer in the United States. Daily guests could enjoy continuous service until midnight, made easier by the kitchen's unique steam dishwasher and cold-storage system. Dick said the Mount Washington Hotel's dining room was so successful that it drew guests away from other hotels and set the dining standard for the entire region. "Many hotels eventually built their own octagonal dining rooms in order to compete," Dick explained. "If you were really grand in those days, you had to have one."

With the life of the hotel revolving around the dining room, the Mount Washington Hotel operated almost around-the-clock from June to October. To do that, it hired 350 employees every year, many of whom were students at some of the East Coast's finest schools. "They hired these kids because they were on the same social level as the guests and could relate well to them," Dick said. "It was a very clubby society." The rest were either local people or seasonal employees of the grand hotels of Florida and New York.

Most employees lived in the on-site dormitories—one for women and one for men—and worked a six-day week, although it wasn't uncommon to work seven days. The array of jobs at the hotel at that time is remarkable, with many falling firmly in the category of "personal service." There were porters, hat checkers, barbers, and musicians; coffee boys, firemen, switchboard clerks, engineers, and gardeners; manicurists, chiropody specialists, tailors, and chambermaids. Everyone offered a job received a letter of employment and "assignment of wages," which ranged from $2.50 per week for busboys ($45 today) to $55 per month for butchers ($1,000 today) to $450 per season for chefs ($8,000 today).

The dining room and kitchen staffs worked the longest hours, often starting at 6:00 A.M. and finishing for the day around 8:30 P.M. Many worked all three meal shifts—no small feat considering that every meal, seven days a week, was a formal, multicourse affair. For example, a typical breakfast included fruit, cereal, fish cakes, veal cutlets, steak, eggs, and french fries. Lunch usually offered a soup course, a meat/potato/vegetable course, or cold meats for lighter fare, a fruit or berry pie for dessert, and cream cheese and crackers with coffee or tea. Dinner was even more extravagant, presenting soup; salad; several choices of meat, potatoes, and at least four types of vegetables; more salad; cakes, pies, or ice cream; fruit, nuts, and figs; and a cheese assortment with crackers. Guests, many of whom were accustomed to servants at home, expected every course to be served in high style and with precision.

Despite the long hours, it wasn't all hard work. Between shifts employees enjoyed social activities planned specifically for them that often included games and other competitive endeavors, such as baseball. Guests greatly enjoyed cheering for their favorite employees or occasionally joining in the fun themselves. And everyone—guests and employees alike—looked forward to the once-weekly staff entertainment night. All employees were expected to participate by displaying any talent they might possess, or by otherwise creating one. It was all in good fun and contributed to the sense of community many guests and employees said they came to feel over the course of a long summer at the Mount Washington Hotel.

But what is life like as an employee of the Mount Washington Hotel today? To find out, I spoke with staff of the hotel's small human resources department, who have the formidable job of keeping approximately five hundred jobs in sixty categories filled year-round on all of the resort's properties— no small task in any location, but complicated by the relative remoteness of

Bretton Woods. They used the word "pride" a lot, as in "we're so proud to work here."

After over a hundred years of continuous operation, the hotel has certainly seen its share of employees come and go. But I'm finding out that, once here, many stay on for years, mostly, it appears, because they feel a strong connection with the history and tradition of this place. And it's always been that way. Working here isn't like working anywhere else, I'm told. It's the guests who set the rhythm and pace in the hotel, and guests change daily, as do events—making a day in January at the Mount Washington Hotel decidedly different from a day in July.

Employees say that so much cultural and seasonal diversity enriches their work environment and keeps an older hotel like the Mount Washington both vital and invigorated. "The values in this hotel are different. It's more relaxed, more comforting here than in more modern hotels in urban settings," a human resources associate told me. "When you're in this type of natural environment, you have a greater sense of inner peace and satisfaction. In the city you have smog, alarms, cars, and other distracting sounds. Here you have nature. No matter how long a day you've worked, you come outside and you're surrounded by mountains. It makes a difference."

Although 80 percent of the employee base is now local, the hotel has sometimes found it challenging to entice area residents to apply for employment. One of the reasons for this could be because, for many years, the hotel didn't seem like a place for "regular folks"—either as employees or guests. Now the hotel is trying to break that perception by presenting itself as a good place to spend one's career. For example, the human resources department is working with a local high school to set up culinary internships so that kids interested in food service careers are able to make a connection with the hotel.

I'm wondering how important it is for employees to know the history of the hotel, and I'm told that it's essential. "Employees need a thorough knowledge of the history in order to do their jobs," an associate told me. "We want that pride, those same values, to continue. They need to know about the tradition here and share the desire to make that tradition continue into the future. When people work here for a while, they have the pride. And that's what guests see. Pride is the wave we're all riding on."

Right now, that means working toward a fourth diamond through the American Automobile Association (AAA) Diamond Rating System, which is involving all of the Mount Washington Hotel's employees in some way (with the exception of the dining room, which already has its four-diamond rating). When a hotel wishes to be included in the rating system, it applies to AAA to be evaluated and is then visited anonymously each year by one of AAA's national tourism editors. The editor evaluates the property, prepares a written report for management, and awards a rating of one to five diamonds, with five being the most prestigious (only about 75 of AAA's 30,000 evaluated properties have achieved this rating). Each year's evaluation starts fresh and can result in a property maintaining, downgrading, or upgrading its rating.

At the Mount Washington Hotel, the idea is to upgrade only from three diamonds to four, which could take several years to achieve, and then leave it at that. "This place was built as a summer cottage for America's elite," says Bonnie MacPherson, the hotel's public relations director. "People come here for New England hospitality and that comfortable North Country feel. We can't forget who we are." What it comes down to is this: the Mount Washington Hotel would rather let its junior guests play on the carpeting and watch its adult guests loosen up than shoot for the stars. "That's what we're about," Bonnie says.

It's also a question of perception—and expense. Bonnie explains that five diamonds can "scare people" and sometimes deter them from visiting the property, because they perceive it as so upscale that relaxing is out of the question. Five-diamond properties also require costly upgrades such as evening housekeeping services, a full-service spa, a variety of on-site first-class shops, and a fax machine in every room. There comes a point when a property must weigh whether it's worth it, as well as whether its guests will object to the increased cost of their stay.

I'm wondering, though, how big a difference there is between a three-diamond rating and a four. The thirty-six-page guide I received from AAA says the difference is between "very good" and "excellent" regarding many, many factors in the following categories: exterior, public areas, guest rooms, amenities, bathrooms, and guest services. Bonnie tells me that for the Mount Washington Hotel, the jump between three and four diamonds would not be that great. Off the record, AAA has hinted that, servicewise, the hotel already is operating at the four-diamond level.

"It's a very refined system. It's funny how little things can affect your rating," Bonnie tells me. For example, a recent AAA report said the hotel missed the fourth diamond because, among other details, it needed to install full-length mirrors in all the rooms. The evaluator also noticed that pine knots were showing through the painting on some baseboards and that there wasn't a pen in his room. "We're really talking about some physical attributes," Bonnie says.

. . .

During any stay, no matter its length, a guest of the Mount Washington Hotel will at some point come into contact with the housekeeping, dining room, and guest services departments. I talked at length with the managers of these areas because I wanted to find out how great a role the traditions of this hotel still play in its everyday operation. Suzanne Russell, a fifteen-year employee of the hotel and its director of housekeeping, told me guest expectations are everything. "The room is unfinished until it's clean and every item is in its place," she said.

Year round Suzanne manages sixty employees that include housekeepers, room inspectors, and lobby and laundry crews. "I look for nice, open-minded people with good references who can work with guests and get along well with people," she replies, when asked about the ideal employee. "My big question is always, 'Why do you want to housekeep?' The answer has to be, 'I like to clean.' If they don't, the pride won't be there." She says she shows job applicants the suites, which either scare them or make them want to be part of the team. "I tell them this is the standard they have to keep up every day."

I ask Suzanne to compare the housekeeping standards of the hotel in the early 1900s to those of today. She thinks they are the same. "It's the details that are very important—from where the towels are placed to the bedspreads. Every room must have the same high standard," she says, firmly. "That first impression really counts. It's rewarding when guests go out of their way to compliment us on how clean and nice everything looks. I want guests to think, Everything is beautiful—not even a smudge."

In a modern hotel, Suzanne's housekeepers would have a different job. For one thing, the checklist for each room would be much shorter. Here, Suzanne says, cleaning intricate woodwork, radiators, and custom furniture requires more time than "your basic little modern room that just has a chair." Which leads to another important difference. Suzanne doesn't set a time limit for cleaning each room. It takes the time it takes, she says, which is usually thirty-five to forty minutes for a basic room and up to an hour and a half for family suites.

But despite its attention to tradition, the housekeeping department does indeed notice trends. They've put duvets with triple sheeting on the beds in some rooms, retrofitted other rooms with ceiling fans, and installed gas-operated fireplaces—all of which you might find on the pages of any upscale home furnishings catalog. Behind the scenes, the hotel recently spent close to $500,000 to upgrade its laundry equipment and can now handle seven hundred pounds of laundry per hour. Before that, the hotel relied on antique machines and outside laundry services, which sometimes threw a wrench into the daily routines of Suzanne's department.

Routine, however, is precisely what the new dining room manager, Diane Southwick, is building into her forty-person department. Diane is originally from Northern Ireland and has a sharp sense of comic timing that beautifully illustrates her assertion that the dining room is, in fact, theater. Her twenty years of restaurant experience have taught her there is no substitute for doing things properly and, yes, actually, it *is* possible to impose order in the naturally chaotic environment of a seven-hundred-seat restaurant.

When it's especially hectic, she says, she coaches her staff to, above all, keep calm. "The key to chaos is communication" she says. "I tell them, 'We're all actors and each table is a separate play.' We talk a lot about pride and how that transmits to the guests. If a guest is rude to a server, I tell them they can't take it personally. If they do, it's like a poison that spreads through the ranks." Thankfully, however, it appears the vast majority of guests are delighted with their dining experience at the Mount Washington Hotel.

When Diane first started her job, she says she spent the first three weeks pouring water for guests so that she could "feel how the room moves and watch how people work together." It's the way all of her new employees start, eventually working their way up to the job they were hired for. She says it gives all of her staff a chance to observe and appreciate what everyone else is doing. "If we don't work as a team, we can't be successful," Diane tells me. "It's not about us. It's about the guests. Everyone needs to know what they're supposed to do, but no one is allowed to say, 'It's not my job.'"

I ask Diane how she regulates traffic flow in an octagonal room, where one side is occupied by the orchestra and the other is filled with different sizes of tables. My eye doesn't see a pattern, but Diane assures me there is one. She points out a grid as well as a walkway that wraps around the outer edges of the room. But the way her staff lays out the room each night depends on whether they are serving groups or "social guests," as the hotel quaintly calls its nongroup diners. (Sixty percent of the hotel's business comes from groups.) Interestingly, all seventy tables are in a fixed location. To accommodate more two-person or four-person parties, the staff simply changes the tabletops. No one is sure when this system came about in the hotel's history, but they do know there are few—if any—systems like it in the world.

This can also be said of the dining room itself. It is decorated in a refined art deco style with leafy green plants hanging from white columns and muted floral-patterned carpeting that doesn't make you dizzy when you walk across it. Mountains fill the windows on the right. The walls are painted a creamy beige-pink, which is so restful that it tends to lull diners into a blissful state over the course of an evening. A small orchestra usually plays in front of an ample wooden dance floor.

"A lot of people tell us they feel they should be in costume from a century ago when they dine here," Diane tells me. But in case any gentlemen have forgotten old-world conventions, the hotel keeps a selection of jackets on hand. "We don't have to tell the ladies how to dress," Diane says, laughing. "They already know."

Is food service, then, really about etiquette and standards? "Yes," Diane says, definitively. "It's a dying art form. I tell my staff to anticipate what the guests will want. Yes, they'll need more bread. Yes, they'll want more water. I tell them to think of it like they are waiting on their close friends. It should be like the invisible arm that brought the food," she says, extending her arm toward me as if holding a platter. She says one of the best waiters she ever knew didn't even communicate with his guests. "He didn't have to. He watched and knew exactly what the guests needed without them ever having to ask."

If the dining room is the heart of the hotel, then guest services is surely its face. Guest services manager Jim Drummond even calls his bellmen "the eyes and ears of the hotel." Jim is the third generation in his family to work for the Mount Washington Hotel, and he has been here every season since 1970. He says he's done many jobs over the years, from lawn mowing to busing tables to lifeguarding. He's been guest services manager since 1985 and also owns a ski shop down the street with his brother. On this day he is wearing a red tie with mini–New Hampshires all over it. "I love this state," he tells me fervently.

Besides the wait staff, Jim's twenty-two employees probably have the most consistent daily contact with guests. These are the folks who greet guests as they walk up the front steps, run the hotel's single manual elevator, change lightbulbs, keep the fires burning, deliver room service orders, and handle valet parking, transportation, baggage, newspaper delivery, and any special requests. They also keep the front-door area clean and swept down. Like Jim, many of his employees have worked at the hotel for decades. "It's not just a property to them. It's a huge part of their lives," he says.

I ask Jim how the hotel and its clientele have changed in the nearly four decades he has worked here. He says it's more of a family hotel today and that many families are starting their own traditions by coming here each year for a full week's vacation. The most significant change he has observed, though, is that people are more self-sufficient now than they were thirty years ago, which has required the hotel to make a number of service-related changes to accommodate this new mentality. For example, rooms now include irons and ironing boards. Guests who wish to wheel their own bags to their rooms are welcome to do so. Golf carts have replaced caddies and, most recently, the hotel installed an ice machine in the second-floor lobby. Before that, guests had to call for ice, which was making many people uncomfortable. "We always go back to service," he says. "We always offer it to let them know it's there for them if they want it. We don't push it."

Jim says his house is filled with photos, paintings, and other Mount Washington Hotel memorabilia, and he even keeps scrapbooks of articles published about it. "This hotel has been my life," he says. "Being here thirty-three years, it's like my home—through the good times, the bad times. You feel good that you stuck it out. These are some of the best times this hotel has ever seen."

## 15

## Currier Museum of Art

---

## "Our Collection Is Our Legacy to New Hampshire"

When the Currier Museum of Art in Manchester celebrates the opening of a new exhibition, the atmosphere isn't at all stodgy, as some might expect from a premium small museum that is part of the national art scene. On such an evening in summer, if you drove down the packed residential street where the blockish museum sits, you might think you were witnessing a neighborhood gathering, or perhaps a lawn party. If you parked and walked up the front steps, you would be greeted with a tray of hors d'oeuvres.

Inside, after you'd had a look around, you would probably marvel at the cool spaciousness of the building's interior and then begin to wonder how long it took to stage the exhibition. Three months, maybe six, you might guess. After all, how much work can there be in a place that appears to change the pictures on its walls only a few times a year?

This is an amusing idea to the sixty-five Currier staffers and their small army of 150 volunteers. Any one of them will tell you it takes two to three years to stage a major exhibition. And during that time, the actual hanging of the pictures, which is done in the final three weeks before the opening, requires the least exertion of all. In fact, there is so much to it that you really have to go back to the beginning to get a sense of, well, the complete picture.

Three years out, you'll find Currier director Susan Strickler with her senior staff tossing around ideas in the charcoal gray Victorian mansion across from the museum where she and other administrative staff work. It's not an unusual scene. Like many museums its size, the Currier stages two major shows between October and May every year, plus a summer show and several smaller exhibitions in between. While this is marvelous for New

Hampshire, it puts staff on a constantly rotating Ferris wheel of generating ideas and nurturing them to full fruition.

For example, say that staff are discussing what type of show to offer during the winter exhibition season two years down the road. One of their first questions is, Should we mount a new exhibition from our own collection or should we host a traveling exhibition and adapt it? The answer depends in equal parts on which exhibitions are available over the next few years, how much they cost, and how well they fit with the Currier's New Hampshire–oriented educational mission. This last point is especially important because, despite the fact that the Currier is commonly considered one of the finest small museums in the United States, it views itself as a New Hampshire cultural institution first.

If the museum decides to host an exhibition, it can do so from any one of several traveling exhibition services in the United States, which periodically publish colorful catalogs listing available shows offered by member museums. The Currier could also go directly to large museums like the Smithsonian that have active traveling exhibition programs themselves. Costs vary, but hosting a show isn't cheap. For example, in 1999, the Currier gambled on an exhibition that featured the works of New Hampshire artist Maxfield Parrish, which, at $135,000 (not including installation, events, programs, advertising, and staff time), was at the high end of the budget. The show was considered so relevant, however, that staff struggled for months with the economics in order to make it work. In the end it did. The Parrish show was one of the Currier's most successful shows ever.

"Canned exhibitions arrive on your doorstep ready to go," Currier curator Andrew Spahr explained to me. "We then have to decide if the interpretation of the exhibition is right for our audience. We might supplement the exhibition with works from our own community or permanent collection. Or we might alter the interpretation to give it a more regional slant. Basically traveling exhibitions are good because they give museums and their audiences access to art that they otherwise wouldn't have."

Andrew brings up an interesting point. It used to be that many art museums regarded themselves more as research and collecting institutions, and gave less thought to playing an educational role in their communities. They didn't need to. Financial support often came from a handful of well-off families that automatically cut a substantial check with each new generation. It almost didn't matter if patrons walked through the doors.

All of that has changed. With a redistribution of wealth in American society, museums have been forced to broaden their base of support to ensure

Director Susan Strickler uses a hula-hoop during one of the museum's popular family days. This particular event was called "Blast from the Past." (Photo © 2000 by L. C. Fernsworth.)

their very existence. "Our patrons are our stakeholders, and there are certain expectations that go with this," said Susan Strickler, referring to the importance of museums to reach out to their communities. But museums are also competing with everything from shopping malls to football games for visitors' time. It's not easy for any museum to entice patrons through doors once considered too hallowed for regular folks.

This is one of the reasons why no museum these days, no matter its size, can afford to ignore the so-called entertainment factor, which looms like a bird of prey over its educational mission. Susan has been grappling with this issue for twenty years—fourteen as a curator at the Worcester Art

Museum in Massachusetts. "As a museum, you have to demonstrate that you want people to come . . . but there are people who never will," she told me. "Museums offer enrichment, education, and entertainment—not necessarily in equal dosages, but there needs to be a measure of all three in every exhibition. We look for a balance. There are four or five museums in the region I go to for my own entertainment, so I don't see entertainment in itself as a bad thing."

The entertainment factor has affected all museums—both small and large—but it's in the latter that it is especially conspicuous. In the last two decades, museums like the Metropolitan Museum of Art in New York and the Museum of Fine Arts in Boston have staged "blockbuster" exhibitions that allow them to leapfrog over their peers and compete directly with Broadway plays, professional sports teams, and high-end restaurants for patrons' time and money. In smaller museums like the Currier, which often work around stricter space and budget limitations, it takes a bit more creativity to marry entertainment with enrichment. But the result is all the more stunning because the effort is often that much greater.

A good example was the 2001 Edmund Tarbell exhibition, a forty-painting show that the Currier built around three significant Tarbell canvases in its permanent collection. (Tarbell was a prominent American impressionist painter who lived in Boston but summered in New Castle, New Hampshire, for over forty years. Many of the paintings he created in his New Castle studio captured quiet scenes from his family's daily life, and eventually defined an important period in Tarbell's career.) The exhibition was four years in the making, requiring Susan Strickler (who curated it) and her staff to research and carefully select the additional thirty-seven works that completed the show. Then they hunted down the treasures and eventually borrowed them from collectors and museums located all over the country. The result was a New Hampshire–style blockbuster that also generated quite a bit of national interest.

"Exhibitions like this one, which are developed in-house, can really tax the staff," Andrew told me. "But the advantage to putting on your own show is that you get exactly what you want." At a total cost of $350,000, the Tarbell exhibition was one of the most ambitious ever for the Currier. To attract a wider audience, it sent the show as a traveling exhibition to the Terra Museum of American Art in Chicago and the Delaware Art Museum in Wilmington in 2002. As a result, a total of about 100,000 museum-goers saw the show—four times the number that viewed it in New Hampshire.

. . .

Beneath the spacious galleries of the Currier is a series of narrow, winding hallways that lead to the small, stuffed offices of most of the museum's staff. Above, it is quiet, cool, and light. Down here, it's busy. At the end of a corridor, I'm deposited at the door of Andrew Spahr, who is typing rapidly to finish an e-mail. A minute later, he gets up from behind his desk and pulls two chairs over to a small table crowded with books. Clearing his throat, he sits back, hands folded on his lap. Ready.

Colleagues describe Andrew as "incredibly articulate," which in my experience with him hovers near understatement. It is obvious that Andrew cares deeply about his profession and its role in preserving and interpreting humanity's artistic history. When I ask him to explain what a curator does, he bristles slightly and tells me it varies depending on the size of the institution. In larger museums, there can be many curators, each focused on a specific era or type of art. At the Currier, Andrew is a generalist, responsible for researching, managing, and growing the museum's high-quality permanent collection that also includes the Frank Lloyd Wright–designed Zimmerman House.

In addition to all that, Andrew curates exhibitions. This means he selects the works to be shown and supervises everything from what goes into the catalog to how the paintings are hung on the walls. He also spends a lot of time with budgets, but is quick to point out that the Currier doesn't choose exhibitions according to what staff believes will attract funding. If they decide to stage an edgier exhibition, they simply create a budget that draws more from fund-raising than from corporate or other sponsorships.

Working from a spreadsheet, Andrew reads through the line items of a recent show to give me an idea of the types of expenses—and tasks—that arise to support an exhibition:

- Traveling expenses for staff to view artworks under consideration for inclusion in the exhibition
- Photographs of the works
- Travel expenses and insurance for loaned works (a major expense)
- Books and other research materials on the exhibit subject
- Production of the catalog
- Production of a video about the artist
- Educational programming (school visits, lectures, concerts)
- Docent training programs
- Signage and banners outside the museum to announce the exhibition

- Labels for each work and text panels for each gallery
- Installation costs for mounting the exhibit (additional staff, paint, construction of walls)
- Additional security staff
- Gallery lightbulbs
- Food and drink for several hundred people for the opening
- Lenders and funders dinner (held a few days before the opening)
- Construction of wooden crates to contain the works when they travel to the next venue (these cost about $1,000 each and are lined with foam to prevent damage from moisture, creating a microclimate in each crate)
- Shipping materials and additional staff to pack up the exhibit
- Travel expenses for staff who accompany the works to the next venue

"My last budget item is usually the Dumpster," Andrew tells me, looking up. "It takes everything away if the walls have been changed in the gallery. It's expensive. It costs about a thousand dollars to rent a Dumpster." But even through the more mundane tasks of curating, Andrew can't lose sight of the overall scope of an exhibition. At the end of the day, curating is about using the collection to create a continuous narrative of untold stories—about specific artists, for example, or even entire periods in art history. "Being a curator is about balance," he tells me. "What is the story you're trying to tell? What is the quality of the works you want to present and where do they fit into an artist's career? What is the best representation from that artist's life and what will it look like in the gallery—visually?"

Andrew says he and his two assistant curators don't find it difficult to select pieces to include in an exhibition, because it always comes down to choosing the artist's best works. Selecting them is one thing. Locating them is another. When a museum organizes an exhibition around specific artworks from its own collection, it normally must borrow related works from other institutions to create a more complete show (although some large museums are able to pull complete exhibitions together from their own collections, or by pooling resources with only one or two other institutions). Andrew and his staff spend a lot of time not only researching and tracking down works owned by other museums or collectors, but convincing them to loan the pieces to the Currier.

"We have to keep following leads. We also let our peers know what we're looking for. You have to get the word out and hope for the wonderful surprise of finding paintings that haven't been exhibited in years," he says. "The thing is, we want to give the public first-rate material. It makes no sense to show second-rate work if you're trying to introduce an artist. Size and space are also important considerations. We normally use an airy installation style so that the works don't look crowded."

If you visit any large art museum, you can't help but notice that the period rooms are arranged in a very different style than, for example, the rooms that hold huge modern-art "installations." Likewise, rooms displaying religious art may have a somberness or darkness to them that contrasts with the lightness of galleries displaying landscapes. This is deliberate. Besides considering the tone of an exhibit, museums vary exhibit styles from gallery to gallery to accommodate space needs for educational programming and traffic, as well as the amount of wall space any given show will use. But, Andrew tells me, whatever style a museum chooses for any particular room—whether it's the modern "white box" approach or a sculpture garden—the works in the room must clearly relate to each other.

What Andrew is getting at here is the issue of accessibility, which in the world of art museums means providing some type of interpretation, or context, for the works so that anyone looking at them will have a greater appreciation, as well as understanding, of them. For example, say you saw a picture of a tree on a museum wall. "Nice tree," you'd probably think, and move on. But if you knew the artist loved this tree and had painted it every day for a year through the seasons, this knowledge would give you greater access to what the artist was thinking and feeling when he painted the tree.

It's this type of interpretation that creates a connection between the artist and the viewer and enhances the viewer's *ability* to better appreciate the art. Like most museums, the Currier uses a battery of tools to help it do that, including videos, handouts, catalogs, gallery talks, text panels, labels, concerts, and special events for families. But there's no formula here. Andrew recalls several exhibitions where the Currier had to be especially inventive. One was the *American by Design, 1930–1960* exhibition in 2000, which featured three decades of American consumer products. There was no catalog for this show, so the museum prepared extensive labels and overview panels. It also ran radio and television programs from the era and set up sitting areas where visitors could relax and listen.

Andrew smiles when I tell him how much I liked this exhibition because it gave me a glimpse of what my parents' life was like when they were young. The trick, he says, was making the show accessible to all age-groups. "For older people, many grew up with the items in this show and could relate to them in a personal way. For younger people, we had to find a way to bring across the economics and ideas from that period."

Another example comes from an exhibition of Soviet-era dissident art the museum hosted a few years ago. It was an unusual show for the Currier and presented challenges of a different kind. Staff recognized that there was an entire generation of people born too recently to understand Soviet repression or the art that came from that time. "We wanted people to understand the artistic and political conditions under which the works were created and why an abstract painting could earn the artist a prison term," Andrew explains. So staff put aside the museum's usual airy exhibition style and hung the paintings and prints close to each other, floor to ceiling. The intent was to give visitors a sense of the small spaces and conditions under which the works were originally created by mimicking those conditions — as much as was possible — in the galleries.

Both of these examples are interesting because they show a museum's ability to "think outside the box" and use interpretative methods other than merely the visual. Art, however, is art, and visualization is a key ingredient in the way most curators prepare galleries for exhibitions. "I don't see a slide show of an exhibit in my mind," Andrew says about how he plans gallery space. "I see how objects relate to each other and to the structure of the gallery. Sometimes it's hard to get this across, so there's some give-and-take. I might decide that two pieces go together conceptually, but then I see they don't work visually. So our gallery preparator, who is also a sculptor and has architectural training, will move it to another location nearby that works better." Ultimately, there has to be a logical sequence in the overall grouping of works, Andrew says.

When the paintings come down and the walls are being readied for the next show, I wonder what criteria Andrew uses to measure an exhibition's success. What tells him that it went well — or didn't? "It's a success if it makes a unified statement about the art being presented," he replies. "Does the installation support the art without overwhelming it? Does the interpretation support the topic and make it accessible? The artist and the work displayed should come alive for people." He pauses. "Before the exhibit opens, I can say to myself, This is the way I want the exhibit to look. But during the exhibition I want to know that the interpretation is helping people to understand it. It may look great, but it's not a success if people don't understand it."

While Andrew and his curating team are preparing an exhibition, there is an entire wing of staff who work in tandem with him, in essence, to make the show happen. Development brings in the sponsors, programming interprets the ideas, marketing delivers the crowds. It's a neat quadrangle of interdependency that works particularly well because the people who carry out these tasks at the Currier believe there is too much to be done to waste time on discord.

One of the museum staff's cornerstones comes in the form of Tina Andrade, who, as director of development, handles fund-raising. Tina tells me about the Currier's funding, which comes from a complicated mix of sources. About 55 percent of the $2.5 million annual operating budget comes from the interest on the institution's $63 million endowment. (This amount is staggering for a small museum; compare it to the Guggenheim Museum's $58 million endowment, an institution many times larger.) The rest comes from individual and corporate memberships, admissions, annual fund drives, auctions, state and federal money, and private foundation grants.

Tina's involved, in one way or another, with every dollar. In the highly competitive fund-raising arena, it's no longer good enough to be able to put on a well-attended event, although that's certainly still essential. Today's development director must be a business-savvy matchmaker who understands that building partnerships is the key to a nonprofit's survival. Not only must Tina open doors, she must—subtly—take them off their hinges. In equal measures, her job is part psychology, part sales, part chutzpah.

Despite this, I'm surprised to learn that Tina finds asking for money particularly difficult. "It's the hardest part of my job," she tells me. "It's also a tremendous hurdle for our trustees. No one wants to call their friends and ask for money. But having a strong sense of mission helps. When you understand the value of what you're giving the community and you believe in what you're doing, it does make it easier. What helps me is my own enthusiasm. People need to catch your excitement, but you also have to recognize that what you're actually doing is selling your institution."

One of the reasons exhibitions are planned so far in advance is to give the museum's development team the time it needs to secure the funding. For example, if the museum needs $15,000, Tina begins looking for the funds a year from the exhibition opening. If it's $250,000, she'll start about three years out. Either way, she approaches two types of sponsors: programmatic, who will fund special programs, and exhibition, who will help defray exhibition-related costs such as the catalog, extra staffing, and travel expenses for loaned paintings.

Working from a groomed list of five hundred individuals, foundations, and corporations, Tina attempts to match exhibitions to the interests of supporters. "With our corporate benefactors, we try to give them the most visibility so they get the most for their dollars," Tina explains. "To do this with integrity, we analyze how an exhibition might be a good fit for a corporation and who is their constituency. We do this before we ask for money."

What a company chooses to fund, Tina says, depends to a large extent on its corporate culture, its image, and how it markets itself. Educational programs for children are popular, but so are "big flashy things" like major exhibitions. For example, she says, a manufacturer might be more inclined to fund special programs because they are something it can offer to employees as a benefit. A bank, on the other hand, might be more interested in sponsoring a high-profile show because of the media exposure. "As a development office, we're aware of these differences," Tina says. "So we combine corporate marketing, constituency, image, and culture together into one package to give sponsors the best value for their money."

Institutions like the Currier compete with dozens of other worthy nonprofits around the state for what often amounts to a small piece of a relatively small pie. In New Hampshire there are only a handful of foundations capable of giving up to $50,000 to a single organization. In addition, Tina says, there are only a few corporations that regularly sponsor cultural and human services programs. "These are the two tiny little worlds where everyone is competing for the same money," she says. "Some foundations focus on funding human services programs, and it's hard to make a case for the Currier with them. We never want to put a sponsor in the place of deciding either-or. But it's not a question of one group being more deserving than another. We're interested in quality of life for all, and that includes the arts."

In another office, Currier deputy director Susan Leidy expresses a similar view when she talks about the importance of art history in New Hampshire's school curricula. Susan is responsible, among many other things, for the museum's educational programming and has been with the Currier for over fifteen years. "Kids might be learning art in school, but not always art history," she says. "So one of the things we're doing is offering refresher courses to teachers on art history. We want them to feel comfortable teaching this subject and we want them to use the Currier as a resource to do so."

One of Susan's tasks is to work closely with Tina Andrade to find grants that help pay, for example, the busing costs for the 8,500 schoolchildren who visit the Currier each year. The museum sees these visits as integral to its mission and goes out of its way to reach as many schools, and children, as it can. "If we can get every fourth grader from Nashua, for example, or every fifth grader from Manchester, maybe twenty years down the road they'll come back," Susan tells me. "It's definitely a long-term commitment, but it seems to be working. We're starting to see kids giving their families a tour, and we hear the words of our docents coming out of their mouths. It's very moving."

Pulling in adults, however, is a different story. "History museums may be more accessible than art museums because they relate to things people have in their homes," Susan explains. "But not many people have expensive art in their homes. It's more of a challenge to reach adults than kids. Kids are more open-minded when they come to the museum. Adults sometimes feel like only insiders know and understand what's in a museum—like someone is winking behind their backs. And they don't like it."

To counter this, the museum is trying to interact more with its adult visitors and empower them with the idea that art is important. A few years ago, as an experiment, staff put out an empty book and asked visitors to fill its pages with thoughts about their favorite art pieces. "The idea was to say to them, You don't need a Ph.D. in art to give your opinion about an artist's work," Susan says. About 250 people wrote in the book over several months, which she considers a good response. "What we learned was that visitors need to be encouraged to talk about art and be given the tools to do so. We also learned we need to create more opportunities for this to happen."

One population the Currier hasn't always spent a lot of time wooing is the "young adult" crowd, mainly because chasing this audience segment is expensive. A few years ago, however, staff started noticing that twenty-somethings were showing up in ever increasing numbers at the museum's occasional Friday night gala openings. It surprised them, but when they looked closer they could see that the changing demographics of southern New Hampshire—which indicated an influx of young professionals had moved into the area—were starting to impact museum programming. Clearly, this segment was looking for events of its own. What to do about it is an issue Susan and her staff are still struggling with. This age-group wants costly programming like film festivals, jazz concerts, and wine nights, Susan says, all of which are labor-intensive and can't be held during the museum's normal operating hours. "The question is this," she says. "Will people get a good museum experience, or could they do this activity in a bar?"

Although it may be less expensive to put on a lecture during museum hours and leave it at that, Currier staff members say they use every exhibition to reach out and pull in new audiences. "This isn't Boston," Susan says.

"We don't have five art museums to choose from on any given day. The Currier is one of the only independent art museums in the state. We're also true believers, and it's our obligation to introduce everyone to the wonderful world of art. The quality of our collections is extremely high."

When the former New Hampshire governor Moody Currier died in 1898, his will stated that his fortune should be used for the endowment of an art museum. Interestingly, he was neither an artist nor a collector, but he greatly valued the role played by art in the development of human civilization. Currier's will further stated that the museum building should be erected on the Currier estate in Manchester at the site of the family mansion on Orange Street. His wife, Hannah, agreed with her husband's wishes and made similar provisions in her own will. She then managed the estate so well that after her death in 1915 there were sufficient funds available to promptly establish the museum. It was only a few years later that the Currier Gallery of Art, as Mrs. Currier specified it be called, was chartered by a joint act in the New Hampshire State Senate and House of Representatives in 1919. (In 2002, the institution changed its name to the Currier Museum of Art because staff felt it better recognized the Curriers' true mission.)

For the next six years, the institution's trustees spent much of their time reviewing and rejecting proposals from some of the most well-known architects of the day. At last they settled on a New York City firm with extensive experience designing libraries and museums. Three years later, on October 9, 1929, the Italian Renaissance–style museum opened its doors to a waiting public. Over 1,400 invited guests toured the galleries that evening to the soft strains of chamber music, and then enjoyed a reception attended by local and state officials as well as distinguished guests from the East Coast art world. The Curriers had left few instructions in their wills for the fledgling institution, but one wish was clear: the museum should serve as a vital art resource for the people of New Hampshire.

When I talked with Susan Strickler about the museum's strengths, she told me, "Our assets are our small size and the quality of our collections and programming. We don't have the ambition of being a Museum of Fine Arts, although we will grow. We need to grow. Through meetings around the state we have learned that the intimate experience we provide visitors is a valuable alternative to larger museums. But small size can also be a disadvantage. People say your collection isn't big enough, or they only come once a year. So we're working on two main fronts—we're improving our visitors' experience without losing the intimacy and strong sense of community here, and we're continuing to improve our programming. It's these two areas that generate new audiences for us."

Susan is one of the new class of museum directors who have as much training in management as in curating. (When I suggested she was perhaps running the museum like a business, she corrected me. "No," she said, matter-of-factly. "I'm running it in a businesslike way.") Susan spoke at length about the museum's goals to build on the Currier legacy by continuing to add to its 11,000-object permanent collection, which has always stood out for its excellence. To the outsider, it may appear that museums see something they like, buy it, and hang it on a gallery wall, but this isn't at all what happens. Most museums, including the Currier, follow a detailed collections plan that shows them precisely what they own and where they need to build.

For example, several years ago, the Currier purchased a 1635 Dutch painting because it wanted to fill out its Dutch collection. In the future, it may consider purchasing another impressionist work to give context to the Monet already in the permanent collection. Thanks in part to a major bequest in 2001, the Currier can now afford to spend about a million dollars a year adding to its collection. While this may appear to be a lot, prices in the art world have continued to rise in recent years, putting many valuable pieces out of the Currier's reach. "We don't have endless resources for acquisitions," Andrew told me earlier. "We can't have depth in all areas, so focusing the collection on areas of strength makes the most sense. Over time we can build on what we've already been doing."

Making these kinds of decisions has proved problematic for museums in the last few decades. Some have stopped trying to be all things to all audiences and started focusing on specific genres, or categories, of works that relate directly to their mission. The somewhat surprising result has been a tightening of collections, with some museums selling off pieces that no longer fit within their collections plan. The Currier isn't in that group, but the institution is going through an evaluation process. Staff members say in the future they intend their exhibitions and collections to better reflect the population diversity New Hampshire is starting to see.

Collecting in and of itself is only part of the game. As the Currier adds more significant works to its collections, it becomes more valuable to its peers as a loaning institution. In fact, the quality of the Currier's permanent collection is such that, for a small museum, it receives loan requests fairly frequently. "We try to be cooperative because we know there will be times when we need to borrow works from other museums' collections," Andrew told me.

From time to time, however, the museum turns down loan requests. Staff members feel strongly that the museum's most important paintings should be available to its own audiences. "Our permanent collection is the legacy that we leave to New Hampshire," Andrew said. "Exhibits come and go, but they don't mean much to the community in the long run. The paintings in the Tarbell exhibition may never be in the same place at the same time again, but we have three great Tarbell paintings here that are part of our permanent collection."

Susan Strickler echoes this sentiment. "We never want to lose sight of our standards," she said. "Our public deserves the same caliber of art that they would see in a large metropolitan area and should be able to enjoy it in a welcoming environment. When people leave here, we want them to feel refreshed and positive about human achievement, that they've had a good experience, and that they've visited a valuable and valued cultural resource in their community."

# Bibliography

*The Art of Violin.* Partial text from a documentary film produced for *Great Performances.* Alexandria, Va.: Public Broadcasting System, Pierre-Olivier Bardet and Stephen Wright, 2000.

Belman, Felice, and Mike Pride, eds. *The New Hampshire Century: Concord Monitor Profiles of One Hundred People Who Shaped It.* Hanover, N.H., and London: University Press of New England, 2001.

Buchanan, Rita. *The Shaker Herb and Garden Book.* Boston: Houghton Mifflin, 1996.

*Bugle of Bretton Woods* (daily newspaper). Bretton Woods, N.H., October 1, 1902.

Carr, Frances A. *Shaker Your Plate: Of Shaker Cooks and Cooking.* Hanover, N.H., and London: University Press of New England, 1985, 2002.

Casanave, Suki. *Natural Wonders of New Hampshire.* Castine, Maine: Country Roads Press, 1994.

Cummings, Thayer. "Strawbery Banke: The First 25 Years." Unpublished manuscript, Portsmouth, N.H., 1982.

Dobbs, David. *The Northern Forest.* White River Junction, Vt.: Chelsea Green Publishing Co., 1996.

Eaton, Aurore Dionne. *The Currier Gallery of Art: A History, 1929–1989.* Manchester, N.H.: The Currier Gallery of Art, 1990.

Fennelley, Catherine, ed. *Country Stores in Early New England.* Pamphlet Series, Old Sturbridge Village, Inc., Sturbridge, Mass., 1955.

Flam, Judy. "Evaluation of Dunaway Store and Kingsbury House Store." Report presented to the Guild of Strawbery Banke, Inc., Cambridge, Mass., June 9, 1989.

Garvin, Donna-Belle. "The Warp and Weft of a Lifetime: The Discovery of a New Hampshire Weaver and Her Work." In *Textiles in Early New England: Design, Production, and Consumption,* edited by Peter Benes. Boston: Boston University, 1997.

Garvin, James L. "The Creation of New Hampshire's Temple of History, 1900–1911." *Historical New Hampshire* 47 (spring/summer 1992).

———. "From a Single Stone: The Portal Sculpture of the NH Historical Society's Building." *Historical New Hampshire* 47 (spring/summer 1992).

———. "Strawbery Banke: Agent of Change, Agent of Preservation." *Strawbery Banke Newsletter* (November 1998).

Heald, Bruce D. *Boats and Ports of Lake Winnipesaukee*. Vols. I and II Charleston, S.C.: Arcadia Publishing, 1998.

———. *Mail Service on the Lake*. Weirs Beach, N.H.: Winnipesaukee Flagship Corp., 2000.

Hood, Laura. *Science-Based Stewardship: Recommendations for Implementing the National Wildlife Refuge System Improvement Act*. Washington, D.C.: Defenders of Wildlife, 1998.

Johnson, Laurence A. *Over the Counter and on the Shelf: Country Storekeeping in America 1620–1920*. Rutland, Vt.: Charles B. Tuttle Co., 1961.

Komanecky, Michael K., ed. *The Currier Gallery of Art Handbook of the Collection*. Manchester, N.H.: The Currier Gallery of Art, 1990.

Lantos, Steve. *New Hampshire Handbook*. Emeryville, Calif.: Moon Publications, Inc., 1998.

Lindsay, Bertha. *Seasoned with Grace*. Woodstock, N.H.: The Countryman Press, 1987.

Mahoney, Kathleen. *Wisdom from a Shaker Garden*. New York: Penguin Studio, 1998.

*Miss America*. Full text from a documentary film produced for *The American Experience*. Alexandria, Va.: Public Broadcasting System, Clio Inc. and Orchard Films, 2001.

Northern Forest Alliance. *Protecting Northern Forest Wildlands: Landscape Conservation for the 21st Century*. Montpelier, Vt., 2001.

Roy, Karl, and Alex L. Shigo. *Violin Woods: A New Look*. Durham, N.H.: University of New Hampshire, 1983.

Starbuck, David R. "Canterbury Shaker Village: Archaeology and Landscape." *The New Hampshire Archaeologist* 31 (1990).

Strickler, Susan. *Impressionism Transformed: The Paintings of Edmund C. Tarbell*. Manchester, N.H.: The Currier Gallery of Art, 2001.

Swank, Scott T., and David R. Starbuck. *A Shaker Family Album*. Hanover, N.H., and London: University Press of New England, 1998.

Tardiff, Olive. *Molly Stark: Woman of the Revolution*. Canaan, N.H.: Phoenix Publishing, 1976.

Thompson, Darryl. "Shaker Cooking: Edible Philosophy." In *In the Spirit of Shaker,* Brasstown, N.C.: John C. Campbell Folk School, 2001.

———. "The Structure of Canterbury Shaker Daily Life." A training paper for tour guides. Canterbury Shaker Village, Canterbury, N.H., n.d.

Tolles, Bryant F., Jr. *The Grand Resort Hotels of the White Mountains: A Vanishing Architectural Legacy*. Boston: David R. Godine Publisher, 1998.

Tree, Christina, and Peter Randall. *New Hampshire: An Explorer's Guide*. Woodstock, Vt.: The Countryman Press, 1997.

Wasson, Joanne F. *Deerfield Fair: A History, 1876–2001*. Henderson Printing, Inc. Deerfield, N.H.: The Deerfield Fair Association, 2001.

## Contacts

Ballet New England
135 Daniel Street
PO Box 4501
Portsmouth, NH 03802
603-430-9309
www.balletnewengland.org

Canterbury Shaker Village
288 Shaker Road
Canterbury, NH 03224
603-783-9511
www.shakers.org

Currier Museum of Art
201 Myrtle Way
Manchester, NH 03104
603-669-6144
www.currier.org

Daughters of the American Revolution, National Society
1776 D Street, NW
Washington, DC 20006
202-628-1776
National Society DAR: www.dar.org

The Deerfield Fair Association
PO Box 156
Deerfield, New Hampshire 03037
603-463-7421
www.deerfieldfair.org

Lake Umbagog National Wildlife Refuge
PO Box 240
Errol, NH 03579
603-482-3415
http://northeast.fws.gov/nh/lku.htm

Miss New Hampshire Scholarship Program
18 Folsom Road
Derry, NH 03038
603-437-9027
www.missnh.com

Mount Washington Hotel & Resort
Route 302
Bretton Woods, NH 03575
603-278-1000
www.mtwashington.com

New England Marionette Opera
PO Box 267
Hancock, NH 03449
www.marionettes.org

Pats Peak
Box 2448
Henniker, NH 03242
603-428-3245
www.patspeak.com

Story Land
Route 16
PO Box 1776
Glen, NH 03838
603-383-4186
www.storylandnh.com

Strawbery Banke
PO Box 300
Portsmouth, NH 03802
603-433-1100
www.strawberybanke.org

The Tuck Library
30 Park Street
Concord, NH 03301
603-856-0641
www.nhhistory.org

UNH Violin Craftsmanship Institute
UNH Division of Continuing Education
24 Rosemary Lane
Durham, NH 03824
603-862-1088
www.learn.unh.edu/violin/geninfo.html

Winnipesaukee Flagship Corp.
PO Box 5367
Weirs Beach, NH 03247
603-366-5531
www.cruisenh.com